To each of you that has touched and has been touched by Norquay, may your memories endure with the beauty of this mountain.

Photo Credits

Bruno Engler
22, 28, 30, 31, 65, 92, 93, 98, 159, 163, 166, 169, 181

Whyte Museum of the Canadian Rockies
1, V, VII, 8, 11, 15, 156, 162

Gavin Young
10 (fire)

Lloyd Harmon
 5, 6

For additional photography I would like to thank Cliff White, Veijo Tiesmaki, Jack MacAulay, Dave Spence Sr., Clarence Hakkenstad, Norm Rault, Don Waters, Murray McCullough, Jean Kelly Shafto, Doug Robinson, Barb Whyte, Jean Herbertson Wright, Bill Round, Ron Duke, Alex Emond, Inez Peyto, Chess Edwards, Simon Hoyle, Ken Baker, Mike Chan, Beth Woolley.

*Author's Note: I supplied about 100 pictures, mostly from a family collection.
I didn't want to include too many photos of my family, however if other people or scenes were featured, they were included.*

About the author

E ddie Hunter was born in Edmonton, Alberta. The family moved to Banff when he was eight. Except for about fourteen years divided between California and Calgary, Banff has been his home. In Calgary television he hosted a live children's show, a ski show and a late night (*Late Knight*) talk show.

In Santa Barbara, California he studied photography and worked as a photographer in Squaw Valley, California. As a freelance cinematographer Eddie has travelled to most major countries of the world.

Eddie Hunter's greatest pleasure: his two daughters and four grandchildren.

THE SPIRIT OF NORQUAY

Published by Banff Mount Norquay Ski Area
Suite 7000, Box 219
Banff, Alberta
T0L 0C0
Canada

Canadian Cataloguing in Publication Data

Hunter, Eddie, 1926-
  The Spirit of Norquay.
1. Banff Mount Norquay Ski Area (Alta.) – History.
2. Skis and skiing – Alberta – Norquay, Mount – History.
3. Ski resorts – Alberta – Banff National Park – History.
I. Banff Mount Norquay Ski Area (Firm)
II. Title.
GV854.8.C3H86 2000   796.93'5'09712332   C00-911000-3

Cover photograph by Jack Hayes
Copy editing by Anne Evely
Design by Mark Robichaud
Printed in Canada

Contents

rosty mornings that start with dry humour and the snap of a binding. Layered conversations with friends that dissolve into powder. That one last turn making one so full of the moment that only a yell, a cross between a wrangler's command and a mountain yodel comes close to expressing how good you feel. The free will of a child's first turn or the trained skill of a World Cup racer, combined with emotions that run out of control; everything from "I'm going to quit this stupid sport," to "Hey, I'm pretty good." Norquay has seen it all.

Norquay has been our community hall. Other towns and cities in western Canada had halls where parents did community activities and the kids ran around. Norquay was our hall and we skied around. It became a part of our schooling; part of our life that developed into a passion for skiing.

This isn't a first person story. It's more like a first and last person story. Firstly I spoke with Chess Edwards who was born in Banff in 1910. He was one of the first persons to ski the Norquay area when he was ten years old. Just about the last person I spoke with was Maureen Lefaivre who currently co-ordinates children's ski

programs while her two children, Brodie and Mackenzie, ski around in the Norquay tradition. In between the runs made by Chess Edwards and the Lefaivre family lies a world of, well, to

In the 1920s the winter carnival encouraged skiing on the streets of Banff.

It was up to Mt. Norquay to add a downhill thrill to their lives. Twenty-five years later Gordie Morrison and Lois Woodworth were two of the best.

Banff Ski Club 1929. Front row left to right, Cliff White and Chess Edwards. Second row: Edith Ashton, Cyril Paris and Mildred White. Back row with pipe, Dr. Quigley.

Beth Woolley's style in 1999.

Dorothy Michael's style in 1939.

use some of your words, joy, passion, fear, love, sharing, excitement, emotion, gratification, etc., all experienced in the spirit of sunny frosty days that can be felt better than explained. Days that cover more than seventy-five years of riding snow crystals on Mt. Norquay.

Recently I was skiing with the current owners of Mt. Norquay, Kika Grandi and Peter White, and Peter's wife Mary. Several months earlier they had put out an invitation to Norquay skiers to send in a Norquay experience, hoping the many tales would provide a starting point for a history of the mountain. I asked, "How did it go?" A number of submissions had been received. A little later I heard the question, "Why don't you write the history of Norquay, Eddie; after all you and the ski area are about the same age?" I had to admit this was true, so here I am applying the first and last person to skiing Norquay, with the help of all of you who skied the years in between.

I started with the oldest skiers I knew. After Chess I spoke with Bill Wellman. When Bill was nine years old in 1928, he was lucky to hitch a ride on one of Ike Mills' horses that Ike used to haul logs for the first Norquay cabin. In May 1999, I spoke with Ted Keith of Banff who had worked on the construction of the road up to Norquay in May of 1934. He had lived in a camp on Stoney Squaw where he had received food, clothing and $5 a month. I spoke with Lloyd Harmon in February 1999. He had taken outstanding action photos in the 1930s and 40s in the Harmon tradition. I also spoke with the man who has taken more photos on Norquay than any other photographer, and annually heads the veteran's race that carries his name, Bruno Engler. I even spoke with a lady who refused to ski Norquay after they put a rope tow on the hill!

I am about the same age as Norquay: I skied it in the thirties. I was there when you climbed for over an hour to the start of the downhill in the Bowl. Your equipment fought you on every turn, but you loved it. I was there when you tried out the first rope tow that twisted arms and clothes into a helpless mess, and you loved it. The first chairlift was a 6-minute ride after a 36-minute line-up, but for the most exciting 1300 vertical feet of skiing in the world. Mark Crozier controlled the line-up like a sergeant major, and you loved it. I watched Banff skiers go on to national titles. I saw Nancy Greene train and then go on to World Cup titles. I watched the hard-core guys ski the big chair until their legs yelled for mercy. There were the "hot

In March of 1929 the Banff Rotary Club climbed to Norquay for lunch, aided by horse drawn sleighs and the dog teams of Ike Mills.

dog" freestyle years. There were wood, metal, plastic, long, short, fat and parabolic skis that got you feeling so good that you thought you could do it all on one ski, so you dropped in on a snowboard.

The Norquay story that follows is divided into three sections. The early pages speak of people and a Government envisioning only the summer season. The people were trying to survive with limited work, enjoying the mountains when they could. The government, as guardians of the National Park, did not see the future too clearly. When the people decided that winter should also be enjoyed, the government was very supportive. This support was shown in Park regulations that licensed ski areas and for many years financed the development and servicing of these areas. There were snags that occurred along the way, but for the skiing public they were optimistic times.

The second section of the book deals with the owners that experienced those years. It is set on a mystic stage, as all the caretakers and owners are brought together to discuss the seventy-plus years that were Mt. Norquay. The stage is unreal, but the words are true.

The final stories of Norquay come from the people who have skied Norquay for over seventy years. The happy days are mixed with some tragedy, but the stories do not deal with the extreme groups that would like to see skiing eliminated from Banff National Park.

I lived many of these pages. I researched many, but most of them come from you. I thank you for that and the spirit in which you pass them on. My greatest fear is missing people that should have their memories documented. I know this will happen, and all I can say is it's similar to trying to have that perfect run. We do our best, but it's never quite perfect.

Eddie Hunter Squaw Valley, 1951.

I f mountains have personalities, does that personality develop because of what they do to us, or what we do to them?

The mountains that encompass the town of Banff are quite different, one from another. William Cornelius Van Horne, the builder of the Canadian Pacific Railway, once targeted little Tunnel Mountain when he said that to follow the river with the tracks up to the site of the planned hotel, he would have to cut a tunnel into the southern slope of that mountain. Tunnel Mountain was spared as he took the tracks around the northern side of the mountain. The personality of Tunnel Mountain remained unchanged.

The rugged peak of Mt. Rundle echoes the stern voice of the Reverend Robert Rundle. He ran the first mission church here in 1841. In a visual way, an arc of snow blowing off the summit will tell us of a coming Chinook – a warm westerly wind that will change the air from winter freeze to spring breeze in just a few hours.

Sulphur Mountain can boast of hot and cold running water. It was that sulphur spring that changed the personality of Banff when the surrounding area was set aside to form Canada's first national park.

Cascade Mountain stands ever clean, as it guides the spring run-off and the sudden storms of summer. The passing of time seems to have had no effect on this mountain.

Other mountains surrounding Banff share too in honour and pride, as they were named after people who discovered or pioneered the Bow Valley: Mts. Bourgeau, Palliser, Brett and Brewster, along with the Sundance Range, which celebrates our native heritage.

Last but not least are two mountains with very different personalities. They share their seasons and their slopes with us, while we admire and share our joy of the outdoor experience with them. Above all, we respect these mountains. They are Mt. Norquay and Stoney Squaw.

Norquay ski area 1936.

Norquay ski area (artist's concept) 1999.

Chapter One

A New Reason for a Winter Season

A native legend tells of a peaceful tribe that spent their summers in the small valley between Norquay and Stoney Squaw. They called it Spirit Creek. They believed the spirits of the area made them invisible to their enemies. Here the Elders had time to tell tales to the youth of the tribe. It was a

Lodge on 6 December getting ready for the 1995/96 season.

time to study their crafts and tipi painting. The warriors practised for the autumn hunt that took place before travelling the river back to their winter camp.

It must have been a grand morning hundreds of years later when John Norquay stood looking up at the peak that dominated the site of the legendary native camp and said, "I must climb that mountain." Norquay was a Métis. An employee of the Hudson Bay Company, he carried his white blood from the Orkney Islands of northern Scotland, his native blood from Manitoba. John Norquay, the first Premier of Manitoba, weighed over three hundred pounds and he was not a young man in 1887 when he decided to

Lodge on 7 December 1995 destroyed by fire. *(photo Gavin Young)*

climb the mountain. The spirits would surely have to help him. But Norquay was a man who had overcome many obstacles in his life. He spoke French and English as well as three native languages. His name lives on in Manitoba as it does here with the mountain that proudly bears his name.

Early in the twentieth century a resident of Banff, Mr. Stan Ward, carried on a logging operation on Norquay and Stoney Squaw. He had built a small log cabin for his caretaker, Bill Davis, who was known as Nigger Bill, a name that would not be acceptable today. It wasn't meant in a derogatory way; Bill was highly thought

New lodge 1996/97.

Bruno Engler arrives from Switzerland to try Canadian snow (1939).

of in the community, and known as a man who could do twice the work of an ordinary man.

Near the base of Stoney Squaw stood another small cabin with a big fireplace. It was occupied by an English woman who had been sent to the Rockies to paint postcards for a large British publishing house, Tucks of London. Nora Drummond shared her cabin with a horse, several cats and the Airedale dogs that pulled a small wagon in summer and a sleigh in winter into town for supplies. The Rockies and the wildlife had a great influence on her art as she went from postcard format to huge oil paintings that were larger than her five-foot frame. In the twelve years that she lived here she became well known and found time to teach her craft in Banff schools. Peter Whyte, who himself was to become a famous painter of the mountains, and co-founder of the Whyte Museum, took classes from her. Sometime during her stay in the Bow Valley her husband came from England to see what she was up to. It would appear he did not 'take' to the mountains, and the mountain folk did not 'take' to him. The town people said of him, "He had a flair for doing nothing." I have a feeling his visit didn't last too long. Several years later Nora Drummond moved to Victoria, sending her former employers a postcard telling them of her change in life-style. I would be surprised if her husband received one! She continued her successful career on the West Coast until her death in 1948. For years her larger paintings graced the walls of the Lux Theatre on Banff Avenue, as they did the dining room of the Mount Royal Hotel. Some of her paintings can still be seen in Calgary's Glenbow Museum.

In the early development of Banff National Park, Ottawa aimed to create a spa-type town in the European tradition. Advertising by the government and the Canadian Pacific Railway catered to people of fashion who wanted to be seen at a popular place in the right season. Sir John A. Macdonald in a speech said, "A portion of the Park offers some beautiful sites for villas and I believe they should be leased to people of wealth, who will erect handsome buildings upon them." That only happened in a small way on the south side of town, which was considered the elite area. With this in mind, Lord Strathcona had requested the name Siding 29 be changed to Banff.

The history of skiing in Banff and eventually on the slopes of Mt. Norquay is rather vague. It is believed a couple of Finnish workers, around 1885, who either toiled on the railway or at the Silver City mines west of Banff, made their own skis and used

Erling Strom in classic Telemark (circa 1930).

them to do extensive hunting in the Simpson Pass area.

Officially, in 1894, George Paris who had been working at the Brett Sanatorium (located on the present site of the Government Administration Building), was sent a pair of skis from a guest who had observed him going around Banff on snowshoes. That man, from Kalispell, Montana, had told George that mailmen there were using them with great success. The skis, when they arrived, were pretty basic with slight tips and leather toe pieces. It sounded like a very shaky start to skiing in Banff. George Paris did impress the locals with a few runs off the slope from the sanatorium, however when he attempted a faster run from Middle Springs down to the Banff Springs Hotel he went from being Banff's first skier to Banff's first ski casualty. One ski was broken, the other ran away and George went back to his snowshoes after his week recovering in the sanatorium.

In 1910 the Austrian climber/skier, Conrad Kain, was responsible for the construction of a jump on the slopes of Tunnel Mountain. At that time Jack Stanley owned a boat company and a lumber mill near Lake Minnewanka. He was making skis cut from a Norwegian design. A young Cyril Paris, George's son, was lucky to get a pair for Christmas.

The pioneers of skiing were not all male. Banff ladies Pearl Moore and Jennie Edwards were active skiers. A few years later, in 1929, two lady skiers from England set one of the first slalom courses on Mt. Norquay. In 1931, Cameron Stockand wrote, "The practice of a slalom became a regular feature on Norquay and practically every weekend two or more courses were 'flagged out.'" (A term that lasted even less time than it took to knock down an old course.)

Banff in the winter virtually closed down. This problem was discussed on a long winter's evening by Norman Luxton and Barney Collison, neither of whom worked for the government or the Canadian Pacific Railway. They discussed the condition of the growing town and how they could get people to visit the area in the winter. They were not looking for high society types, they just wanted outsiders to come and compete against Banffites in the winter games. In the winter of 1916/17 the Banff Ski Club was formed and in February 1917 the first Banff Winter Carnival was held. It was a success right from the start. It drew people from all the western provinces and the state of Montana. Each year the carnival queen would be chosen from a different city. In the beginning skiing played a minor role. It was largely hockey (both ladies' and men's), speed and fancy skating, curling, some swimming events at the Cave and Basin and a variety of street events, including a toboggan slide that came off the side of Tunnel Mountain down to Banff Avenue. The only skiing events at early Banff winter carnivals were jumping and cross country skiing, as well as ski-joring behind a galloping horse. This was done with a rider and skier, but a lone skier trying to control the horse and ski provided the most excitement. The young ladies of Banff enjoyed ski-joring as many had equestrian backgrounds. Jennie Edwards won the Brewster Ski-Joring Cup on more than one occasion. Other competitors included Edith and Lorna Wellman, Ethel 'Tillie' Knight, Elsie Brown, Pat Stirling, Ruth Lane and Mrs. Bessie Harvey. Edith and Lorna Wellman's younger brother Bill was to become one of Banff's leading alpine racers after Mt. Norquay had been developed for downhill skiing. Lorna Wellman Oliver passed away in Banff in early 1999.

The original jumping event at the carnival of 1917 was held on Tunnel Mountain

Rupe Edwards and Peter Vadja in powder.

behind the old Harmon house. Gus Johnson, from Camrose, was here for that competition and also for the 1919 event, which was then held on a more challenging hill by the buffalo paddocks east of town.

It was quite a 'leap' from the Tunnel Mountain jump to the new buffalo paddock area jump. Peter Whyte wrote, "Two of the best jumpers competing on the new jump were Gus Johnson and Adolph Maland. Johnson was the only one to stand as Maland found the jump too abrupt." Judging at that time was not too much different from today. One to twenty points were awarded for style or character, and one point for each foot of distance. You lost thirty points for a fall and touching the ground with both hands was considered a fall. Touching with one hand, the jumper would lose fifteen points. A tape measure was used for measuring distance. According to Roy Andersen, who carries on the Norwegian influence in Banff, and Colin Capel, a former member of Canada's Nordic Olympic Team who won the Canadian jumping championship in 1992, judging isn't that different from eighty years ago. Today there are five judges. The top and bottom scores are discarded so that only three count. Points are still awarded for style, and therein lies a changing story. Early jumpers would windmill their arms hoping to get extra lift while maintaining their balance. Then followed an aerodynamic style with arms behind the body. Then an unstable position with arms out over the tips. Today's jumpers are affected by technical rulings; one being that the length of the skis cannot exceed a certain percentage of body height. In the air, the present style is to ride the skis in a reverse snowplow position, creating lift and distance. This, combined with new clothing material providing less drag, creates even further lift and distance. The new technology has meant that many existing jumps such as the 70- and 90-meter jumps at Norquay are outdated. On them today a jumper would exceed the critical point on the hill and land on the outrun.

Gus Johnson stayed on in Banff where he passed on his love of the sport to young skiers. He was attracted to Norquay where he became one of the first to clear land with skiing in mind. Unfortunately he had failing health. As the Crag & Canyon in 1926 stated, "Gus Johnson, the Swedish jumper and father of Banff skiing died following a lengthy illness and a variety of complications." He was still a young man at the time of his death.

John Bird, Bill Wellman and Bob Bryant, spring skiing. (photo Lloyd Harmon)

Before his death in 1926, Gus Johnson, along with some of his skiing students, had cleared a run which cut up to the avalanche slope. While doing so he had stockpiled timber for a cabin, however people unknown to the ski club had removed it. Finally in the fall of 1928 enough timber had been collected to start a cabin. Bill Wellman, a young skier of that time, remembers getting a ride with Ike Mills' horses when they were dragging logs for the cabin. In October of that year Cliff White asked for permission to start construction, which was granted by the Parks Department in November.

The new cabin gave the skiing community a place of focus, and a new place to party. It was located about 20 metres below and to the north of the 1940 lodge which still stands. Mr. W. E. Round, writing for the Crag & Canyon at that time said, "The second skiing party of the season was held last night at Mt. Norquay. Another great success as some forty members of the club left town at six o'clock. After having dinner at the camp they attended to several miscellaneous items as yet not finished, then skied until midnight. When the clouds obscured the moon they hung a lamp on the cabin, which gave good light to the lower part of the slide. Dancing and entertainment followed, where the phonograph, Cliff White and Louis Trono and their banjos were kept busy."

The official opening of the ski cabin was made during the winter carnival on February 3, 1929. The program suggested that people wanting to go up for the opening in a four-horse-drawn sleigh, should buy their tickets by twelve noon. The price was $2 for the ride and lunch. The sleigh would leave from the King Edward corner at one o'clock. The program added that if you would like to walk it would take 45 minutes from town if you didn't stop for photography. The spirit generated by that little cabin seemed contagious and the Banff Rotary Club decided to hold their luncheon at Norquay in early March. Mr. Noble was president of Rotary that year. He was also one of Banff's leading photographers.

Apparently there was some problem with the sleighs on the road to Norquay, as a report states the first arrived an hour and a half before the second. Some of the delay was caused by the second group stopping to view the mountain sheep, which had been missed by the first group. Evidently 'Doc' Kennedy and Bill Keely had a wager going concerning a threat that would see one of them walking down. However after the late lunch, a tug of war between the ski club and the Rotarians, followed by a few trying to ski, all bets seemed to disappear with the fading light. One gentleman, Mr. A.E. Horst, of Rock Island, Illinois, a guest of Rotary that day, said, "I am most impressed with the construction of this cabin, as I understand it was built largely by volunteer workers." That statement came from a man that was in the construction business. He was also impressed with Banff. He and his wife had been travelling around the country looking for a winter experience. They had gone to Yosemite in California, then to Grouse Mountain near Vancouver, but it wasn't until they came to Banff that they found a real 'winter resort.'

This was the beginning of Banff's winter trade. Up until that time all the advertising that had been done was for the summer visitors. Except for some carnival advertising, the Norquay area would for awhile rely on word of mouth.

The winter of 1929 did seem pumped with activity. The landing of the first aeroplane in Banff added to the excitement. A five-passenger plane from Calgary's Great Western Airways piloted by flying ace Captain P. McCall, did a slow-motion bank in the thin Banff winter air before a spectacular landing on the frozen Bow River. Environmentalists of the 1990s would not have been impressed with the good captain's landing. Coming in from the north to the south in low evening light, he couldn't stop before going over the small pontoon bridge used by pedestrians for crossing the Bow River to get to the skating and curling rink. When he hit the bridge he took to the air briefly, landed at an angle and continued on in a skid. Witnesses said it was only the pilot's ability that stopped the plane before he hit Mather's boathouse. The next day the departure held even greater excitement. Just as they took off from the river, with apparently no snow on the ice, a strong gust of wind blew the plane to the right. It happened that there was an opening at that point where Echo Creek enters the Bow. Once again McCall manoeuvred his plane to safety as he dodged the trees in that small opening until he had enough 'air' to make his escape. Sharing that dramatic exit was one of the originators of the carnival, Norman Luxton.

Meanwhile back at Norquay skiing was great, but the builders of the cabin were now realizing (if they didn't know it before), that they had partners in the Parks system of Canada. In many ways the government was eager to promote skiing as part of the National Park experience, but at the same time they were reluctant to let people make money because of the park's existence. They just didn't want to see all this natural beauty go commercial, or they at least wanted to keep control on it. With several government departments involved, this at times became confusing. Flash ahead seventy years to the nineties and add the conservationist forces to the mix, and you will realize that the thirties were relatively calm. Norquay was born with love and spirit and the blessing of the Park system. However a couple of years later the government was put to a further test.

The Banff Ski Club had been formed in the winter of 1916/17. It remained as such until 1931 when the name was changed to Banff Ski Runners of the Canadian Rockies. Tex Woods is given credit for the change. It was his suggestion a club be formed similar to the Trail Riders of the Canadian Rockies, an organization that gave pins and awards for distances covered. His idea was to encourage high country touring, and not only to be a Banff club, but also to include other areas like Lake Louise and Jasper. This idea came about while on a trip to Ptarmigan Valley with

Cliff White, Fulton Dunsmore and Cyril Paris. Shortly after his trip Cliff White applied to Parks for permission to build a lodge in the Skoki Valley. The 1930 application was received from Mr. Clifford White, President of the Norquay Ski Club. (I excerpt from official government correspondence of that time.)

The Superintendent was under the impression that Mr. White was making application on behalf of

Newspaper ad for ski train.

the Norquay Ski Club. Instead, it was learned that Messrs. White and Paris intended to operate the Skoki Valley project themselves because the Norquay club was unable to assist in financing the scheme. As the Department did not wish to have two private citizens operating a project of this nature within the Park, their application was refused. The Parks Canada correspondence went on to say, "Later, however, Messrs. Paris and White assisted the club financially and application was made on behalf of the Mount Norquay Club to build a cabin at Skoki Valley." A license was issued to Mount Norquay Ski Club for a period of five years from the first day of August 1930. Further correspondence stated that Mr. White wanted a twenty-one year lease as protection for their expenditure. Then it goes on "…It now appears that the SKI CLUB OF THE CANADIAN ROCKIES, LTD., have entered into an agreement with Mr. and Mrs. Peter Whyte, whereby the latter have leased Skoki lodge from the Ski Club, to operate a high class ski camp."

Calgarians arriving on ski train. Prominent skiers John Southam centre, and Allan Carscallen, far right.

The Skoki area went on to have greater conflict with the Parks office in Banff and Ottawa. They extended their operation into summer, which wasn't covered by the license issued to them. The Skoki area situation really became a 'sticky wicket' when Sir Norman Watson from England entered the scene. But I'll let Rodney Touche, in his great book, *Brown Cows, Sacred Cows*, tell you that story, which led to the beginning of skiing at Lake Louise.

Around this time Mt. Norquay was also ready to improve the cabin and ski hill hoping the government would assist them in different ways, one being to complete a road to the area and then a new ski jump to attract the best jumpers and large crowds.

Norquay wasn't just a Banff story. Skiers from Canmore, Calgary, Edmonton and many small towns had started to enjoy a weekend in the mountains. In the late thirties the Edmonton versus Calgary feud took to the ski slopes of Mt. Norquay. Calgary won for many years until somebody in the Edmonton camp said, "We had better learn to turn these ...darn things." In time, Edmonton had their share of victories.

John D. Southam was a leader of Calgary skiers. John, a new Calgarian sent from the slopes of Ottawa to work at the Southam Company's *Calgary Herald*, saw two fellow Calgarians, Dudley E. Bachelor and Gordon B. Moodie, floundering on skis with a copy of Hannes Schneider's *Wonder of Skiing* in one hand, and a piece of cake in the other. (Some say that piece of cake actually had a label and a cap on it.) A bite, or whatever, would be taken from time to time, for relaxation. Anyway, through the organizing skills of John D. Southam that lost group got whipped into the very proud Calgary Ski Club. The second president of the C.S.C. was Allan Carscallen. He loved the mountain experience and came to the high country on many occasions. One such ski tour, the first ski attempt of Mt. Balfour, was with Victor Kutschera, photographer Lloyd Harmon and his friend Gordon Moodie. An account of this was in the *Canadian Alpine Journal* of 1935.

At this time in Banff jumping was a big attraction. Some of the world's finest jumpers had competed on the jump overlooking the buffalo paddock. In one of the final contests held on that jump, Nels Nelsen, of Revelstoke, who had held a world title not long before, was in town to help convince Parks that a new jump at Mt. Norquay was needed. It would be a great source of entertainment for visitors to Banff National Park. Ben Woodworth and a group of young men had already started to prepare an area for the jump. They had hoped the government would come through with enough money to make a structure large enough to support jumps of over 300 feet. There was a delay, but Ottawa finally came through with $500, which was enough to construct a jump allowing leaps of over 200 feet.

By 1935 the road was almost completed. It had taken five years and had been a slow job because during the Depression the government would only put crews to work when money was available. They were called relief crews, as in unemployment relief. Pay varied from $30 a month to $0.25 an hour. All work was done with pick and shovel. One story out of that project had the foreman, Rosie Powell, explaining to one of the workmen, "You wouldn't be so cold if you did more work." The alert answer came back, "I would rather go home cold than tired."

The number of races increased on Norquay after the completion of the road in 1935. Banff was quickly developing some of the finest racers in the Dominion. This was understandable because Norquay was by far the most challenging ski hill in the country. Skiers in other areas looked to Banff for the best skiing. The rest of the world was impressed too, but looking back at a day of racing on Norquay in 1935 with today's vision, the race was more amusing than competitive.

If Banff was developing some of our early stars on skis, the local *Crag & Canyon* was developing one of the first ski writers in W. E. Round, who had a feeling for the sport and humour in the reporting of it. The following is an account of races held on Saturday and Sunday, March 16 and 17, 1935:

"The senior open events were held Sunday afternoon, the first one being the downhill race for the Brewster Cup. The start of this race is up at the foot of the cliffs on Norquay, the course having an 1800 vertical feet drop to the finishing line. The competitors were started one minute apart so as to avoid the possibility of collision. It was a thrilling sight to see the competitors making wide sweeps across the face of the mountain so as to break their speed. Stan Ward was the first one sent away. Chess Edwards followed and next came Vic Kutschera. The latter from the start swept almost straight down the mountain side for several hundred yards and quickly overtook the lead of Chess Edwards, who had met with a tumble that took a little time to get himself straightened out. Vic took several tumbles in his course but he overtook Stan Ward on the trail that runs across the face of the mountain through the timber; Stan was down and Vic had to throw himself in order to avoid a collision. These two skiers took some time in extricating themselves, and the latter finally got away and came across the finishing line in the lead, his time being taken at 3:26,1/5 and it was the best time of the day."

The racers competing in that downhill of 1935 had to climb to the starting gate. The climbing time would vary, depending on snow conditions, but it was generally an hour and a half, after which the skiers had to wax their skies for the run down. It would be a few years before a small cabin with a stove was constructed. It would be another fourteen years before a chair lift was added.

Ted Paris followed Vic Kutschera in that early race, in a time only a few seconds more than Vic's approximately three and a half minutes. Then came Herb Paris, Rupe Edwards, Norman Knight, Stan Ward, Bud Kennedy, Chess Edwards, Lloyd Harmon, Austin Standish, W. J. Ross, Bob Bryant, and H. Snelson. They were all Banff skiers except Calgarian Ross. The time of the last racer was almost eleven minutes, three times that of the winner. There hadn't been too many previous downhill races, so naturally experience was hard to gain. To practice running a full downhill on Norquay was unheard of. The only experienced racer in Banff at that time was Vic Kutschera, and he had moved here from Austria.

The ladies were racing slalom for the Atkin Cup. Gladys Atkin won it in 1:44, which was 38 seconds ahead of M. Read, followed by K. Jennings, M. Crosby, A. Grant, J. Atkin, E. Browne and D. Wood.

On the same weekend, Bill Wellman was the first junior winner of the Paris Trophy. Second on that day was Lloyd Harmon followed by E. Madsen, R. Crosby, Stan Ward, J. Robertson, Jack Anderson, Bill Round, T. Greenhaigh and Robert 'Steam' Watt. Rob Crosby would go on to have three consecutive wins in this race, which entitled him to keep the main trophy for good. In the future Eddie Hunter would become a double winner of the Paris Trophy.

Another column by writer W. E. Round: "…prettiest sight of the day was Norm

Walter Ringer, German team, wins the MacFadden Trophy. (Norquay 1938)

Knight's junior ski team in action. These juniors, Frank and Bud Gourlay, Robbie Crosby, Don Lewthwaite, Gordon Hoggard, Gerald Locke, Arthur Andrews and Jack Hayes, are on their way towards going places, and going far. There's more than speed and skill in their work – there's rhythm and poetry."

The Canadian Amateur Ski Association (C.A.S.A.) did not recognize the western clubs for many years with good reason: the western clubs had not united in their efforts for recognition. Dave White, representing the Ski Runners, finally held a meeting with other divisions in Alberta and British Columbia, and shortly afterwards Nels Nelsen was appointed vice-president of the C.A.S.A. Several major events were then awarded to Banff and Mt. Norquay.

The Dominion Championship of 1937 raised the level of Canadian skiing to new heights as a spectacle, and was an inspiration to young skiers. A young Swiss team put on a wonderful display of competitive skiing and another Swiss, Walter Praeger, who was coaching at New Hampshire's Dartmouth College added to their exhibition. The best showing by a Canadian was by Louis Cochand, from the Laurentians. Pierre Francioli was the outstanding Swiss skier, winning the slalom and downhill. The outstanding jumper was Alf Engen, the American Champion from Utah. Not far behind was the Canadian Champion, Tom Mobraaten, from Princeton, B.C.

In 1938 the field would be just as strong. In fact the visiting German team would beat the downhill record of 1937. Francioli, the Swiss skier had had a time of 2:26.08 the previous year. Franz Machler, of the German team had a time of 2:14.00 in 1938. Sigfrid List, who had won the cross country race, had a good chance of winning the combined trophy until he decided to climb Cascade Mountain the morning of the slalom race. He had a successful climb, which was perhaps the first winter ascent of Cascade, but didn't make it back in time for the race!

At this time there was another surprise competitor in town. Peter Vadja, a Hungarian national who had been attending school in Switzerland and racing for that country, arrived along with the German team. He had been unable to make the trip in 1937 because of exams. Peter was a strong stylish skier who was to stay on and live the rest of his life in Canada.

Probably the best slalom racer to come off the Norquay slopes in the 1937 - 38 period was Rupe Edwards. He along with Norm Knight, Ted Paris and Victor Kutschera went to a major meet at Mt. Rainier, Washington State. A Seattle paper reported, "Rupert Edwards of Banff, Alberta, as brilliant a slalom racer as has ever been seen in Washington, today had the crown of Pacific Coast slalom-racing champion – and 2000 Washington skiers were today convinced he earned the title." Kutschera placed second. A Vancouver skier, Ken Hague, placed fourth. The other Banff skiers placed highly in either the downhill or slalom.

The skis of Dominion champion Gertie Wepsala, in 1939.

Recreational skis, 1999.

The Canadian skiers were doing well against the Americans, but that had not been the case against the Swiss team of 1937, or the German team of 1938. Western skiers were good natural athletes, however they had no coaches, and training for a race, well, that didn't exist. When you had to climb for each practice run, not many were possible. Mt. Norquay didn't have a rope tow until 1941.

Other problems were becoming obvious at this time. The mountain wasn't always safe. Because not many people skied the upper slopes, like the steep Bowl, the snow did not compact or stabilize. Vic Kutschera, who had had some snow training in Austria, submitted a report stating that certain snow crystals were present in the snow layer that would be unstable for skiers. Due to the danger of an avalanche, the hill was closed on January 18, 1938, the first action taken by authorities to close a slope on Norquay.

There was need for another service as well. Because of the injuries that were occurring, Drs. Atkin and Worthington had conducted classes for some of the Norquay staff to prepare them to treat minor ski accidents on the hill. Some Calgarians were doing the same, or taking St. John's Ambulance courses. An average Sunday on Norquay would see two to three hundred Calgarians skiing. A ski patrol was the next step.

The years between 1937 and 1940 had been extremely competitive ones at Mt. Norquay. During that time two Dominion Championships were held, plus other major races. The little cabin could hardly hold the crowds that were showing up on weekends. The operators were trying to make some money from the skiers and visitors, with the government not in accord. In the middle of this circus, the cabin burnt to the ground on a cold night in January of 1938. W. E. Round wrote in the *Crag & Canyon*: "Two scorched sentinel-like chimneys; a few smouldering logs; two ash-covered stoves; rows of neat tin-foil bundles – caskets for chocolate bar

Quite often these dinners would be held when George Encil returned after a successful hunting trip.

Victor Kutschera, Jack Anderson, Steam Watt, Bill Wellman and extreme right with paper hat, George Encil.

Veijo Tiesmaki, Jim Morrison, Margaret Morrison, Jim McLeod, Bud Gourlay and back to camera, Dick Pike.

corpses…fantastic glass relics in the snow…little heaps of ashes with toe-irons protruding…shapeless glass 'blobs', once candy jars…skeleton of the cook's knife bent like a corkscrew…charred frames of a few cameras…scorched ski wax cans dotting the ashes…fireplace and chimney leaning as if sorrowing…front door handle lying on the door step…ashes and cinders to the top of the Lone Pine slope." The Norquay cabin as seen on Monday morning January 30, 1938.

E. S. (Sid) Duncan, manager of the camp, said he had left the cabin at about five o'clock, with all fires well dampened. It was about nine o'clock when Bill Wellman, Archie Dick and Bill Stenton, coming out of a downtown hotel noticed the red glow off the Stoney Squaw skyline. They rushed to the area, but could only grab a few pairs of skis from an outside locker. Almost sixty years later a much larger Norquay lodge would burn down, and on the morning of December 8, 1995 I would think the ashes looked very similar, more plentiful, but pretty much the same.

The spirit and co-operation that had existed in 1928 when the Norquay cabin had been built appeared to go up in the smoke of the fire that destroyed the cabin nine years later. Looking at that period after sixty years, it is hard to get a reading on it. However, from the correspondence that was exchanged between the government people and a variety of others, either representing, or wanting to represent Mt. Norquay, the situation looked very unsettled.

It must be remembered that Banff had originally been conceived as a spa in the European tradition. Something had gone wrong if this was meant to be the government's plan for it. Certainly Sir Norman Watson was trying to adhere to this 'elite' option for the Lake Louise area. A letter written by Sir Norman on July 5, 1937 to The Hon. Mr. T. A. Crerar, Canadian Ministry of Mines and Resources, Ottawa, is quite demanding. In part he says, "It is necessary we have exclusive rights to the area, secondly we require a road up to the half-way cabin from Lake Louise." He goes on to add, "Should this scheme have your favourable consideration, which I most earnestly desire, I will carry the matter a stage further by again communicating with Sir Edward Beatty and Sir George McLaren Brown and possibly Sir Edward Peacock." In sharp contrast to all the 'Sirs' gathering their wealth together for the Skoki area, the people at Norquay were asking the government if they could charge 50 cents for daily admission to special ski events. The reply came back, "…Section 6 of the Lord's Day Act states it is not lawful for any person to engage in any public game or contest for gain or for any prize or reward. The same section also states it is illegal to impose an admission fee, either direct or indirect on the Sabbath." Eventually, Ralph Harvey, president of the Ski Runners of the Canadian Rockies, was given authority to charge for special ski events during the Winter Carnival and the Dominion Ski Championships of 1937.

And then in contradiction, a letter from Superintendent Jennings on February 11, 1938 stated, "At present no authority whatsoever has been issued from this office authorizing a charge to be made for those events. The department is looking into the matter for special skiing events, but under no conditions will charges be made on Sundays."

The original Banff Ski Club had dissolved into the Ski Runners of the Canadian Rockies. Then a new club called The Ski Club of the Canadian Rockies Limited, seemed to exist sponsored by The Norquay Ski Club, who were basically the same people. Shortly a new group would appear with a more business-like name, The Canadian Rockies Winter Sports Association, Inc. But it too carried names from the previous clubs.

On January 19, 1938, ten days before the Norquay cabin burnt down, this letter was written by P. J. Jennings, Superintendent of Banff National Park, to his superior F. Williamson, Controller of Parks: "Mr. E. S. Duncan called at my office today. He stated he had been charged $25 for the Norquay clubhouse license. He thought that was excessive, because they didn't operate in summer. He also said there should be some control in the parking lot. He then said he couldn't look after the ski accidents on the hill, but thought a first aid tent with a competent man should be installed on the hill. I told him the department had expended a large sum of money in the construction of the road, the parking lot and on the jump, as well as clearing slopes, and felt that it was now up to the clubs concerned to take care of the rest." Mr. Jennings closed the letter by saying he was going to have a phone connection nearby in case a doctor was needed, and would probably have an officer in the parking lot on weekends.

It would appear the local government office was being fair in its dealings with Norquay. But then the lodge burnt down and new problems would arise.

A letter on March 9, 1938 from Superintendent Jennings to his superior: "Messrs. C. White and A. Mather called on me yesterday and stated that they were delegated by their company (Ski Club of the Canadian Rockies, Ltd.) to discuss officially the situation with regard to undertaking further development of their leasehold property on Mt. Norquay. They didn't want to go ahead with plans for a new lodge until the following issues were satisfactorily resolved:

1. The management and control of the skiing slopes.
2. Authority to charge for the use of the grounds maintained by the club.
3. They could charge a membership fee, which would include the use of the

grounds and clubhouse.

4. Major competitions if organized by other societies, would have to have their consent.

"Mr. White added, 'We at present have company capital of $20 000 and about all shares have been subscribed, but if we get the go ahead on this, we could raise our capital to $50 000.' Mr. Mather pointed out that; '…their club is comprised of young men who were the pioneers in skiing around Banff.' He added they (The Ski Club of the Canadian Rockies) were responsible for the original clearing of Norquay. Also, it was their members and associates that developed Ptarmigan and Skoki lodges.

"During the discussion I pointed out to the gentlemen that the present arrangement was unsatisfactory; the public were not being cared for in the manner expected in a National Park. That any new lodge would have to be run in a much more efficient manner."

He added, "To summarize the content of this letter. It is obvious one or two actions should be taken in the interest of the Park.

(1) That we construct suitable accommodation and take over and operate the skiing area at Norquay, or

(2) Ask the present leasee company to operate the area and charge for the use of their leasehold. We must approve of the clubhouse.

"If we go with number one we would have to cancel the existing lease. But apparently they are not prepared to spend money on the care and maintenance of the skiing area for the general public, free

Norquay Cabin completed in late 1928.

of charge. There would therefore be no objection raised to cancellation, in fact it is expected that they will voluntarily give up their lease if existing conditions and terms are enforced."

It was obvious the government wasn't too eager to take over Norquay and build a new lodge. If the Ski Club of the Canadian Rockies thought they could make money, they would have to be thinking of a ski

Destroyed by fire January, 1938.

shop, dining room and rope tows. What else was there to an area in 1938?

Mr. J. O. Apps, General Executive Assistant of the CPR, wrote the next piece of correspondence that I found. It had been sent to the government to lend support to

Mr. White and the Ski Club of the Canadian Rockies. It told of White's previous accomplishments, and that he was associated with prominent men of substantial means in Canada, the United States and England who were fully impressed with the opportunities of the Skoki/ Red Deer areas and prepared to offer financial support to any well considered development plan. "I understand that Mr. White has drawn up plans for chalets, huts, ski tows and other features, but any further development is entirely dependant upon transportation from Lake Louise to the head of the Ptarmigan Valley. If the National Parks Department can be persuaded to construct a passable road to start with…" This was not the Norquay problem, but it dealt with the same people. This letter was obviously written to put pressure on the government by those with influence. Then this surprise letter of August 23, 1938 from Dave White, Jr., President of the Ski Club of the Canadian Rockies Ltd. "At a meeting of the Ski Club of the Canadian Rockies Ltd., we have unanimously decided that all rights to the areas on the easterly slope of Mt. Norquay, outlined in license dated the first day of April, 1935, be relinquished." It was apparent from that letter that the Ski Club of the Canadian Rockies was going to put all their efforts and money into the Skoki/Temple area, with the hopes they could get the government to build a private road into their area of development.

This must have been a set-back for Cliff White who had worked so hard to advance Canadian skiing in the Rockies, along with his friends Fulton Dunsmore, Cyril Paris, Tex Woods and other members of the White family. His talents had been in many domains, including early touring trips into the Columbia Icefields where he had pioneered the art of documentary ski cinematography. In 1936 during a talk to the local Rotary Club after returning from a trip to Europe where he had toured the leading ski areas with Sir Norman Watson, he mentioned that the rich were not

Peter Vadja and Betty Gentles. (1939)

Peter and Betty in 1999.

going to the elite hotels of Switzerland because of the war clouds that were gathering over Europe. However the less expensive hotels were still busy. He also mentioned the narrow gauge railway at Davos that took skiers to the 9000-foot level for a run down of 3000 vertical feet. It would be another fifteen years before Norquay had anything coming close to that facility.

Meanwhile new people from Banff and Calgary were talking with Parks officials and making plans for a new Norquay lodge, which this time were successfully carried out. This company was known as the Canadian Rockies Winter Sports Association, Inc. The Banff members were Dave White Jr., Jim Morrison and L. S. Crosby. From Calgary were a Mr. Dailey, Manager of the T. Eaton Company, J. Cross, President of the Calgary Brewing Company and a Mr. Dawson, District Passenger Agent of the CPR. The company that they formed was to have capital of $10 000 divided into 1000 shares of $10 each. Of these, 600 were offered to the public and 400 held as Treasury stock. This was all happening in the autumn of 1939, just as Canada was going to war in Europe.

On January 20, 1940 to the ballroom music of Jim Hutchins and his Cascade band, the new Norquay lodge welcomed skiers and its new owners just in time for the Dominion Championships that were once again to be held in Banff. This lodge still stands today, at the foot of the North American chairlift.

An excellent programme was published for the Dominions of 1940. Lloyd Harmon who was obviously developing a keen photographic eye, similar, but with more action involved than his famous father, Byron Harmon, took most of the photographs. In that same programme, Don Lewthwaite, a top junior skier, wrote an article on the formation of their junior team and the coaching provided by Norman Knight. It was the first concentrated training given to young Banff skiers. Don said, "It was amazing how much we improved. When the race season started it seemed like we on the team took turns in winning." Rob Crosby, Bud and Frank Gourlay, Art Andrews, Jack Hayes, Gerald Locke, Gordie Hoggard and Don Lewthwaite were on that team. If it hadn't been for the war, these boys would have been Canada's top skiers. Instead, they all went to war. Gordie Hoggard and Don Lewthwaite didn't return.

The Dominion Championships of 1940 did not have the international competitors the 1937 and 1938 races had had. However the new lodge made the event much more pleasant for racers, officials and the public, especially on Sunday March 3, when over four thousand people came to watch the jumping.

The new lodge had been built by the Canadian Rockies Winter Sports Association, Inc. They were more business people than skiers. President at the time was L. S. Crosby of Banff. Directors were Calgarians J. B. Cross, W. Dailey and J. W. Dawson as well as Dave White of Banff. Margaret and Jim Morrison were managing the lodge and dining area. Betty Gentles, a Vancouver girl who worked for the Morrisons the following year, said they were wonderful, generous people. She recalls the morning ride to Norquay in the back of Jim's truck. It was hard to get any colder and still survive.

Ted Paris of Banff won the Downhill at those 1940 Dominion Championships. Art Coles of Vancouver won the Combined, and Gertie Wepsala, Vancouver, won the Slalom. Dorothy Michaels of Montreal won the Ladies' Combined. Eleanor Boyle, Lake Louise, won the Junior Ladies' Slalom and the Downhill. Bud Gourlay, Banff, was first in the Junior Boys Slalom and Downhill.

There were many young skiers from Banff who competed in the races, but because of the lack of tows before 1941, they didn't progress very rapidly. Veijo and Hannu Tiesmaki were two brothers who had arrived in Canada in 1933 from Finland at the ages of 18 and 16 years respectively. They had lived there in a skiing area, but didn't learn to ski until they came here. They learned some of their skiing the hard way, carrying heavy packs of supplies into the high country of Assiniboine and Skoki. They improved enough to compete in the Dominions of 1940 with a great feeling of accomplishment.

The ski train special from Calgary to the Dominions in Banff cost $2.10 return. There were also special trains from Vancouver. Travelling to Banff at a much slower speed was Don McCrea who skied 500 miles on a route from Revelstoke, over the Big Bend highway (closed in winter) and up to Jasper where he joined his brother Bill McCrea and Jim McDonald. The three of them then skied down to Banff stopping enroute to climb Snow Dome at the Columbia Icefields. It had been a light snow year and much of the trip from Jasper to the Icefields was made walking.

Other happenings around Norquay:

Bud Gourlay makes a 'Schuss Cycle' from a bicycle frame and two half skis. It

Who can forget the speedy Memorial rope tow!

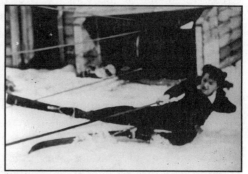

It always took your gloves to the top but not you.

Good old Jerk and Twist.

had no brakes and the report was Bud didn't teach it to snowplow. It was a wild ride, apparently very much like Bud's skiing style.

Peter Vadja, Hungarian by birth, who had arrived in Banff in 1938 along with the German team, had won several races in the period leading up to the 1940 Dominions and was expected to be one of the top runners. Just a few days before the races were to start Peter was skiing the old trail from Norquay to town. It crossed the road in several places. At one of those crossings that came upon the road suddenly, he hit a bus going down the road. It was a serious injury as he fractured a femur, thereby missing his chance for a Canadian title. (An interview with him in February 1999 at his home in Sidney, B. C., is found elsewhere in this book.)

Charlie Biel, Banff's famous cowboy artist made two new trophies for the 1940 Dominion Championships. J. B. Cross and J. I. (Jim) Brewster sponsored them.

Artist's early concept of little skiers.

Pint sized boardercross 1999.

That winter the Calgary Ski Club held their races at Norquay. Harry Armstrong was the winner followed by Ken Thompson and Harry's Brother, Bill Armstrong.

A problem was discovered at the mountain at about this time. On weekends when there were so many skiing, descending and ascending skiers failed to stay in the proper up and down lanes, resulting in a lot of them meeting up with people they didn't want to meet!

It was also about this time that the last senior races were held as during the war years there were only races for juniors. (A senior race at that time didn't mean for those of advanced years, as it does today.) In one of those last races Ted Paris won the Slalom and Bill Wellman won the Downhill. A young Rob Crosby defeated Art Coles in a slalom held at Jasper following the 1940 Dominions where Coles had won the Combined.

The war of 1939 - 45 changed skiing on Norquay: in competition, the races would be mainly high school meets. As the war progressed, Australians and New Zealanders came to sunny Alberta for air training. The sport of skiing was new to most of them. When they tried skiing on the slopes of Norquay their air training seemed timid by comparison. Turning, or banking, just didn't happen for quite awhile. It looked as if they might be encouraging injury to lengthen their leave! They did enjoy the Rockies and were well received in the Banff area.

The war effort needed healthy well co-ordinated young men, just the types that were skiing on Banff's junior team. For awhile the war had certain glamour as young men decided in which uniform they would look the best to become a hero. Hollywood had already exploited the scene. The hero survives, returning home to his loved ones as the theme music with one hundred strings reaches an everlasting crescendo. That same movie may have involved a death somewhere along the way, but it was all a mistake, a small mistake that would never happen again.

It was pretty much like the only death that had occurred at Norquay up until that time. Shortly after the jump had been completed in 1935, a young Sandy Thompson was ready to join the ranks of Banff's fine jumpers. Eager to experience the thrill of the new jump he misjudged his landing, or perhaps it was a sudden cross-wind that blew him off balance, or it might have happened the way Jimmy Deegan saw it several years later when he wrote the poem, "Tragedy of Sandy":

The binding parted on the take-off,
Vaulting Sandy through the air,
Like a wounded bird he toppled,
To a savage landing there.
We rushed on to the out-run,
Saw Sandy crushed upon the snows.
Spine fractured, he lay unconscious.
The lamenting chinook wind blows.

(This is part of the poem by J. Deegan, from *Timberline Tales*.)

Following the accident and until his death two years later, the route of all parades would make their way in front of the Thompson house so that Sandy could see them.

Lives were now to be lost in World War II. At the end of the war there was a memorial giant slalom trophy put up for competition with the names of the fifteen members of the Ski Runners who had lost their lives: Don Lewthwaite, George Oxborough, Hannu 'Joe' Tiesmaki, George Walls, Jack Wilson, Bud Williams, Jim Watt, John Bird, Doug Calder, Eric Chisholm, Rupe Edwards, Jim Erickson, Hans Gunnersen, Gordie Hoggard and Malcolm Calder.

Following the war Norquay was still the most popular ski area in the Rockies.

Climbing in the year 2000 (Magic Carpet).

Sunshine, operated by the Brewster family, had gained skiers following the completion of a private road to the area in 1941. Skoki never did get the road they had wanted. Temple did; however it would be another ten years before the Temple/Whitehorn area would make moves to become a major ski area.

George Eisenschiml, later to be changed to George Encil, came to Canada before the war from Austria/Czechoslovakia. He had been brought up in a family that had made great wealth making fabric gloves, even doing business in Canada with Eaton's and Morgan's stores, but he didn't like the business. Because the Jewish people were being prosecuted at the time, his escape route with the family wealth was rather vague, but apparently international intrigue at its best, just one step ahead of Hitler's Gestapo. Encil had been told he could get his money out to North America, but in the end escaped with only $50 000, and with that had to bring a sister and mother to Canada. His mother, who had been a concert pianist, and also an amateur botanist, lived for many years in Banff and is buried here. Most of his life would be spent collecting art, studying the ski business and the techniques of some of the early ski instructors that introduced the Hannes Schneider method of his fellow Austrian. After Encil arrived in Canada he spent several years in the Canadian Air Force. Many of his fellow cadets called

Herring-bone steps and earning turns in the 1930s.

him Eisenhower because they couldn't remember Eisenschiml. That encouraged him to later shorten his name. In time he purchased the Norquay lodge shares held by Banff and Calgary people, after which he built the chairlift that opened in December of 1948. The community sentiment for Norquay took a bit of a jolt because of this sale, but not enough to take away the family feeling that Banff had for the area, and one that was still growing in Calgary and Edmonton.

For the next fifty years, Norquay was to be controlled by six major groups, along with the Parks system of Canada. From 1947 to 1960 the operator was George Encil. Walter Fisher took over in 1960 until 1968 when he sold to Bill Herron. In 1978, the Sulphur Mountain Gondola organization took over and managed Norquay until Brewster Transportation joined them in 1990. The most recent sale took place in June 1995 at which time Kika Grandi and Peter White became the owners.

Peter Van Wagner, Norquay instructor 1953.

Chapter TWO

White Snow and the
Seven Owners

First owner George Encil 1946.

Second owners Eva and Walter Fisher 1960.

Third owner Bill Herron 1968.

Arthur Haenni (Sulphur Mtn. Gondola) 1978.

Dave Morrison (Brewster Transport) joined Haenni in 1989.

Mary and Peter White 1995.

Thomas and Kika Grandi 1995.

Once I started to explore the history of Norquay there was no way I could stop. I kept meeting people who had had some touch with the mountain in the past, and they in most cases would lead to someone else with whom they had shared those experiences, which was exactly what I wanted. I was, however, finding that one day remembered by one person was completely different from the way another person recalled it. I wondered where I could go to find out what really had happened. The thought occurred, if I could get all the past owners of Norquay together for one meeting, surely the truth would come out.

It actually happened in early April 1999. In fact it was the first day of April when some trickery is to be expected. The weather was a little unusual that morning. It was a beautiful spring day with small clouds appearing one minute, and then disappearing, almost like little puffs of snow that are made when the upper slopes are bombed for snow stabilization. The Norquay staff was busy getting their day underway. It was about a week before season closing. I got the idea many of them were thinking about the wind-up party.

There has always been a mystique about Norquay. It could have started with the native spirits of centuries ago, and then been reinforced in the sixties when grooming crews on more than one occasion witnessed strange lights from the invisible forces of other worlds. This April morning came with other images. I was sitting in Norquay's new Cascade Lodge, in Kika's Lounge, which wasn't open, and was the only person there when all of a sudden one of those exploding clouds appeared outside the lodge's big windows. From it came figures, moving quickly as if they had been rehearsed. First came a man carrying very long skis. He was smiling and obviously very happy to be here, then he disappeared. My thought was of Gus Johnson, the first man to pick Norquay as a ski hill. Then came two men with very large Banff Ski Club crests on the front of their sweaters. I recognized them as being Cliff White and Cyril Paris. They were chatting away, but they didn't disappear. They sat down in front of me and continued to talk. I was wondering if I should say something when George Encil sat down next to them. He had a big leather brief case from which he pulled a mound of papers. Then came in order the rest of the people who had leased this small valley between Mt. Norquay and Stoney Squaw: Walter Fisher, Bill Herron, Art Haenni, Dave Morrison and the present owners, Kika Grandi and Peter White. They all sat in a circle with me in the twelve o'clock position. A man whom I felt must represent the government took the ten o'clock position. The eleven o'clock seat was empty.

I was still trying to decide if I should say something, or if I would just be talking to myself when Cyril Paris looked straight at me and I thought he said, "Hello Eddie." Before I could respond, he said, "I have come up to Norquay today to see if I can find a location for a kid's jump." I wanted to say, "Cyril, you did that about sixty years ago. It was a beautiful little jump. Some of the kids you built it for still talk about the happy times they spent on it." But then Cliff White spoke up, "I skied with Cyril today as I wanted to check out the kitchen in our new cabin. I was thinking of having Austin Standish and Cyril's brother, Herb Paris, manage it for the rest of the winter. I understand the Calgary Ski Club will be starting a ski train to Banff, which should increase the numbers coming to Norquay." Cyril added, "Cliff and myself are going in from Lake Louise next week to tour the Ptarmigan Valley. It would be nice to have a cabin up there and we already have a name for it. How does Skoki sound?"

Then they all started to talk to one another and all of a sudden George Encil jumped to his feet. It would have been a short jump! George had changed his name from Eisenschiml to Encil and apparently had held a party to announce the change saying, "You take the 'p' out of pencil and you get my name, Encil." George had arrived in Canada in the late thirties and because of his Austrian/Czechoslovakian background had a heavy accent when speaking English, especially noticeable when he replaced the 'th' with a 'z'. He had several friends, but just as many people who didn't understand him. As George stood up it was obvious he was addressing everyone that surrounded him. He was excited, which accentuated his accent and distracted from the message he wanted to give. In general he was saying how much the owners should thank him for really getting Norquay going. "Everyone was just standing around afraid to take a chance when I came in and built the chairlift. Then in 1950 I brought the first North American Ski Championship to Banff with all the leading European skiers. With great vision I purchased the Sunshine ski area in 1952 to turn it into the 'Sun Valley' resort of Canada. I thought the government encouraged me, and then what did they do in 1959?" He got very excited and pulled some papers from a heavy leather case he had brought with him.

Then the person sitting in the government chair spoke up. "I would like to refresh your memory, Mr. Encil. The Minister of Mines and Resources, The Honourable J. A. McKinnon, came to Banff to officially open your new chairlift, at which time he thanked you on behalf of the department for what you have done in this first great national park in Canada." Encil acted as if he didn't hear him. He continued on saying, "Look at all the jobs I gave, there is Ted MacAulay my manager, Red Crozier, Louie Louis and in the summer the Banff boys have jobs putting banners on the bumpers of cars advertising the summer ride on the lift. When I built the lift I had Pete Jacobs, an engineer I met while in the Canadian Air Force, come and do the job. I also made three ski movies here in the Rockies, *Ski Pro's Holiday*, *Rhythm on Snow* and *Mount Bulyea*. One of the skiers, Jim McConkey who had fallen into a crevasse while filming on the Columbia Icefields and broken a collarbone, later came to work for me in Banff. I wanted him to be my manager in summer and winter. He was an excellent skier and golfer, and was a great promoter for Norquay. I employed Ray Wardell as my construction and maintenance superintendent. He was an excellent engineer and it was his decision to build my upper terminal Tea Room to withstand a severe avalanche even though others thought it foolish to spend extra money to guard against an avalanche threat that didn't exist. People in town said, 'How foolhardy it was, after all the building is built on a ridge.' But only four years later a huge cornice did break off the summit. The amount of snow was far too heavy to stay in the regular avalanche path and it shot down the ridge hitting the Tea Room right where Wardell had predicted a possible avalanche could hit. Veijo Tiesmaki discovered the mess going to work at the top of the lift on the morning of March 26, 1956. It had happened somewhere between 6:00 p.m. and 9:00 a.m. and the damage was nothing compared to what might have happened if the Tea Room had not protected the upper terminal."

All of a sudden the owners broke into applause. It took Encil by surprise. The

Stan Peyto (Mr. Mountain).

Parents help out. Left to right, Jack Wilson, Ev
Crosby, Elden Walls in Hudson Bay coat.

government 'seat' spoke. "My name is B. I. M. Strong and I was Superintendent at the time. I remember that very well. I also sent a letter to Ray Wardell thanking him for the excellent report he sent to my office following the avalanche. It was gratifying to see the terminal had withstood such a test." George seemed a little flustered with the response he was getting. It had been his plan to impress the other owners, and for the moment he was doing just that.

Then a deep voice from the eleven o'clock chair was heard. "Excuse me, I don't mean to intrude, I do agree with you Mr. Encil that the North American race you brought to Banff in 1950 was an impressive event. However, I wanted to say something about a race that started a year before you even built the lift. My name is Bob Freeze. The competition I am talking about is the Intercollegiate Ski Meet that started in 1947 and ran for twenty-five years. I was at university in Edmonton when I discussed with my friends Norm Rault and Maury Van Vliet, what they thought of an international inter-varsity ski meet. The University of Alberta backed it and for a quarter of a century it became the major college four-way ski competition in North America. During those years we had up to sixteen schools competing in a single year. It usually took place in late January and early February on the slopes of Mt. Norquay. The cross-country event was held down in the valley. The ski jump was still the original, but it was an excellent test for the Scandinavian jumpers who were exchange students, many of them Olympic team members. I remember the first downhill, which took an hour to climb. I was the second to start. In front of me was a student from Montana State by the name of Jack Davis, whom I will never forget. He had apparently put on slow wax and his jacket was open, but he schussed the whole course falling briefly on the cliff and still won the race. I also remember that Jerry Monod had set the slalom course. Stan Peyto always played a major part in staging the event and was at our twenty-fifth reunion." As he sat down, and at the same time faded away, the owners all said, "Thank you."

George Encil was still standing when Bob Freeze had finished. Before he could continue on with his Norquay years, Bob Dawson was standing where Freeze had been only seconds before. "Hi! My name is Bob, and I just wanted to add that you didn't do all the work, George, when it came to putting on the North American event. I had worked for you as a welder when we built the lift. I also acted as a ski patroller in the year before the government put Frank Gourlay, and I believe Bill Round, in that position. In the summer of 1949 I stayed on the mountain in a tent with Jimmy Deegan and we worked with the crew that was cutting the new North American downhill." Then he disappeared.

Fred Wonnacott (Mr. Cigar,) a great friend of parents and racers with an appropriate thermos for each.

Glen Tooke, always willing to help with races. (Roland Fuhrmann in the gate.)

George Encil looked at everyone as if seeing them for the first time. He relaxed enough to realize he didn't impress the other owners the way he had wanted. He went on to say, "In answer to Bob Freeze who just spoke, yes, the Intercollegiate Ski Meet was a wonderful event and it ran long after I left Norquay. I also realize there were many people to help me with the North Americans in 1950. I know of the work you did, young Dawson, on the lift and cutting trails. You acted as a patrolman along with other duties before an organized patrol was formed. You see, I remember. In the planning of the North American downhill, for the actual run itself, I can thank Harvey Clifford and his instructors, Ted Hunter and Rick Hamburg. After Clifford I brought Franz Gabl from my hometown of St. Anton, Austria, to Norquay. He had won a silver medal in the Olympic downhill of 1948. It was an amazing comeback for him after having to spend many horrible years on the Russian front during the war. Franz stayed in Banff and Norquay for about three years. He has told friends that it was the highlight of his life. He has since become a very good writer chronicling the war years, and the period up until his Olympic race. Gabl is now writing of his life in Canada and the United States.

"Also at the time of the North American race in 1950, John Southam, publisher of the *Calgary Herald,* helped me raise money to bring the European racers up from Colorado where they had been competing in the World Championship. Senator Cameron at the Banff Centre was a big help as he gave lodging to the skiers. I would also like to mention that it wasn't just a European show. Canadian Sandra Tomlinson was 3rd in the Ladies' Downhill, only 8/10 of a second behind the winner, Janette Burr of the U.S. Erika Mahringer of Austria was 2nd, 4/10 of a second behind Burr. A Banff girl, Lois Woodworth was 9th, a very good showing. Gordie Morrison of Banff was 15th in the Slalom. In a field of 48 starters, Andy Tommy of Ottawa placed 15th in the Men's Downhill. The big winner that year was Zeno Colo of Italy. He won the Downhill in 2 minutes 3.3 seconds over Austrian's Egon Schopf and Christian Pravda. He also won the Slalom, defeating Swiss star George Schneider. The Ladies' Slalom was won by Dagmar Romm of Austria."

At this point I decided to say, "Excuse me, George. I don't know how you and all the owners came together, but I think it's great as I am doing research on the history of Mt. Norquay. But I don't want to see this turn into a trial where anyone is criticized for what they have done on this mountain." And then from the government chair, "I agree. My name is J. Smart. I was Controller for the National Parks Bureau, Ottawa, in 1947. Mr. Encil, you operated Norquay at very trying times. I have correspondence here that indicates that to be true. We in government for awhile had trouble trying to decide who was in charge at Norquay. The lodge concession and the rope tow installed in 1941 were operated by the Canadian Rockies Winter Sports Limited, however the actual managers of the lodge seemed to change quite often. And frankly it wasn't operated to our satisfaction. I even had an assistant controller who suggested we not renew the concession. The total profit we received for the year 1947/48 was $60.33. That was the year before you put in the chairlift. In early 1947 I had received a letter from the company secretary, Mr. Eric Harvey, giving a similar report. He said that their company was subscribed by private citizens and organizations whose primary, if not sole object was to encourage skiing in the Banff and Calgary area. They had shown very little profit, something like $1200 in six years of operation, and no shareholder had received dividends. At one point it appeared as though they would develop Norquay, then they changed their minds and sold their shares to you. We had some problems with each other, that was natural, but I felt we worked them out to a mutual understanding here at Norquay, and later when you took over Sunshine. You did an excellent job on the upper Tea House, and we worked together in building the restrooms and developing the water supply for Norquay. It must have been quite a shock to find out how we operated in the Park, but I feel you had the pleasure of bringing in some of your friends, like Hannes Schneider, whom you deeply admired, then Franz Gabl, and finally Mr. and Mrs. Walter Fisher who operated Sunshine, and then bought Norquay from you in 1960. You must have many good memories."

"Thank you, Mr. Smart. Yes, I do. I met many people who helped me including Mr. J. A. Hutchinson of your office. Mr. Eric Harvey became a friend and he actually made me a member of his club in Calgary. I think it was a Scottish club. I enjoyed help from Jack Douglas at the Bank of Commerce in Banff and took the bankers up to Norquay to show them what we were doing. They weren't very comfortable and felt shaky on a very steep slope. If I had asked them for any amount of money at that point, they would have said, 'yes.'"

As I sat listening to the owners and the government people, I found some of it interesting, but I was hoping more skiers would appear to talk about the families that automatically went to Norquay every weekend. That was how the strong feelings for the mountain started. It was Stan and Inez Peyto, the Beckers, Morrisons, Tookes, Woodworths, Whites, Hendersons, Kellys, Monods, etc., Banff families that would soon be joined by families from Calgary and Edmonton, plus all points in between. They didn't all come here to enter a race. They would all ski, but it was also a time to be with friends in conversation, or in the warm spring sun. The young ones would be brought to the mountain and released by their parents, similar to a bird pushing her young from a high nest, giving her baby a brief second or two to learn to fly. It wasn't that extreme, but it was that natural. I have been told by many of you, that your folks would leave you knowing that there was always someone from town to look out for you. There were Calgary families that would stay overnight in small campers in the parking lots. All these activities grew with Norquay. It wasn't a big mountain that dominated you. People felt comfortable there and still do.

I couldn't help but think of Jim Reeves. In the time period of which George Encil was talking, Jim would have been out running one of the rope tows. They were made basically from old car parts, the parts that still worked, that is, but never too well. He mentioned a favourite of his, an old Buick motor that leaked too much to hold anti-freeze. On cold mornings he would start the motor and get it pretty warm before he put the water in the radiator. If he put it in too soon it would freeze right up, but you had to get it in before it got too hot. He said, "God, that thing would hammer away, then it would mellow out and run just fine until I attacked it again the next day." Tickets sold four rides for $0.25 or twenty for $1. Jim added, "But for my friends I would just punch where there was already a hole. Sally Becker got so embarrassed because of the big hole in her ticket, she finally threw it away!"

Frank Gourlay, first official member of the Government Ski Patrol in the late 1940s.

Bill Smythe worked on the tows at about that time. Apparently he did the best imitation of George Encil, but done in a friendly manner without malice. Next to the

Norquay Ski Patrol 1954/55. Left to right, John Wackerle, Jimmy Innes, Jerry Johnston, and Ken Baker.

Peter Cooper, Rev. Hollywood, Toni Sailer and kids, 1961.

tow you would have seen this sign. "Any person using this rope tow shall do so at their own risk and agree that the Banff Chairlift Corporation Limited and/or its employees shall not be liable for any loss or damage suffered thereby by reason of the Banff Chairlift Corporation or its employees' negligence or otherwise." The key words were "at their own risk."

Just after the war Dick Pike had received a license to build a rope tow at Norquay. This confused the Norquay operation at a time when direction was needed. He operated it for a while and then sold it to the lodge operators at that time, Canadian Rockies Winter Sports Ltd. Shortly after that things were reorganized and George Eisenschiml became President and Ted MacAulay Secretary-Treasurer.

While George Encil stood talking to present and past owners of Norquay, his eyes made contact with Walter Fisher and Mrs. Fisher, who sat behind her husband. Finally George said, "I would like to introduce Mr. Fisher."

Fisher stood up slowly and spoke even more slowly. "I came to Canada in 1952. I had gone to school with George Encil when we were very young. Then the wars came." Behind him his wife spoke up. "Everything was taken from us when the Communists moved in." Walter continued, "I had designed a new bicycle. A photo had been taken of me and the bike, which ran in a German newspaper, but had also been printed in the Calgary paper. George saw it by accident when he was lighting the fireplace at Sunshine and somehow managed to get in touch with me. I had already planned on coming to Canada with my family as I had been offered a job in a spinning mill in Quebec. My family had been in textiles before we lost everything. But George said, 'Don't go there, come west, I have a job for you.' So Eva and my five-year-old son, Marcel, came to Banff. I managed Sunshine Village and Mt. Norquay for George until I purchased Norquay in 1960, after Mr. Encil had sold Sunshine to Cliff White Jr.

"I managed Norquay when Ray Wardell did all the work on the upper Tea Room. I was there when George and the government people were deciding who was going to build the washrooms and if there would be enough water. We had similar problems at Sunshine." Mrs. Fisher added, "It was awful, he would go down one road and up the other." Walter continued, "Mark Crozier and Louie Louis worked for me on the lifts. They were a wild pair, but still very dependable. Howard Srigley had done some hill grooming at Norquay when he was still working for the government, and then he worked full-time for me. We got better equipment, and it was amazing how Howard could take that machinery so high on the mountain. I was there when the government brought in the German jump designer, Heine Klopher, to plan a new jump in 1955 which was hopefully to be used when Banff got the Olympic Games. The judge's stands were added in 1959. Later, in the sixties, Doug Robinson came to work for me. He was so good at modifying my lifts. He changed the lift to handle gondolas in the summer and back to a double chair lift for the winter. I had already replaced the single chair built in George's time with a double chair. That cut down the line-ups for the big chair. I tried to make it easier for people to go to church and still ski on Sunday by having the Reverend George Hollywood come from Banff to conduct a service in the upper Tea Room.

"It was very hard to make money at Norquay in the winter. During the week there would be very few skiers: some days when it was cold there would only be one or two, and the ski school wouldn't give a lesson for a whole month. Then on weekends it was so busy people couldn't get into the lodge. When we had special jumping events Norquay had up to 7000 people in a day. Buses were still arriving while people were lining up to go back down. Many skiers would bring their lunches, and those who didn't ski would sit in the lodge looking out the window for hours over a cup of coffee. A lift ticket at the time for Calgary and Banff club members was only $4, for the chair and rope tows. That was also the year, 1959, when the Sulphur Mountain gondola and the sedan lift at Lake Louise opened for the summer. That winter Lake Louise opened a poma-lift, and that was the beginning of Whitehorn and Temple areas. Lake Louise was charging $5 for the gondola and poma-lift, and a dollar more for non-members.

"Jerry Johnston had been in charge of the ski school at Norquay, but he went to work for Cliff White at Sunshine, and Heinz Vifian came to work for me in 1961. He headed the school and joined Norm Russell who operated the ski shop. I believe Heinz stayed at Norquay for 13 years. It was he who started kid's programs and Ladies' Day. I changed the chair to a double chair in 1961, and built poma-lifts in 1962 and 1963, and then a T-Bar on the Wishbone slope in 1964, but it was so hard to get money to do these things."

Mrs. Fisher leaned forward, "It was because the government had different leases for each lift and you never knew if they were going to be renewed. They said, 'you don't have to worry,' but they never put it in writing and the banks didn't understand."

Walter came back, "I went to the Industrial Development Bank (IDB) in Calgary for help. I had also wanted to put up a gondola on Sulphur Mountain back in 1959 but things got very political when Claude Brewster and a Swiss company started selling shares to Banff people, and of course they got the contract. Later they wanted to buy me out for $40 000, but I refused. That was close to the time I purchased Norquay from Mr. Encil; $40 000 was about the value of the lifts for iron scrap.

"We also worked very hard to bring the Olympics to Banff. My wife even went over with some of the officials to present Banff to the International Olympic people. It looked like Banff would be awarded the Games for 1972, however negative letters from around the world, including Canada, kept mentioning that Banff was in a National Park. Canada's bid was defeated. The Games went to Sapporo, Japan, which just happened, like Banff, to be in a national park.

"Some people criticized me for frosting the windows so they couldn't sit for a long time with just a coffee and look out at the hill. They didn't like it either when I sent them downstairs to the basement to eat lunches they had brought with them. I don't know what else I could have done; it seemed almost impossible to break even operating the day lodge."

Some new voices:

Canada's '68 Olympic Site

IN 1955 A GROUP known as the Calgary Olympic Development Association was formed to raise funds and develop Canadian skiers of Olympic caliber. By 1957 CODA was thinking about bringing the Olympic Games to Canada. In 1959 they submitted a bid to host the 1964 Olympic Winter Games at Banff, Alta.
CODA officials did not expect the International Olympic Committee to give their bid serious consideration. They regarded it as a necessary forerunner for their more serious

CODA: Calgary Olympic Development Association, 1968.

"Excuse me! My name is MJ. I am Norm Russell's wife. We operated the ski shop at Norquay during the 50s and up until the time Mr. Fisher sold it to Mr. Herron in 1968. We also operated the ski school with Heinz Vifian. I just wanted to say we have no regrets, in fact those Norquay days for us still live on. We started ski programs for children back in the mid 1960s working with Malcolm and Sheila Cullen, who did so much to teach skiing to children. We still arrive each week with our Weekend Warriors from Calgary. We generally have three buses and about twenty-eight cars. I would just like to thank the Mt. Norquay Ski School and in particular Maureen Lefaivre, who I think is a real crackerjack when it comes to organizing our young skiers."

"I too have some information pertaining to the operation of Norquay at this time. My name is Harry Dempster. I was Superintendent of the Park during the period about which Mr. Fisher is speaking. At the time you were trying to control people who brought their lunch to Norquay, the Calgary Ski Club held a survey of their members. I have the results of that poll and a comment from the club president who said, 'I think you will agree that there is no possible doubt from the results of these questionnaires about the inadequacies of the present facilities. Also that if a public lunchroom were provided it would certainly be appreciated and used.' It was signed by Jay Joffe. I would also like to say, Mr. Fisher, that it was difficult to understand your attitude when in 1958 you threat-

Banff and Calgary interests worked hard to bring the Olympics to Banff. The final try and defeat was announced in 1966. The winner in 1972, Japan.

ened to keep Sunshine closed until March if we didn't plow the road for you. In the same year you released false information to a Calgary newspaper regarding development at Norquay in the Forty Mile Creek area, which was a watershed area for the town. We had a telephone conversation just prior to this release, and you said nothing about it, so I can only assume you did it to raise a controversy, for whatever reason." Dempster sat down in Seat No.10, just as MJ faded from Seat No. 11. Fisher had one final word. "You can call it controversy, but the government was the one that went back on it's word when you gave the lease to the Swiss people after indicating to Mr. Encil that he would face no new opposition. The gondola on Sulphur Mountain killed Norquay's summer trade."

Then, out of Seat No.11, the seat next to where I was sitting, "I don't believe this conversation is reflecting the good times I remember of the late 1950s and 60s. My name is Bob Meggs, and I remember Norquay at that time as being a marvellous place. I realize you owners wouldn't have the same view as the people who skied the mountain, and those of us who worked at Norquay jobs we enjoyed. I worked on the patrol when it was still managed by Parks. John Wackerle was my boss. John insisted on patrol members that were well trained and in good shape to carry out their duties, whether it be bringing in a casualty, or tramping the length of the mountain, which was the way we groomed the mountain before Howard Srigley and the Tucker Snowcat showed up.

"In the winter of 1953/54 Jack Pugh came to head the patrol. He had some good ideas and was responsible for adding a braking system to the toboggan, so that a single patrolman with a casualty could control the descent. Fritz Frey was before Jack, and the first woman on the patrol was Mary June Miles; other patrol people like Frank Gourlay, Bob Dawson, Bill Round, Jimmy Innes, Marcel Ferraris, Jimmy Masterson were folks who loved being on the mountain. I know other people working for the government in town thought we were a bunch of characters who only wanted to ski, but we were serious about our jobs, and held in high esteem by other Norquay employees and naturally, the skiing public.

"I do remember that just to satisfy the people in town including Mr. Encil, Mr. Fisher and the people at the Parks Administration building, we would start our day tramping the slopes which were visible from town, so that they would see we were working and not just enjoying a run in the powder.

"Harry Dempster was the most enthusiastic Superintendent as far as skiing went. We noticed that after a fresh snowfall he always arrived on the mountain for an inspection. Harry enjoyed a powder run as much as anyone. What I mean to say here is that all these people did a great job and enjoyed sharing these days with one another. Unlike you owners, we didn't have to get involved in the politics. Our days ended talking over a cup of coffee, or we repaired to the local pub for a brew. If I haven't thanked you in the past, I will now. Thank you!"

Bob Meggs was about to sit down when he changed his mind, possibly because he appeared to have the attention of the owners. "It wasn't just myself and the patrol people who thought that way. After Jerry Johnston and George Capel had the ski school, Heinz Vifian took over for the next thirteen years. Heinz was also a neat and very organized person. I'm not sure if it was by choice, or if these people just happened along, but they were the wildest, most talented group of skiers you could find on any mountain. Before extreme skiing became the thing, these guys were looking

The summer trade that once supported Norquay was discontinued after the winter expansion of 1989/90.

for the unusual slopes. Franz Gabl was followed by Rudi Gertsch, Norbert Wiegele, Sepp Renner, Jim Davies, Siri Strom, and Irwin Tontch. I can also tell you that in the years to follow, the Banff kids born about this time continued this beautiful style of skiing, which could go wild when least expected.

"Having been around Norquay for so many years I couldn't help but notice how their personalities were reflected in their skiing styles, especially if they were timid, or on the wild side. Many of them worked for you, Mr. Encil, or you, Mr. Fisher. I know they respected you both, but because you came from a much different society they were tempted to do things that might have confused you. Your method of communicating with people was different from the way we were accustomed to in western Canada. Some people took offence, while others might have made fun of it. I do hope it wasn't a personal problem for you, or a European vs. Canadian thing. These people would have reacted to a similar Canadian boss the same way, and of course many of them were European themselves. I just want you to know they were all good people.

"I have talked to many Banff families that spent every weekend of the winter at Norquay. They seemed to be less affected by the changes in ownership than staff were. Because they were used to being there, they kept on doing what they had always done. You probably noticed this as being quite different from the ways in Europe. Banff families still go to Norquay the same way they did fifty years ago. To these families it is not your average ski area, it is their back yard. In a matter of minutes, families, school classes or individuals can go for a few runs and return to town to do other things. There are not many places in North America where you can do that. Excuse me for talking so much. It's just that Norquay has given me a lot of pleasure. Thanks again."

Walter Fisher stood up again. "As disappointed as I and my wife Eva were about the Sulphur Mountain Gondola development, we decided to keep Norquay going with an improvement of our own. Making the lift into a double chair in 1961 eliminated the long line-ups on weekends in the winter. It also improved the summer operation because summer people were less nervous about the ride if they had a friend sitting next to them, which the double chair allowed. We had fewer people riding in the summer after the Sulphur Gondola started up in July of 1959, but we always thought we had a superior view to Sulphur, and that in time people would realize that.

"In the next two years following the chair conversion, I built the two Lone Pine poma lifts. I sold the lodge in 1962 because it was so hard to make money with so many skiers bringing their own lunches, and staffing was always a problem. We tried coin operated machines for awhile, but people didn't like them. We had an excellent ski shop and ski school operated by the Russells and Heinz Vifian.

"With the installation of the Wishbone T-Bar in 1964, we opened a new area that was good training for the racing groups. There was a time when I had some trouble with the new T-Bar and I asked Doug Robinson, who had an excellent record in building and modifying lifts, to come and look at it. After he fixed the lift, I asked him if he would be interested in staying on. We talked about changing the chair lift to a gondola style for the summer, and back to a regular chair for the skiers. Doug said he could do it. He drew up plans and took them to Ottawa as he figured it would be faster than trying to explain the concept and get approval over the telephone. I got the money from the Calgary branch of the Industrial Development Bank (IDB) and we got the okay from Ottawa and went ahead with the gondola. Doug planned it so well that we lost very little time. He worked out a system where he used trackline, which basically used the old lift to raise the new one. It was a major operation with new towers, and the upper terminal had to be completely re-designed. In summer it carried six groups of three gondolas, and worked out very well. It went into operation in the summer of 1966. That date sticks in my mind because it was not long afterwards that we got the word that the Winter Olympic Games had been awarded to Sapporo, Japan, for 1972. I operated Norquay for another two years and sold it to Mr. Bill Herron in the summer of 1968."

As Walter Fisher sat down, taking the hand of his wife, all eyes slowly turned towards Bill Herron. This meeting, if you could call it that, had no agenda: it was obviously ad lib. If Herron had decided not to address the group I don't know what would have happened. I thought for a moment that Peter White had a question. I don't know to whom he would have addressed it and that was probably his thinking too as he sat back down again.

Looking back to the summer of 1968, Pierre Elliott Trudeau had appointed Jean Chrétien Minister of Indian Affairs and Northern Development. (At that time it was the ministry in charge of National Parks.) Later that same summer while addressing the Senate, Senator Donald Cameron, Director of the Banff Centre said, "I live in a company town, or should I say I live in a government town. When I say 'company town' you will know what kind of authoritarian rule I am equating with." I wouldn't put those words in Bill Herron's mouth, but I think it's quite possible he had similar thoughts during the next ten years at Norquay.

Herron stood up. "My name is Bill Herron. I am number four at your table of Norquay owners." He got a little chuckle from the 'seats' that would follow him. "I have a clipping from the *Crag & Canyon* of October 30, 1968. It is announcing my immediate plans for Norquay. I wanted to start with a small lift suitable for children by building a 450 foot (150 meter) poma lift on a lower slope visible from other lifts, so that parents could keep an eye on their children. Clearing was to be done on the Lone Pine, the Bowl and the Gulley Run where it meets the North American. I was also ordering new grooming equipment and a snow vehicle for the ski patrol. My outside manager, Howard Srigley was, I felt, the most experienced grooming equipment operator in the Rockies. With the growing number of racing clubs in the province, we planned on having more flexible rules so that these clubs could set their programs up to get the most out of their time on the mountain. I noted that we had the best area for training, and that included all age groups. I mentioned that my wife Carol, and our children Shelley, Brent and Brian had enjoyed skiing here in the past and that it was our hope to make it more enjoyable in the future.

"Following the opening in 1968 I added a T-Bar on Stoney Squaw. That provided the first skiing on that mountain since ski pioneer Cyril Paris had put a jump on that slope for the kids of Banff.

"If I may digress for a moment, I have the feeling that some of you owners that followed me are wondering why Mr. Fisher or myself didn't have a lodge built with accommodation. If I may read in part a letter I came across in old Norquay papers, I will give some answers to that question. The paper from which I am quoting is headed 'History.' It is hand-written, but does not include a signature. It starts, 'Mt. Norquay Village (Banff) Ltd., present owners of the Norquay Lodge, purchased and began operation of the said lodge on July 1, 1963. There were originally three partners in the company:

John Slupek, dry cleaning plant owner and operator, Edmonton.

R.P Wekherlien, real estate salesman and promotor, Edmonton.

M.A. Martyna, oilfield supervisor, Edmonton and Calgary.'

"The account continues: Mr. Stupek and Mr. Martyna had been associated in two business ventures prior to this and were at this time attempting to sell Paramount Cleaners (Edmonton) Ltd., which they owned jointly. It was intended that Mr. Stupek would be the active partner in the operation of the Norquay lodge. Mr. Wekherlien was to assist him by promoting development of a real ski lodge (with accommodation). 'A proposal made by our company to the Federal Government in 1963 was for a lodge costing $760 000. They approved it only in part; they will not permit us to develop accommodation.'

"Later in this report it said, 'Present Park policy does not permit development of accommodation in the new lodge. However, this rule has been broken before and will eventually break for Norquay. A major reason for this restriction on accommodation is the supply of adequate water. The government estimates it will take $76 000 to build adequate water supply lines to the Norquay site. If a developer were willing to pay these costs the decision might be reversed. We feel the Olympic decision in two years time will favor Banff and result in an easing of these regulations.' The letter went on to explain what happened to the unfortunate partnership of these three men. It took three years to sell the cleaning operation in Edmonton which presented problems in trying to operate the Norquay lodge during that time. They had great plans for the lodge in summer and winter. They noted that Banff at that time had no activity for young people; that dancing and nightlife hardly existed. The letter also said, 'Should the Banff Chairlift go on the market, we have the right to first refusal. Should we find a buyer for our lodge, Mr. Fisher has the option to buy first.'

"It sounds like these people were willing to build a day lodge without the accommodation if their partnership had been successful, or perhaps it was because Banff didn't get the Olympics that they changed their minds. Anyway, that answers in part how the government felt about a lodge with accommodations at that time, and it hasn't changed since.

"My first winter at Norquay was a real test. It started out with lots of snow, but then turned cold between Christmas and New Years, very cold, and stayed that way all of January. I don't believe Heinz Vifian's ski school gave a lesson that whole period. It's a helpless feeling owning a ski area with no one there except you

The Tin Man from the Wizard of Oz?

and your staff. It gave me a lot of time to think: I decided to have a promotional film made. Eddie Hunter had just returned to Banff after working in television for several years. He agreed to make a 12.5-minute, low budget film. It turned out fine and we used it for TV advertising and trade shows. It also won an award at the Seattle Film Festival. Our grooming equipment was to help business, but I'll let Howard Srigley, my hill manager, tell you about that."

"Thanks, Bill. Well, to start with we had the new Bombardier equipment. It had a wedge-shaped track that was firm and ideal for climbing the steep slopes of Norquay. Before I came to Norquay I had groomed at Sunshine, Lake Louise and Norquay for the government. I had used a Tucker Sno-cat that I transported to the different areas during the week to groom mainly their lower slopes. Now being employed full-time at Norquay, my challenge was to groom the steeper upper slopes. I figured I could do it with the Bombardier. It had a high-speed second gear of which I planned to take advantage. To get to the upper areas of the mountain I started by traversing, in reverse, across Rick's cut-back. That section was generally pretty soft,

Banff Winter Carnival and Bonspiel
February 8th to 15th. 1919

Programme
Events and Attractions
B. W. Collison, Secretary

Early promotion for the Banff Winter Carnival, 1919.

which meant I had to run it and get off quickly, which is where the fast second gear came in handy. I would leave it overnight to harden up. It might take me two or three days, but I would continue up the North American and cut back to the upper part of the Bowl, which took me to the top.

"The greatest trick was clearing the snow from the treads when you were headed downhill. The build-up of snow turned it into a toboggan, a toboggan with no control. To regain control I had to brake to one side, which put me on the diagonal and hopefully cleared the treads. But until the moment they did clear, you held your breath. I remember teaching that manoeuvre to Dean Christou and Don Howe with them at the controls: somehow just holding my breath wasn't enough! They of course turned out to be excellent operators.

"I had been concerned over other equipment. I recall a strange sound coming from the big chair that varied with the number of people on the lift. When I finally found it I almost panicked. The cable looked awful! I quickly ordered a new one out of Vancouver and Bill and I worked overnight to replace it so as not to lose too much time. When I had the old cable checked it was still 50% efficient which gave us a safety factor of 2.5 to 1. There was no real danger, it just looked much worse. Naturally, if there was any doubt at all, the equipment was replaced. Bill, being an engineer, was always sensitive to the condition of our equipment."

Bill Herron acknowledged Howard, and continued on, "We were booked to run the World Cup races in 1972. They were to be slalom and giant slalom races run off the top of the mountain from the big chair. In 1971 we decided to replace the two poma-lifts with the Cascade chair and within the next two years I upgraded the Wishbone Hall T-Bar to a Doppelmayr T-Bar.

"We still had a small staff, only sixteen being permanent, but they were good people who really wanted to be there. Klara Huser had joined us: she was a great asset and would stay at the mountain long after we had left. Klara was friendly with everyone with whom she worked and demanded the same attitude from the staff towards the customers. We always insisted that the staff not talk down to the customers. This was at a time when the word 'Gorby' was used to degrade tourists. One day Klara overheard a staff member use the word to describe a customer on whom she had waited. Klara approached her, mentioned that the staff had been warned against this type of thing and said, 'I will relieve you. You can go to the office and pick up your cheque, you are through.' Klara had started as part-time help. She had always had a happy demeanour right from the start when she was helping little kids on the poma-lift, and especially when she worked special events on the mountain.

"I feel I should mention another lady who worked at Norquay almost as long as Klara, Magdlena Korndorfer. She sold lift tickets in the winter and worked the summers managing the upper Tea House from 1959 to 1979. A quiet little lady who was always 'on the job.'

"We had built up a good relationship with the other ski area owners, Cliff White and John Gow at Sunshine and John Hindle at Lake Louise. The help that we got from the army and General Brown was amazing. Because of their co-operation we staged their large international meet following the World Cup. During this period the General had landed a large helicopter at Norquay. Parks' people complained to me, but I asked them how I was to disagree with the Army? Not that I wanted to.

"I say we staged the World Cup races. We had done much of the course preparation with Howard grooming the upper slopes, but the local Ski Runners plus dozens of Alberta and national members of the Canadian Amateur Ski Association ran it. Rob Crosby was Chairman of the organizing committee and Doug Robinson was Chief of Race. Chief of Course was Brian Skrine for the Giant Slalom and Leo Berchtold for the Slalom, with so many others helping including Stan Peyto on timing, George Capel gatekeeping, Imo Von Neudegg, accommodation, Don Hayes, transportation, and Mel Ferrari, Treasurer. Lorne O'Connor was the Technical Director from the C.A.S.A. and Al Raine was here as Head Coach of the National Ski Team. And so many others that found themselves preparing for the most important World Cup ever held in Canada. As it happened, to make the job more difficult, Banff and area recorded a record snowfall that year.

"Being the owner of Norquay I was responsible for all the skiers who came here. It was a great pleasure to be able to hold World Cup events, but we still had skiers coming who didn't know or care about the competition, they just wanted to ski, especially that year with so much snow and ideal conditions. During the training period I found some of the international racers cutting into the lift line ahead of regular customers. They were used to doing this in Europe where as racers they are held up on a throne. I explained to them that they couldn't do that here and that if they continued their numbers would be taken from them. Karl Schranz was here but in an unpleasant mood because the International Ski Federation had just told him he couldn't race because he had been racing for financial gain. I'm not sure if they let him ski at the Olympics in Japan that year, but he didn't race here.

"Erik Haker of Norway won the Giant Slalom and Andrzej Bachleda from Poland won the Men's Slalom. Austrian Anne-Marie Proell won the Ladies' Giant Slalom and Britt Lafforgue won the Slalom.

"In 1975 we hosted the North American jumping competition. Jumpers from Finland and Japan competed with the Canadian and American teams. A member of the Canadian team, Tauno Kayhko, made the longest jump, 81 meters off the 80-meter jump.

"We had an outstanding Ski School in 1977 who were also good racers. Jim Montalbetti, Dave Larkin and Dave Grierson won the Molson's Fifth Annual C.S.I.A. Pro Team Race at Silver Star ski area near Vernon, B.C.

"I believe somebody mentioned that I might have had some trouble working under the controls of the National Park because I had been used to working in a free enterprise system under provincial rule. Well, perhaps you could say that I did the odd time. I remember that we needed a workshop to work on equipment. If your equipment isn't in shape accidents can happen. Because the approval was slow in coming we decided to go ahead and build the work shed. It was a 40- by 70-foot building that we had been able to erect in a day by using a crane. When the government people saw the action, we were just about to put the door in place. Of course they said we had to move it. Then a lengthy discourse followed as to where it should be moved. There was another project, and we lost out on that one too. I had planned installing a new double chair for the new Wishbone run. In order to have the lift ready for the short construction period I had ordered it before the final signatures had been applied. The lift lay on the ground for two years and the government never gave the final approval. We sold the lift. The government always has the last word, and it was quite often not what you wanted to hear."

Moose checking out construction of the first lift.

Carol Herron, Bill's wife, stood up and with a big smile on her face said, "At times it really was something, but we have good memories too. I remember friends like Catharine Whyte, and Harry Dempster, who was Superintendent when we first arrived. I also remember Harry's races against Dr. Ian Wilson: they were always having fun races. Bruno Engler, like so many other Banff people, was so very supportive of our efforts at Norquay. I remember the good spirits of our staff and some of the funny things they did. I don't know why I recall them having shovel races, but I guess it was part of the fun. I can still see the torchlight parades off the big chair at New Years. I can feel the pleasure that my children had while learning to ski on these slopes. Brian and little Shelley who still is skiing in top form at the ripe old age of 35! Brent is still interested in the history of the area and once did a school report on it. I remember one frosty night with a full moon when Bill was going out to check on one of the lifts. It was such a beautiful night that I decided to go with him and all of a sudden we had a moose charge us. As we were making our escape I thought I heard Bill say, 'I wonder which government office told it to charge us?' Speaking of charging, the government did bring a lawsuit against us. They had given us permission to cut on the Wishbone slope. The Banff Ski Runners were helping us as it was to be a training area for their club. Anyway, Parks said we had over-cut, so they charged us and we were convicted and fined $1. However the big charge came when we were not allowed to put up the chair lift we had already ordered, and that probably cost us a million dollars. I guess it was government hassle that made us decide to sell in the end. I heard someone else say here today how difficult it was to plan. Parks didn't seem to realize that costs and labour were always increasing while they were involving us in a lengthy review process before we could increase lift prices. The government has so many 'arms' that sometimes they get in their own way, like the time the Army landed helicopters at Norquay during their own races and the Wardens complained to us. I guess the Wardens didn't want to fight the Army. To end on an 'up note,' we were fortunate when we operated Norquay because the government still plowed our parking lots. In fact we were third on their list right behind the Trans Canada Highway and the fire roads. I understand that the next owners had responsibility for clearing the parking lots themselves. It wasn't easy for us, but all in all it was a good experience; but then it wasn't easy for the people working for the government either. It has to be a give and take situation. The memory of friends though, will remain forever."

The Dr. Ian Wilson, Harry Dempster Challenge, 1975.

Mrs. Fisher was smiling as Carol sat down. Without getting up she said, "Your moose experience was funny and reminded me of one we had with sheep at the upper Tea Room. I was in the Tea House not really paying much attention to the sheep because they were always there anyway. But this day was to be different. All of a sudden the front window just seemed to explode. I jumped back when I realized a sheep was coming through! There was glass everywhere. When I telephoned the insurance company later on, they thought I was either drunk or crazy while trying to explain how the ram had seen his reflection in the glass and charged it."

Mrs. Fisher's remark was unexpected, but I thought it helped bring the group a little closer together, at least the Herrons and the Fishers, or was that just my imagination?

As unreal as this little meeting seems, it is similar to the way I felt when I interviewed the Norquay owners. Talking to them, and then talking to all the people who had skied and snowboarded there over the past sixty plus years, were really light years apart. The difference between owner and customer should be easy to understand, but the difference between the owners was a surprise. Had I given it more thought I shouldn't have been so surprised. After all, we have only six main groups that have operated Norquay from the very beginning. During that seventy-five year period the world of business (and pleasure) went through many changes. This meant that each owner operated under different conditions than the previous one, which is why the owners around the table today don't appear to understand one another. What could George Encil, who spent around $175 000 to bring Norquay up to date in 1948, say to Art Haenni and Dave Morrison who spent around $10 million only

Art Haenni checking the new Mystic expansion of 1989.

Area manager Pat Coté checking the upgrading of the Cascade chair 1999.

forty years later, to do the same thing?

The last two sets of owners met with similar conditions. When Mr. Haenni, representing Sulphur Mountain, took over Norquay in 1978 from Bill Herron, the banks were in a very giving mood. In 1995 when Kika Grandi and Peter White became owners at least one bank, the Alberta Treasury Branch, was similarly inclined, prompted by much different conditions. But I'm getting ahead of myself.

The group was still intact; the next speaker should be from seat six, Art Haenni, unless a speaker from the government or the open seat next to me, suddenly appeared. No, Mr. Haenni was going to speak.

"That's true, in 1978 all you had to do was phone the bank and they asked how much you wanted. So when we bought Norquay money was no problem. When Bill Herron asked us if we were interested I had to go to my shareholders to ask them. Some were in favour and some were not, but in the end they all said okay. Part of our reasoning was to protect our business on Sulphur. There was talk that there were people interested in developing Norquay by extending the lift to the top of the mountain and down to the Timberline Hotel. That would have been a big project, but as I said, money was plentiful in those years. We decided to go ahead with both summer operations, and to save skiing in winter for the people of Banff.

"It has always been our policy to have our equipment in top condition, which we had with the Norquay lifts. We also started the first snowmaking on Norquay. Danny Cox had been hired to install a small hand lift and I asked him to stay on to see what could be done to make snow. After overcoming the problems of water shortage and lines that would freeze up, he decided to build a large reservoir underground. I believe it was 70 by 70 feet, and 12 feet deep. We then ran pipes down to Forty Mile Creek deep enough that they wouldn't freeze. This was much later when we did the major development into the Spirit and Mystic areas. By then Banff no longer depended on Forty Mile Creek for it's water supply.

"Before all that happened, which was for most of the 1980s, we had had to decide what to do with the summer operation. How many people were required to operate the lifts, how many for maintenance and most importantly, what did our customers want? We tried everything. We tried gondolas, and then said to ourselves, well we have gondolas here on Sulphur, so we tried chairs. The people said, 'are you nuts, I'm not going to ride on a chair,' so we tried gondolas plus chairs, and even that didn't work. Also the view, although it's tremendous, after five minutes you have seen it and there isn't anything else to do. It isn't a 360° view like on Sulphur Mountain. In addition, the bus drivers hated the drive up to Norquay compared to the straight road on the way up to Sulphur. It didn't make much sense to keep Norquay running in the summer with only 10 000 to 15 000 people a month when we would have that many in two or three days on Sulphur. So when we faced giving up the summer operation for new skiing terrain, the decision wasn't much of a problem.

"I might add that in the early 1980s we had several years with little snow, and the little bit of snowmaking that we had at the time didn't help very much. About that time we, or our ski club, had started promoting ski packages out of Great Britain and Europe, but it took a while for it to build up, so business was pretty low. This brought us to a time of decision on plans for the future. We even thought of closing down completely, but the costs of removing everything to return the area to its natural state were prohibitive, so the only other course was to expand. We had to make a decision, but kept holding off because there was work I had to do on Sulphur Mountain. Norquay had only limited appeal in those days and the skier count wasn't as good as it is today. So you have many thoughts about what could be, and how much money it might all cost.

"We had looked at upper Wishbone, but it wasn't really intermediate skiing terrain. Then we looked at the Mystic area and beyond. I still really favoured Stoney Squaw as it had always been a vision of mine to see it developed with a lodge, a small lake where you could do some curling, and even with some small houses along the top of Stoney Squaw that could be seen from downtown Banff. I know that wasn't very realistic, but the idea had originated back years before when Dave Leighton from the Banff Centre and I had talked about a sports center at Norquay for training instructors in their chosen sport. Getting carried away with dreams like these, mixed with some practical thinking, doesn't always include the government viewpoint.

"Then comes the political bargaining.

"I still favoured Stoney Squaw for many reasons but it had several hidden ridges that would need blasting. The government didn't like that aspect. They wanted us to give up the North American run so that it would grow back in and look nicer from town. If we gave it up and the summer gondola operation on the big chair, we would get access to intermediate slopes somewhere. We didn't mind giving up the lower North American, it wasn't used that much anyway, and we didn't mind giving up the summer operation, as we didn't need two summer operations and we had the best on Sulphur. So we got our intermediate ski slopes in the areas that would be known as

Mystic and Spirit.

"Before this could happen I had to go back to Europe to talk to my shareholders. I got a surprise when they didn't go for it, telling me that if I wanted to go ahead with expansion I had better find a partner. I didn't want to quit on this because in the back of my mind were the 13 million dollars that were available from the government because Banff hadn't got the Olympics and because they had built Nakiska which was taking business away from Norquay, Sunshine and Lake Louise. Our share of government money in any development would have been $2.5 million, but of course we would have to match that figure. So we talked to Brewsters, whose president Dave Morrison talked to his owners Dial Corporation, in Phoenix, Arizona. They were looking to increase winter bus and tour activity so we teamed up, and Norquay took on a new direction. The master plan took quite a while as we decided on runs, the increased snowmaking program, and a day lodge. We had many people working with us on this."

All of a sudden I was aware of someone in the guest seat. "Mr. Haenni, Jim Buckingham here! Excuse me, I just wanted to back up some of the points that you made earlier, and possibly throw more light on the situation at Norquay after my arrival in November 1983. It was quite a small area when I came, with one big chair, the smaller Cascade chair, the children's hand tow and two T-Bars, one on Stoney Squaw and the other on Wishbone. I believe the skier count at that time was between 30 000 and 40 000. Sunshine was getting between 350 000 and 400 000, while Lake Louise was going up to 500 000. It was obvious that the Sulphur Mountain operation was subsidizing Norquay.

"When I arrived I was so impressed with the condition of your lifts. I learned that nothing was too good when it came to keeping equipment in perfect working order. The snowmaking program that Danny Cox had initiated was impressive, especially when you consider the limited water supply he had at the time. It really changed the area when expansion took place and he was allowed to use water from Forty Mile Creek with lines deep enough to prevent freezing, along with updated pumps and hydrants.

"I recall how you wanted to develop Stoney Squaw until we discovered the hidden rocky ridges. We then realized the proposed lift would have to go along a ridge and the runs would drop off on either side away from the lift. After studying the contour map I discovered the slope from the top didn't have the vertical drop that we thought it had. We also researched the Gulley run. If it had snowmaking and a chair lift from near the Timberline Hotel a lot of skier traffic would result. I believe I can say that Parks' people disliked the Gulley idea even more than the Stoney Squaw plan. They figured the snowmaking equipment and the lift would become a barrier to wildlife travel. Excuse me for jumping in, I just wanted to add that those were exciting years for me leading up to the expansion, but nothing compared to taking part in the expansion itself. I felt that you made Norquay into a viable operation, and I am also proud that we always kept the environment in mind."

"Thank you, Bucky. There were many people who worked hard for Norquay during that time, Klara Huser, Jim Montalbetti and Danny Cox just to name a few.

"Dave Morrison, do you remember when you were with Brewsters and we discussed plans which you took to your head office at Dial in Phoenix, Arizona?"

"Thank you, Art. Yes, it was a very exciting time. My company was willing to invest in the Norquay expansion. We had researched the Alberta ski scene. We even had a letter that said Nakiska would either be turned into a training center or made viable as a resort. We thought that if the former was the case, those customers would be drawn to Norquay, but that didn't happen. Also the destination skier traffic from Europe took a little longer to develop, or perhaps we just quit too early. As you know, we installed the finest equipment to draw skiers, but we just didn't get the expected increase from Calgary. Club Ski will tell you the increase for Norquay destination skiers has now gone from 6% to 12%, but the regional market has not grown much.

"I don't want to keep going back to Nakiska, but the people that operate that area don't have to pay the government anything unless they show a profit. So you might say they had the free use of a ski area, while we were operating with real invested funds. When you can't see a viable future, that doesn't mean someone else can't make it. When you can pick something up for eight cents on the dollar, or whatever, that relieves a lot of your headaches. That would have been the way the current owners came into Norquay. But it is possible we left them with other headaches, either caused by us, or by the government.

"Following the Bow Valley Study of October 1996, I believe development is becoming increasingly difficult for ski areas. I would guess that it is 10 times more difficult now than it was ten years ago, and ten years ago it was probably 20 times tougher than it was fifty years ago. I would like to wish Kika Grandi and Peter White the best of luck. From what I have heard they are doing a fine job. Thank you, Art."

"Thank you, Dave," Art Haenni continued. "Yes, we certainly do wish Kika and Peter the best of luck. Dave, you said perhaps we left too early. That could be true, but you must remember that I was involved with Norquay for about seventeen years. I believe that is longer than any other owner.

"Going back to 1978 when we purchased Norquay, we paid $750 000 but there was a debt of $500 000. In the 1980s we had some very bad snow years and the snowmaking covered only a small area. Sulphur Mountain was really sponsoring Norquay, however you could say Norquay was protecting Sulphur as far as the summer trade was concerned. There had been talk about other people coming in after Bill Herron with plans to build a lift system that would have been real competition for the Sulphur Mountain Gondola.

"Recently, when Eddie Hunter interviewed me, he asked me if the Grandi family was interested in Norquay at that time. I had no idea that Kika and her family had been interested. Bill Herron came to us and asked, 'Are you interested?' I gave him a $10,000 retainer while I spoke to my shareholders, and that was it. It wasn't until recently that I heard the Grandis had been interested. Maybe they should have taken over then: it might have been better for everybody.

"After the expansion we had a heavy debt load. As Mr. Morrison said, the destination skier traffic didn't pick up until later on. We were almost in the same situation as we had been before the expansion. 'What do we do?' We had just about written off all the 'write-offs,' so we stopped paying. When the creditors came calling for money or the keys, we gave them the keys. That is pretty much the Norquay story as I saw it."

"Thank you, Mr. Haenni. My name is Eddie Hunter. All of us in this mystical cir-

Kika Grandi breaks the news: "I just purchased Mt. Norquay" to daughters Astrid and Vania. The girls were more than a little surprised.

cle are known to one another, some for a long time. It has been a pleasure to search you all out during recent months and to hear the information you have given here today. I realize some of you have enjoyed it more than others. It is very difficult to compare views when they cover such a great period of time. It's also impossible to compare the dollar value of the 1950s, 1970s or the 1990s.

"The concept of meeting in a circle is to bring different views. Your view may also depend on where you are sitting. This would still be true if we were sitting at a rectangular table; it just seems to lend greater continuity to a subject when discussed in a circle. I am not sure if we kept that continuity going today: I hope we did. Possibly I should have mentioned to more of you that I wanted to bring you all together. I think you would have had interesting questions to ask one another, and then again perhaps you would not have shown

Peter and Mary White with sons Adam and Sandy test the early snows of Norquay. Older son Jonathan raced with the Banff Mountain Ski Academy starting in 1991.

up at all! It was quite a stretch for some of you to remember your Norquay days, after all there were a lot of years to cover. Those memories can also be classified as good or bad, depending on your mood the day you left Norquay. I don't know what you would read into it, but Art Haenni told me he hasn't skied since.

"I did mention to Peter White, co-owner of Norquay today, that I would like to bring you all together and if so, would he have a question he might ask any of you. His reply: 'Well, if you ever put that group together, I would be fascinated and would love to attend. But I think I would do more listening than talking, because they have all the experience, and I'm the new boy on the block. To be very honest, what was a wonderful windfall for us was to inherit the development of Spirit and Mystic Ridge, which Art Haenni and Dave Morrison did, and from which we have received much benefit. No previous owner had started with such an advantage. I would have thought that to try and make a go of Norquay strictly with the North American chair, the Cascade chair and the T-Bar on Stoney Squaw, would have been very difficult because you didn't have any intermediate skiing, and modern ski areas require intermediate skiing to be profitable. So it's thanks to Art Haenni and Dave Morrison that we have it here now, and so I'm very thankful for that.' That comment was made in the spring of 1999, not long before the end of the season. We are fortunate to have both of the present owners here today, Kika Grandi and Peter White, along with all their staff."

At this point a voice came from the government seat. "Excuse me, I have a letter that was recently sent to Mr. Charlie Zinkan, Superintendent of Banff National Park. It comes from the Alberta Wilderness Association.

'Dear Mr. Zinkan,

'Proposed violation of the Mt. Norquay ski area long range plan.

'Alberta Wilderness Association members of the Calgary region, have called the provincial board to let them know that the owners of Mt. Norquay ski area are planning to ignore parts of the ski area long range plan. Instead they plan to open the North American chair lift and cliff house for summer use.

'The discontinuance of summer use was agreed to by the operators as part of the long range program.'

"The letter closes, Canadians were even told that the trade-off for getting a long-range plan in place was the approval of an extension that more than doubled the ski operation. Park's values have already paid the price for achieving a long-range plan. Must more Park values be impaired through the undoing of the plan? The Banff National Park and its beleaguered Bow Valley cannot afford the ecological costs. I am just the carrier of this letter, but I thought you may want to answer it."

Peter White and Kika Grandi looked at one another, and then Peter spoke. "I don't believe that deserves an answer. We would naturally like to resume a summer operation with government approval. We certainly don't plan on going ahead without that approval as that letter indicates."

Mr. White, how did you become interested in the Norquay ski area?

"Well, Norquay wasn't my first interest in Banff. I can go back to when I was a teenage cadet attending the summer army camp on the outskirts of Banff in 1956. Later, my wife Mary and I came here shortly after we were married on a Skifari holiday. But it was in 1991 when my oldest son, Jonathan, showed an interest in becoming a competitive skier that we thought seriously of coming to Banff. The Banff Mountain Ski Academy had just started up, so following a good recommendation from a friend of ours we enlisted Jonathan. As he was still very young, the rest of the family decided to join him in Banff as much as possible. We came here for several winters. I had to travel back and forth to Toronto for business reasons, but we enjoyed Banff and I became Chairman of the Academy. Because my two younger sons, Adam and Sandy, were members of the Mt. Norquay Racing Club, we spent a lot of time at Norquay. The rumour was out that Norquay was losing money. It happened that Dave Morrison was my neighbour in town. For a couple of years I approached him asking if he would be interested in leasing Norquay to me. I told him about the ski area that I operated in Quebec with Pat Coté, and that we would be interested in operating Norquay on our own. I suggested we lease the mountain for $1, which meant they wouldn't be losing the million dollars including depreciation they were reported to be losing each year. For a couple of years they declined the offer despite the fact they didn't want the situation to go on forever. Finally the Alberta Treasury Branch decided to pull the plug and the Norquay owners handed over the keys.

"In the meantime our family had become friends with Kika Grandi and her son Thomas who was on Canada's National Ski Team, and an inspiration to the

Academy. I asked her if she was still interested in Norquay, and she was delighted at the prospect.

"The Alberta Treasury Branch had confided the responsibility for the sale to a Calgary firm. They told me they were going to invite bids, that it would not be for public tender. They were inviting bids from Art Haenni, Dave Morrison, Charlie Locke, Ralph Scurfield, a man from Texas who had shown an interest, and me. Now I didn't know what to bid. I was asking practically everyone I knew, 'What should I bid?' You don't want to bid too little, or too much. Don Findlay, founder of the Academy, said, 'I know what I would bid.' Of course he was just kidding, but he said, 'I would bid a dollar more than the other guy.' I laughed, and then thought, gee, could I do that? So I called the person who was handling the sale in Calgary and asked him if he would take a bid that was X dollars higher than the next highest bid. He said, 'Yes, I would take a bid like that. It's been done frequently in liquidations I've been involved with to get rid of the assets in a bankruptcy, and so on.' So I thought, okay, I'll do that, and I asked Marty Von Neudegg, a lawyer who is always interested in Norquay's welfare, to help me. We submitted a bid that was to be $50 000 higher than the next highest bid, but of course we didn't know how much we were bidding, because we didn't know what we were going to outbid. Then one day I had a phone call from Marty who said, 'Congratulations Peter, you and Kika are now the new owners of Mt. Norquay ski area.' I said great, how much did we pay? When he told me $861,000 I thought fine, that is something we can manage. The next highest bidder was Charlie Locke from Lake Louise: I understand he wasn't too happy."

Kika, what recollections do you have?

"I met the White family through the Ski Academy: Peter and his children were involved in the Academy. My son Thomas, who was on Canada's National Ski Team, was a symbol for the Academy, and I believe that is how we became known to one another.

"I remember our families coming together. I believe it might have been in May or June of 1995. My daughter Vania, who is a journalist, was in town and with Peter having newspaper interests, we got together for a breakfast meeting. It was just a sociable gathering, but before Peter left, he said, 'Oh by the way, Norquay is for sale. What do you think, Kika, if I make a bid do you want to jump in with me?' I said, sure, why not? Then I left for Italy. Later while I was still in Italy, I started thinking of what I had said and I was nervous, but when Peter phoned me two or three weeks later with the news, I said 'Okay!' My daughter Vania said, 'Are you crazy? You've never run a big business.' I must admit most of my reasons for buying Norquay were with my children in mind. With Thomas's life being skiing, it seemed natural for him. Vania being a journalist, she could always write promotional stories for Norquay, and Astrid studying child psychology could give advice for the daycare center at Norquay. After Vania said that to me I remember going for a bike ride to think about it. I thought okay, if I'm doing this it's for myself, and not my children. That's what they want me to say.

"Of course Peter White made a very good deal in buying Norquay. I understand Lake Louise wanted to buy it, but they were going to take away the equipment and just close it down. That's what I heard. We wanted to keep it open for Banff skiers, and hopefully for summer business. We wanted to do a 'ski museum,' along with an interpretative centre and a study of the wildlife. Mr. Charlie Zinkan, the Park's Superintendent, said he approved, but when they sent it to Ottawa they said no. So everytime we are almost ready to go with something, they turn us down. It's too bad because it would really be a small operation, and our lease says we can have a summer sight-seeing operation. But we will keep trying. After all, we are environmentalists too.

"To go back a little on something Mr. Haenni said about the Grandi family wanting to buy Norquay a long time ago, it is true that shortly after we came from Italy in 1975 we heard it was for sale, but actually it didn't look too good at that time. There were winters with very little snow, and there was no snowmaking at that time. It's true we wanted to be involved in a ski area; that was the reason we came to Canada, that along with my husband's wish the children become bilingual in English.

"Norquay was, and still is, a wonderful family ski area. I wanted to add some of the Italian feeling to the area, especially in food. I would like to have a regular job at the area, but I do travel quite a lot, perhaps to see my mother in Italy, or my children wherever they are. So it isn't fair to our manager Pat Coté, who likes to keep on top of everything. But I still hope my children and I will become more involved in the future."

Ever since this ethereal round table meeting of the owners and others had started, I hadn't really felt like I was a part of it. Now that we were speaking of the present, I did feel that I could say something. I had asked Peter White and Kika Grandi a question before they had spoken, but even then I didn't know if they were responding to me, or if they were going to speak anyway. Not many days earlier, Mr. White had mentioned that he and Pat Coté were partners in a small Quebec ski area, and now how fortunate he was to have Pat as the general manager at Norquay. I asked if he could enlarge on that and he responded with the following example.

"Well, as you may remember, four days before the planned opening of Norquay under our management, on December 7, 1995 the lodge burnt to the ground. The background to that is that Pat, as a very prudent manager, had called for advice from TransAlta, our electricity providers, to see if we were running the most efficient operation that we could. They told us our heating system could be improved. So we asked what they recommended. They said they could handle it for us and contracted an electrical contractor to install a new furnace. Apparently the installation wasn't properly done, and on the very first cold night with the furnace operating at full blast it burnt its way through the floor, fell into the basement and set the lodge on fire. So luckily for us we were covered by insurance and the fire wasn't our fault, and we got this brand new lodge for next to nothing. It has won awards and I feel it is a real jewel for Norquay. The down side was of course that we had to operate out of portable trailers for that first winter. The good side was that people were very understanding and very happy when they saw the new lodge.

"I would like to add to what Kika has said about the summer operation. We would like to operate in the summer, after all this was the first area to operate as a summer attraction, and to do so without incident. An operation here would take away to some degree from the heavy traffic from which the Sulphur Mountain Gondola suffers in the summer. Also, a ski museum and interpretative centre would add to the historical information that Parks want to pass on to visitors, and at the same time relieve the government of that expense. We would operate in a completely responsible way, and at the forefront of good environmental practices."

The second that Mr. White said, 'environmental practices,' the mist that had carried the group of seven owners and their supporting friends into this unlikely meeting started to lift, and with it the past seventy years of Norquay ownership faded into the bright sun of spring. I asked myself, did it really happen? Then Pat Coté came into the lodge to speak to Peter White and Kika Grandi, and I knew then that we were in the present.

I thought this would be a good time to bring Norquay up to date.

Pat Coté, the present Manager of Norquay, is a very vibrant man who likes to be involved in all aspects of the operation and reflects the energy of the new Mt. Norquay. So I asked him, "Of what are you the most proud?" I didn't have to wait long for an answer. "I am proud of the accumulated efforts we have made over the last four years that are finally paying off. A lot of people had it in their minds that Norquay was steep and icy. That was a big barrier for us to overcome. But now people realize that because of our good grooming and the friendly staff, we offer great value. Skiing by the hour is a fantastic value. I can always sell a ticket to individuals or families who are wondering how long they should ski or are worried they have missed more than half a day. I never have to ask them to come back later as I can sell them a two hour, three hour or a four hour half-day ticket. We are customer friendly and we also have a money back guarantee. If you don't like the skiing in the first hour we give you your money back. But if we do that, I want to know why you didn't like it so I can fix it. In the two years we have had that policy, I believe we took back ten tickets last year and this year we haven't had any returned.

"Much of our success started when we came here four years ago. We invited long-time pass holders to sit down and tell us what they would like to see happen at Mt. Norquay. We listened to our customers. Many of the things you see here today were ideas that came from them. If you can listen to your customers and then deliver what they want, you can't go wrong. People don't have to guess anymore if they should go to Norquay today; is it going to be good today, did they groom? Folks don't have to wonder anymore: they can count on us. We may be the smallest ski area in the valley, but as a result we are also in a position where we can groom all our slopes on a nightly basis, whereas some of the larger areas cannot do that, they just don't have the equipment to do it. You have good choice at Norquay, our snowboard park is excellent, we have programs for children, we encourage ski racing and we still have the locals who love the ride off the big chair. We find an increase in the numbers coming from Calgary that enjoy the two quad chairs that supply intermediate skiing for the Spirit and Mystic areas.

"We are still a family area. Families don't feel like they are going to lose their children. If the parents don't ski, they can sit in the lodge and watch them ski. Perhaps this is sounding a little too much like a commercial. You could go and talk to Clarke and Maureen Lefaivre in the Ski School, or my brother Rob in Marketing."

I should have realized as the interviews advanced to the present owners and staff members that their comments would sound like promotional statements, which would only be natural. Pat Coté, being Manager had, as he once said, "been given a lot of space by CEO Peter White to operate the mountain as I see fit." He was certainly doing that and enjoying it. The ski area in Quebec where he and Peter were partners didn't offer Pat the same pleasure as did Norquay. At the same time, the presence of Kika Grandi at Norquay helped retain the family feeling which the area had always enjoyed, at least to the locals and the people of the Bow Valley. But it was apparent that Pat and Rob Coté were 'in charge.'

Going to see Rob Coté, the marketing manager, I expected to be hit with promotional material, especially if he was as enthusiastic as his brother Pat. My main reason for going to see him was to hear about the special events that take place at Norquay. On my way to his office I ran into one of those 'special events,' the skiing legend, Jungle Jim Hunter. Jim, one of Canada's best known Olympic skiers from the early 1970s, had teamed up with local ski shop, "Ski Stop" for a promotion on Rossignol skis. People taking part got to try the new models for the year 2000, and challenge Jungle Jim in a friendly slalom.

Talking with 'Jungle,' we reflected on the World Cup races of 1972 that were held at Norquay just after he and other Olympic skiers had come from Japan where they had competed in the Olympics that Banff had expected to host. If Banff had been awarded the games for 1972 there would have been problems. That year turned out to have a record snowfall, much of it falling in February on the dates of the Olympics. A giant slalom and slalom were held at Norquay during that time, but not without problems. One might wonder what would have happened if we had had the Olympics? The giant slalom would have been run down the North American, but on a much longer section than used for the World Cup of 1972. The ladies' and men's slalom would have been run on Lone Pine and Wishbone. The whole mountain would have had to be prepared for races overcoming the heavy snow. The downhill was to have been at Lake Louise and the Bobsled run was to be out by the old fireguard, beyond the Cave and Basin. The winter of 1972 was one when most locals left their cars at home and went to work on skis. If we had held the Olympics that year, it could have been the year of the "Great White Elephant."

Rob Coté, Pat Coté's younger brother, is a Level IV Canadian Ski Instructors Alliance instructor, a member of the Interski Team, and had instructed at Sunshine for ten years before coming to Norquay in 1996.

"I have been here since the take-over of 1995 and this winter of 1998/99 has been the best in many ways. The natural conditions of good snowfall, combined with moderate temperatures have made it a great year. Changes made by management in our operation have also helped to increase the numbers skiing at Norquay. Greatly appreciated by skiers and snowboarders coming to Norquay are our ride-by-the-hour ticket sales. We also think our grooming is impeccable. So much so that if in the first hour after buying a ticket you don't like the condition of our slopes, we will return your money.

"There has been an increase in destination skiers, those people arriving in Banff for a stay of more than three days. Currently, 50% of these skiers are from the United Kingdom, with Germany and the United States being good markets as well. The American numbers are increasing, as is the Scandinavian interest. There isn't much difference in hours travelled for the UK people to come here, or go to Austria. It ends up being a day's travel either way. But once they arrive in Canada, the in-resort costs here are so much less, especially in meal service."

I asked Rob about special events at Norquay.

He said, "'The Rude Boys' and the 'Unlimited Snowboard' competitions are the two best attended snowboard events in Alberta. We have a special day with Nissan who call it their 'Ultimate Test Drive Day.' They invite Pathfinder owners to ski Norquay and test drive their new models. We had over 2 300 on that day.

"We have the 'Ronald McDonald Children's Charity Legend's Ski Challenge' that is hosted by Karen Percy and other top skiers. Last year they raised over $80 000. We also have the 'Mount Everest Ski Challenge.' The goal is for skiers and snowboarders to match the vertical of Mt. Everest in one day. It is a team event that takes pledges to raise money for the Red Cross, and the Banff Centre. 'The Ski Stop' has 'V.I.P. Challenge' with Jungle Jim Hunter. This past winter the 31st International Interbourse competition was held at Norquay. Members of stock exchanges from around the globe established it. Each year the race is held at a major ski area in Europe or North America. They have some excellent skiers. The Calgary Exchange won the event in 1996 and 1997. Ken Read organizes another charity race that combines top skiers with teams that compete under the name of SMED.

"Excuse me if I'm seeming to promote Norquay. After all, it is my job, and I find it a pleasure to tell people of the fine facilities of this area and the history of Mt. Norquay that covers 70 years of skiing.

"We have many race programs for young and old. Ray Seguin, a former coach of Canada's National Team, has given new life to older skiers with his 'Rut Runners' program. We even have a senior group that go under the name 'Crack of Noon Club'. Frank Gourlay is a member of it, and he skied here on the first patrol 50 years ago. These are the special events, but we always have our ski school with Clarke and Maureen Lefaivre, along with the Ski and Mountain Patrol headed by John Thornton. I could go on."

But I said, "That's great Rob. I think you are having a good winter, and you haven't even mentioned the snow making or the good natural snow we have had this winter."

He gave me attendance figures that were very encouraging for the winter of 1998/99. On a Saturday or Sunday, Norquay will see about 2000 skiers each day. Weekdays the figures are more like 500. Twenty-five years ago when the area was operated by the Herron family the full-time staff numbered sixteen. Today there are one hundred full-time on the Norquay staff, which swells to one hundred and fifty counting part-timers. As has always been the case they come from across Canada, with a good number from Australia.

So here we are in the final skiing days of spring 1999, seventy years after the first cabin on Norquay opened for skiers. Each caretaker brought a different attitude to the area. In the beginning Gus Johnson just wanted to ski and expose the young people of Banff to skiing. Cliff White and Cyril Paris wanted to do the same, but with the building of a cabin, commercialism started to appear. George Encil laid out big bucks to build a lift, but his direction was vague at times and his relationship with the government ran hot and cold. He did however do a lot for pleasure and competitive skiing in Banff. Walter Fisher, the next owner, also did much to upgrade the mountain but with a few snags that didn't go too well with the skiing public. Both men, Encil and Fisher, came from a European society that was much different from that of western Canada. At times they didn't understand us, and at times we didn't understand them, but they were both honourable men.

Enter Bill Herron, the first Canadian to hold the reins in over twenty years, and kick his spurs into the underside of the government. Bill understood the skiing public and did his best to make Norquay a friendly place with the people he hired, and by bringing in new equipment. In the end, I think he just got tired of putting on his spurs each day and he rode off to a new challenge outside the Park.

Perhaps the biggest surprise happened when Art Haenni crossed the Bow Valley from Sulphur Mountain to take over Norquay. Under his leadership, in the true Swiss way of doing business, everything was upgraded including early efforts at making snow. Fresh from the gold that flowed up and down the Sulphur Gondola, he then found Norquay a struggle to make a few coins. He even had thoughts of closing it down, but the expense of restoring Norquay to the pre-logging days of the early century would have been too great.

At about that time, Dave Morrison was driving by with a Brewster bus full of money. Art took some of his Sulphur gold, they combined it with a few million dollars from the Government's Olympic legacy, and voilà, an expanded Norquay minus the historic North American run. It didn't work, as you all know, but we thank Art and Dave for the new Mystic area, lifts, lodge and new snowmaking. But not as much as Peter White and Kika Grandi thank the Alberta Treasury Branch (the big loser), for the good buy they received. So now, we skiers and snowboarders, sliding into the new millennium, thank you Norquay for the great grooming, Snowboard Park, and new lodge with hot chocolates that almost remind one of the hot chocolates mixed in the original lodge of seventy years ago.

I believe all the owners did the best that they could. Each had different problems and different rules with which to contend. Those rules continue to challenge ski area owners. The part the Government plays has changed dramatically through the years, but most of the challenge has come from extreme environmental groups that are willing to exchange the stroll of a grizzly bear for a family's pleasure and our children's exposure to a mountain experience -- experiences that have done so much to develop what we call a Canadian personality. Those groups don't seem to realize that those of us who live in the mountains live the life of environmentalists, we don't just talk about it. We want to continue living it with our children, their children, and the children that follow, as the original concept of a national park stated.

The following section contains comments made by young and old and covers all stages of the Norquay scene. The comments are much like an ungroomed hill in a variety of conditions; some crusty stories and some as soft as powder. Many thanks to those of you who took the time to share your thoughts.

Kids

Chapter Three

Norquay Spirit

The following are comments about Mt. Norquay made by skiers and snowboarders there during the last seventy years of the twentieth century. Some were terrific at their sport: some were terrified. Most relate moments of joy with relatives, friends and the mountain itself. There were days of great sorrow along with days of happiness that will last the individual a lifetime.

Except for a few early comments and some of the later ones, they are not in chronological order. Memory is involved here, so don't be too critical. One day remembered by one person can sound like a much different day when remembered by another.

That's what makes memories so wonderful, they just belong to us.

W. E. (BILL) ROUND (Mr. Round had written a ski column in the *Crag & Canyon* of the1930s and 1940s. He had a very personal approach to the sport, which always made his articles interesting, especially for that period. He passed away in August 1967, in Victoria, B. C. He was 84.)

Here, in 1929, he described how to get to Norquay.

"At the present time the camp is reached by travelling the west road across the C.P.R. tracks, then, where the road swings to the left to approach the Vermillion Lakes, a trail continues practically straight ahead through the timber. This trail can today be used for half the distance by cars. The balance of the distance is done on foot. Walking the whole distance from town takes about 45 minutes. The popular way is to snowshoe to the camp, enjoy skiing and snowshoe back.

"The Mount Norquay Ski Camp, as the site is known, is not established in the interests of skiing only. Natural springs in the area will provide water for skating rinks. There is a natural toboggan slope that can be developed into one of the most wonderful slides on the continent. Facilities for cross-country skiing are limitless. All forms of winter sports will be fostered there and instruction will be given free in all of them."

(He added this little poem to his column of 10 February1939.)

My Bonnie lies on the ski slope

And lies and lies and lies.

My Bonnie comes down from the ski slope

And lies and lies and lies."

(And from his ski column, January 1950.)

"Skiers of Norquay, please fill in your bathtubs and refrain from schussing when the hill is crowded.

Did you know Cliff White suggested they start building the first Norquay cabin in October 1928? The Park Superintendent agreed in November 1928. It was completed in a couple of months by volunteer labour."

Kendall and Mystee Hunter aged one and four. Frozen diapers helped Kendall stay up, 1966.

CHESS EDWARDS (Born in Banff in 1910. He and his brother Rupe were top skiers in the 1930s. Rupe was probably Canada's best at the time.)

"What do you mean the first cabin on Norquay? The one we built for skiing in 1928, or the cabin Nigger Bill lived in when he was caretaker for the logging company?"

"I believe it was 1937 we started spreading the name of Banff around the west. My brother Rupe had won a major slalom race in the Seattle area. About that time Dave White and Ralph Harvey took four of us, Arthur Williams, Sid Peyto, Carl Oakander and myself to a big jumping meet outside Spokane, Washington. There was an unbelievable crowd of 22 000. We jumped well and got some good cheers for Banff, but in the newspaper write-up they said Banff was in British Columbia. What else is new?

"My brother actually got double coverage in the Seattle papers. Initially the paper had reported the winner to be Hans Grage, an American. Then following an official check by mathematical experts, it was discovered Rupe Edwards of Banff was the combined champion for slalom and downhill. The top team was also from Banff, Norm Knight, Ted and Herb Paris and Viktor Kutschera. Second place went to the Vancouver, B. C. team, followed by two Seattle and one Oregon team. Do you believe you need a math expert to figure out the times of a ski race? When they finally got it straight the headlines said, 'BANFF SKIER IS CARNIVAL HERO. Rupert Edwards of Banff, Alberta, as brilliant a slalom racer as has ever been seen in action in Washington, today has the crown of Pacific Coast slalom champion. Over 2000 Washington skiers were convinced he earned the title at the Third Annual Seattle Junior Chamber of Commerce Sport Carnival.'"

P. J. JENNINGS (Superintendent, Banff National Park, 1938.)

"A good winter season under present conditions only provides 8 or 9 busy weekends. The craze for skiing which now grips the public may not continue."

GEORGE ENCIL (First owner of a chair-lift on Norquay.)

In instructions given to Mark Crozier, his lift manager. "Tell zee boys not to make yellow holes in zee snow near zee Tea House."

KENDALL HUNTER (Writer/Photographer. Grew up in Banff, raced in the 1970s and 1980s. Married name, Maycock, and presently living in Switzerland.)

"Like a perfectly memorized race course, I anticipated every turn of the Norquay road. It has been years since I regularly ascended this route, whether by family car, ski team van, road bike, mountain bike or the sole of my shoes. After years of being away, it isn't the open road that stretched before me but the lure of the familiar. Nowhere did I feel more at home than on this mountain. I could drive this road with my eyes closed, even now.

"There isn't one memory I savour more than the next. Simply, or not … my memories are that of growing up. As I scanned the hill, each place unfolds and reveals a scene of my childhood from the earliest days on skis to the demise of a ski racing 'career.'

"I'm not sure if it's the photograph taken by my Dad or the actual experience that comes to mind, like so many childhood memories. The photo is of my first days on skis: my sister Mystee and I are standing outside the old lodge. At one year, I stand with frozen diapers and bowed legs on skin skis learning to both walk and ski at the same time.

"At seven I first attempted the 'big chair.' I recall accompanying my Mom down the Widow Maker that she aptly rechristened the 'Oh My God.' I can remember having to jump to reach the padded green seats of the creaky orange chair lift. My friend Eva and I would giggle as Nelson, the cute lifty gave us a grin from below a frosty moustache as he held the chair.

"Practising slalom by the Memorial rope tow I pause and take it in. So many feelings are wrapped into that one patch of space; I have a hard time sorting through the memories. Slowly it comes alive, and I hear the gates being whacked, the hum of rope sliding through taped-up gloves as I try to grip it for the twentieth time that day; the searing pain of bone spurs as I unbuckle my 'Lange Bangers' after each run through the course. And Dale Dorion, my coach saying, 'try again, one more time – one more time.'

"I chased a dream with the Percy sisters as we tirelessly skied the slopes. During times when we gave the race course a rest, we'd discover new trails through the trees; cheer each other on as we conquered the 'C' jump and dared each other to tackle the 'B.' In the spring we'd take our bagged lunches outside and smear on the Snick to make us 'Honey bronzed and very, very desirable,' as the tube promised. Take a mountain and peel away the dream that gave it its gloss, and it's the faces of friends and family that remain. One friend (Karen Percy) caught the dream making us all feel like winners.

"Eventually I happened to take myself almost as far away as I could get from the slopes, but no matter how far I went, when I started to miss home, I'd close my eyes and imagine all these things – and the smell of Snick."

Kendall Hunter and Karen Percy chasing the dream, 1981.

BILL WELLMAN (A top Banff skier in the 1930s and 1940s.)

"I saw Sam Evans ski down the slopes of Norquay, go right over the porch of the original cabin and right through the open door. With Sam you never knew if he was out of control or just doing it for a lark. I also remember coming out of the Mount

Royal Hotel in January of 1938 and seeing the red glow in the Norquay sky. We raced up but could only save a few skis from the cabin which burnt to the ground."

GEORGE PURCELL (Banff born resident who worked his teen years with brothers Gordie and Garry at Norquay, late 1950s and early 1960s.)

"I remember a little trick we would play on school teachers we didn't like. While putting them on the poma-lift we would stand on the backs of their skis while the tension built up in the retractable rod, then step off and they would fire away like a rocket, generally ending up in a heap, only to come back and do it again. I was named after George Encil. He and his sister had rented a cabin from my mother when he first came to Banff."

NEWS ITEM (A couple of months before the chair-lift was to open in 1948.)

Frank Gourlay was elected President of the Banff Ski Runners with Don Becker, Vice President, Kay Watt, Secretary and Sid Worts, Treasurer. Council: Doc. MacKenzie, Bob 'Steam' Watt, Bud Gourlay, Rita Hansen, and junior representative, Barbara Whyte. It was also reported at this time that George Encil was trying to get General Eisenhower to officially open the lift.

MR. A. E. HORST (A visitor from Rock Island, USA. He and his wife were touring the west looking for winter resorts. He is attending the first Rotary lunch being held at Norquay, in March of 1929.)

"When I arrived in Banff this morning the sign at the railway station said that Rotary meets on Monday, but after speaking to your President I was informed you had this special today, and here I am with my wife having lunch on top of one of your beautiful mountains. And that sleigh ride up here past the Rocky Mountain sheep was a real treat we will remember wherever we go."

On the same day the *Crag & Canyon* carried this item.

"A snow slide occurred at the Norquay Camp a short time after the Rotarians and guests had left. A spectacular sight as the snow came off the top and funnelled down the slide area to the north of the cabin. Some wild rumours have been circulated about the slide covering the cabin. These are groundless. The slides are annual events and have been expected by ski officials for several days."

GEORGE PARIS (Recognized as Banff's first skier in 1894.)

"The feeling of speed overpowered George on his run from Middle Springs to the C.P. Hotel. That combined with tricky snow, long skis and too many trees, finally ended in a disastrous crash, a broken ski, a sore back and a return to his faithful snowshoes."

GUSSIE JOHNSON (Grandaughter of Swedish ski jumper Gus Johnson who was one of the first skiers to cut runs on Norquay and teach young Banff skiers the pleasures of the sport in the early 1920s.)

"Because my grandfather has been called the father of Banff skiing I feel I should have a family experience from Mt. Norquay. Unfortunately my father, Vern Johnson, was only five years old when his dad, Gus Johnson, died in 1926. The family returned to Camrose, Alberta, for Gus's burial and the family stayed there. The only family history we have from that time in Banff are a couple of photos of my grandfather. I believe he was 41 when he died and the causes of death are quite vague; it could have been cancer. I always wanted to know more about my grandfather, other than the few photographs I have seen in Banff's Whyte Museum. He must have been a colourful skier. The only thing I can add is that my dad had an older brother, Robert Johnson, who was born in 1913."

American Sam Evans has been making visits to Banff and Mt. Assiniboine for over 60 years. The eccentric 89 year old flyer landed his aging Piper Cub on the defunct Banff air strip in April of 2000. The spirit never dies.

GUS JOHNSON (The Father of Banff skiing, won this race and passed away later the same year.)

1926 – Gus Johnson won a five mile Carnival race that went to the Upper Hot Springs and return in 40 min. Cyril Paris was second in 44 min 22 s and 16-year-old Chess Edwards completed the course in 59 min.

DAEM BROTHERS MEMORIAL CUP SLALOM
1934 – Rupe Edwards defeated Hamish Davidson of Vancouver. It was Davidson's first defeat in 4 years.

CALGARY HERALD (November 26, 1929)
"If as expected, the Banff Calgary highway is kept open this winter, it will be possible for Calgarian winter sport enthusiasts to make week-end visits to the mountains as they do in summer. With modern closed cars now in use this trip will be made with a great deal of comfort."

ELWYN SMITH (Worked for the government in the Finance Department.)
"It was my job to go to Norquay and check their ticket sales on the lift, from which the government collects 5%. I did that from 1955 to 1965. First the owner was George Encil and then Walter Fisher."

CLUB SKI formed August 31, 1980. It gave birth to the highly successful Ski Banff Lake Louise joint venture among Skiing Louise, Sunshine Village and Banff Mt. Norquay, which markets the area to destination skiers.

RUSSELL BENNETT, CLIFF WHITE, JOE WEISS
"In 1932 we skied from Jasper to Lake Louise. Bennett was an American from Minneapolis. Joe Weiss was a Swiss guide who lived in Jasper, and myself, Cliff White. I was there to assist Bennett, but I was also interested in doing cinematography in the area."

AL WITHERS, DOUG JEFFREY, FRANK BURSTRUM, VERN JEFFREY, JOE WEISS
"We five Jasper skiers decided to go to the Banff Winter Carnival in 1930, so we

skied to Banff. Enroute we experienced temperatures of minus 55° Fahrenheit. This really slowed us up. We were four days overdue when we arrived in Banff, just as Wardens U. Lacasse and Walter Child were ready to go and look for us."

DON McCREA

"I skied 500 miles from Revelstoke over the old Big Bend highway up to Jasper. There I joined my brother Bill and Jim McDonald and we skied to Banff. It was a light snow year, much of the trip from Jasper to the Icefields was done on foot. At the Icefields we took time to climb the Snow Dome."

PETER VADJA (A Hungarian national who had been going to university in Switzerland. He didn't travel to Canada with the Swiss university team in 1937 because he was writing exams. He arrived the next year when the German team was competing in Banff.)

"I have so many thoughts about my early years at Norquay and in the Banff area. Skiing against the Germans in 1938 and then meeting Bruno Engler the following year when he first came to Canada in 1939. Then the following winter when I had my strange accident just before the Dominions of 1940.

"In 1939 I was coaching Gertie Wepsala who was from Vancouver. At the time she was Canadian Champion, and I believe held the American title too. We were staying in Jasper, because we could drive to the Columbia Icefields for summer training: the road wasn't open from the Banff end at that time. We were training on Mt. Athabasca and some of the time staying in the Icefield chalet operated by Jack Brewster. We were training for the 1940 Olympics that we thought would still be on and for the Dominion Championship in Banff in March of 1940.

"We were preparing for a big Labour Day race at the Icefields. Most of the Banff guys were there, Rupe Edwards, Norm Knight, Ted Paris and many others. Also that was when Bruno showed up: he had just arrived in Canada. They told him in Banff where we were staying, so here he was. I don't know how he got there, but we had a lot of people from Calgary and Edmonton. I remember we were all listening to the King's speech when the war broke out. We thought we were all going to die, so we might as well get drunk and we had a helluva party.

"In the winter of 1940, I was training for the Dominions in Banff. I was expected to do well because the year before at Norquay when I raced against the German team and all the Banff boys, I beat some of the Germans and I was ahead of Rupe Edwards who was the top Canadian. Well, you remember the trail from Norquay that crossed the road in quite a few places on its way to Banff? After training all day I decided to ski down. I was going pretty good when I shot onto the road at a blind corner and wham, I hit a Brewster bus. That was it, I broke my leg. So there I was in the Banff hospital with a broken femur. The doctor wanted to put it in a cast. I had strong thigh muscles at the time and I knew the muscles would pull it right back, but of course the doctors wouldn't listen to me. Anyway, the President of the Edmonton Ski Club said, 'I can't get you out of here, but if you can get out somehow I will get you the best bone doctor in western Canada.' So, with a little trickery a couple of my friends, Ted Zinkan and Art Coles sneaked me out of the hospital onto a late train to Calgary and Edmonton. It was a painful trip, but a Dr. Huckle performed the operation and I spent three and a half months in Edmonton's

University Hospital.

"It is still clear in my mind (1999), just as it was in 1938 when I arrived from Europe, the powder skiing on Mt. Norquay and the moose that would watch the skiers on the downhill course. He would actually watch each racer and look up for the next runner."

BRUNO ENGLER (Cinematographer, still photographer, Swiss Mountain Guide, story teller. Arrived in Banff in 1939.)

"Not long after I arrived in Banff Jim Brewster sent me to the Icefields to set up a Labour Day ski race. He gave me a car but didn't tell me the road wasn't finished. When I finally got there, this guy in a beat-up western hat said, 'It sure took you a long time.' It was Jack Brewster. I didn't know if he was kidding: I didn't speak English very well. I said, 'I don't know, I had to walk a long way.'

"When I arrived there I met the elite of Banff skiers. There was Rupe and Chess Edwards, Norm Knight, Jack Hayes, Don Lewthwaite; they were all there. We saw Peter Vadja and Gertie Wepsala skiing right under an icefall. Peter Gabriel and myself were both Swiss guides, we thought that was crazy. You could see blocks of ice all around, it was moving, so we called them down. Then we had a party.

"At Norquay, I remember a big race in the 60s. I was still in the Army Reserve and I got some of the Army up to prepare the downhill down to the Timberline. That was the year Vancouver skier Ronald Tonnesson was killed in the upper 'S' turn."

Bruno was showing some of his still pictures to Eddie Hunter.

"I have taken so many pictures at Norquay. Look at that jumper! That jump is the most scenic jump in the whole world. Look, see how high he is with Mt. Rundle behind him. That's where the Olympics should have been, not in Calgary with grain elevators in the background.

"This is Toni Sailer when he was here in the early 1960s. He skied here quite a bit and spent a fair amount of time skiing with the young kids of Banff.

"There is a picture of my annual veteran's race. A lot of people used to put costumes on for it. Here is one of Catharine Whyte; she always came for it.

"Remember this one? That was the most famous jump; the day that Rudi Gertsch jumped over the upper Tea House. He was the best skier, but I was afraid he wouldn't clear the small building and the railing below it. I remember the day when Mel Medic came up to Norquay with the new Toni Sailer skis he was selling. He gave a pair to Rudi Gertsch to try out. He said, 'They are zee best.' Rudi ran down the mountain and then cut through the trees and went over the 'A' jump. When he landed, which was on the brow, the skis bent to the shape of the hill. Rudi returned the skis to Mel saying, 'Here are your skis, they are zee best.'

"Here is another picture: I think it is Johnny Pristov when he was on the ski patrol, that was 1970.

"That is the upper Wishbone. One year we made a traverse across to that area after stabilizing the avalanche area. It was good skiing, but Tommy Ross who was assistant Superintendent wasn't too happy with it. I said, 'Tommy come on across and have a good run.'

"He realized then it was safe. Bill Herron ordered a chair for the Wishbone, but he ordered it before he got the government okay. It lay on the slope for a long time: finally he had to sell it.

"This is the best setting in the world for a jumping picture..." Bruno Engler.

"You asked if I was on patrol when Herman Fuhrer was caught in the avalanche? I didn't see the avalanche, but I was there. Frank Gourlay should know all about that, he was on the rescue. I came back from Edmonton in 1955. I was on patrol with Frank in 1956/57; I believe that was the year it happened. After that, when Walter

Perren was in charge we built the avalanche mounds. Walter was called a Mountain Specialist. He was the one that turned Wardens from horsemen to climbers. I remember taking pictures of Wardens looking puzzled as they went from pony roping to climbing ropes. The government decided they should train Wardens to do rescue work after the two major accidents at Lake Louise. In 1954 a ladies climbing team from Mexico lost four lives on their descent from Mt. Victoria. A year later seven lives were lost on Mt. Temple. That's when Walter Perren was brought in to co-ordinate mountain rescue. It was also close to the time the Canadian Pacific Railway decided to discontinue the Swiss Guide service, a service they had supplied in the Rockies since 1886."

Bruno, you have been taking pictures in the Rockies for sixty years. Is there one film in your memory that comes to mind?

"There is a film I shot near Lake Louise for the CBC on Edward Feuz, who was well into his eighties at the time. It had some fantastic footage I shot with basically a soundman and myself. I got Jim Davies to fly us up in his helicopter to Abbott's Pass. When Edward saw the helicopter he said, 'Are we going up in that thing? It hasn't got any wings.' But he loved it. On our way to the pass Jimmy decided to give us an extra ride up the Yoho. When we finally arrived at the pass, Edward didn't want to get out. While we were there Rudi Gertsch came along with a party he was guiding. He was to supply the other half of our story, which was to compare the old climbing methods with the new.

"In between scenes I noticed Edward eyeing the famous Pinnacle at the Pass. He hadn't been up it for a long time, but it was always something he enjoyed doing whenever he climbed in this area. Rudi was really concerned because Edward was now 87 years old. He still wore the old nail boots, 'they were good enough in our time, I don't see why they wouldn't be good now.' But Rudi said to me, 'Is he going up there?' I said, 'maybe, but I didn't tell him to do it. If he does it, it's because he knows he can do it. He's been up there many times; every time he comes to Abbott's Pass he goes up there and yodels.' But Rudi wouldn't listen to me; he went to help him. I can understand Rudi's concern, but I knew how Edward would react. When Rudi approached him he went as red as a gander. He said, 'Young fellow if you don't get away you'll get yourself a face full of nails.'

"Anyway, Edward went up the Pinnacle and stood on the top and then he said goodbye to all the mountains, to all his friends, 'goodbye Schafer, goodbye Ringrose, goodbye Huber, goodbye Victoria, goodbye Peyto, goodbye Hungabee, this is the last time I'll be with you dear friends.' Rudi and I just collapsed. I couldn't see through my camera: I was crying like a baby. When he came down and Rudi was still fighting the urge to help him, I wondered how I was going to finish this scene. In the end, from a low angle, I had Edward kicking steps into a hard cornice that had been rounded off. It looked like he was walking right into the clouds and disappearing into his mountain heaven. Then I slowed the frame speed of the camera, which made the clouds speed up and the audio went to the haunting sounds of the Alpenhorn.

"This year marks 100 years since the Canadian Pacific Railway first signed contracts with Swiss Guides to stay all seasons in Canada. The first guides were Edward Feuz Sr. and Christian Haslar Sr., the year was 1889."

IRENE CLARKE CHOQUETTE
(Grew up in Banff.)

Irene Clarke Choquette: "I was the first person to officially ride the first Norquay rope tow in 1941."

"I was the first person to officially ride the first rope tow at Norquay. I have a picture to prove it, 1941. I loved those sunny spring days at Norquay. This one day when we were all feeling extra charged, Bud Gourlay, who was always doing something wild, grabbed a pair of skis and climbed up to the big jump. We were all watching so he clowned pretty good, but when he landed, the skies went right through the log landing area and broke both skis. He dragged himself back to our group with the comment, 'Boy, am I glad they weren't my skis.'"

NELS NELSEN (Jumper from Revelstoke.)

Nels Nelsen in the mid-1930s had held the world's record jump of 225 feet. He came to Banff in 1935 to help convince the government that Banff needed a new jump. While he was here he competed on the old Buffalo Park jump. It was hoped Parks would give enough money to build a jump where leaps of 325 feet were possible. Ottawa allocated $500. This would probably build a jump for 200 feet. The money was given too late to start construction in 1935, but Ben Woodworth had already started some Banff boys to prepare the jump area at Norquay.

COST OF NORQUAY FIRST ROPE TOW – 1941

Tow line...$396   Gas motor...$350   Cabin, 10 ft. x 12 ft....$201   Fixtures...$300
Cost to ride...four rides for 25 cents

JIM REEVES (Banff High School student during the war.)

"I worked the Norquay rope tows in the 40s. Rather than punch the tickets of my friends, I would punch where there was already a hole. A real cute gal, Sally Becker, finally got so embarrassed at carrying the same ticket all winter, she threw it away and bought another one.

"I remember, with frozen hands, trying to start the old Buick motor that ran the tow. It leaked so much you couldn't put anti-freeze in it. If you put the water in first it would freeze right up. So I had to get it going and warmed up, but not too hot, before pouring the cold water in the rad. God how that motor would hammer and pound away before it realized everything was okay. I think the motor came from one of Mr. Beattie's old cars, that's what the tows were made from, old cars. They used the wheels to run the rope back down the slope. And the way those ropes would twist, it would just grap clothes and mitts, and you went with it.

"I worked on two Norquay tows. The second one was the Memorial tow. It had as many problems as the first, but they were different. It had a Chevy motor with a governor on it. The governor gave it more gas as the load increased, but it wasn't gradual. It would really speed up, people would go up there sometimes faster than they skied down. But they were going so fast at the top many would shoot right through the safety gate, almost into the bull wheel. People would pile up, but they didn't seem to worry about it too much. You could never get away with anything like that today. Some got really good at it; all they had to do was judge their speed and let go before they hit the top, and coast the last 15 or 20 feet."

HOWARD SRIGLEY (Outdoor manager of Norquay in the late 1960s and early 1970s. Had also managed at Lake Louise, and before that groomed at Sunshine, Lake Louise and Norquay as a government employee.)
"Well as you can imagine I have many memories and I think they are all good ones. Staff was always a concern. In the fall when young people came around looking for a winter job, I would always ask them where they were from. If they said Saskatchewan, I always had to ask them several questions before they would tell me they were from a farm. If they did finally tell me they were, I would ask, 'And did you operate your Dad's combine?' If they said, 'Yes,' I would say, 'You're hired.' I knew I was getting a responsible young worker.

"Of course the heavy snow year of 1972, and the World Cup race held during February was a challenge. I was operating a grooming unit up by the 'S' turn on the North American. There was so much snow it avalanched on me and I slid into the trees. No great damage, but there was so much snow and it just kept coming. We had such a difficult time trying to set the snow up to hold for the Slalom and GS races. We finally got large hoses out and soaked the runs before foot tramping and ski tramping them. We started preparing the slopes about three months before the races and were lucky to have the army helping us. I believe it was the following year we tried to return the favour by staging the Army's international competition: we had a great working arrangement with the Army.

"I also remember years when we had rain and not enough snow. I made a mogul cutter, actually got a patent on it. The idea was to cut the tops off the moguls and move the snow into the thin spots. We also used it to bring snow from non-skiing areas. There were many times when the rain would set up a terrific base if it turned cold after the rain.

"I would like to give a plug for the Government's early involvement in skiing. I don't know if people remember that it was the Park that started ski areas. It goes back a long way, but leading up to our bid for the 1972 Olympics, they were very supportive. Before that they had cut runs. They started with 'S-type' runs then realized fall-line skiing was the way to go. They cleared the timber, plowed the roads and parking lots, supplied the Ski Patrol, looked after snow stabilization and even built the jumps and judges' stands on Norquay. I took a Tucker snowcat on a flatbed to all three areas and did the job on behalf of the government.
"I worked many enjoyable years with Klara Huser at a time when the area was

SEASON TICKET 1978-79

Adult prices before Oct. 29th			
Ski Big 3	Lake Louise	Sunshine	Norquay
$270	$170	*all dates*	$115
and after Oct. 29th			
$280	$180	$195	$125
Day Tickets			
	$10.50	$11.00	$8.00

owned by Walter Fisher, and then by Bill Herron."

PAT LEVER (Fresh from England, 1966.)

"Not long after arriving in Banff from England, I was employed at the Banff Centre and my good friend FRAN KELLY and I decided to play hooky from work. We had in mind a beautiful spring day at Norquay, which it was. While riding up on the poma-lift I realized that the man a short distance in front of me was my boss, Ken Madsen. My immediate reaction was a sharp command to Fran behind me, 'We had better get off.' That sudden release of two skiers affected the whole line and everyone fell off. As we scrambled away we were hoping Mr. Madsen was in a position where his vision was obscured."

CHRIS McMURDO (Banff resident, 1999.)

"I enjoy the friendly family atmosphere of Mt. Norquay. It reminds me of my younger years in Val Gardena, Italy. I feel that my seven-year-old daughter, Martina, is perfectly safe skiing here. I know she will always be in the eyes of local people at Norquay."

Martina McMurdo, always at home, 1999.

BANFF WINTER CARNIVAL 1929

The Carnival Committee arranged to have Captain McCall of Western Canadian Airways, to storm Edmonton and Calgary and intermediate points with flyers inviting citizens to the Carnival of February 2 to 9, 1929. It included a discount on the train ride from Calgary to Banff. They also arranged to have two planes do stunt flying while the train was in the Morley flats area. The planes were available in Banff for those wishing to see the Carnival from the air.

JEFF CUELL (Tenor man with "Jazz Suite," rotating Rotary goal tender and local insurance agent.)

"As a jazz man I love playing gigs at Norquay, especially for the Veteran's Race, but MAN it's hard to swing to BRUNO ENGLER'S yodelling."

Marty Von Neudegg and daughter Stephanie, 1999.

MARTY VON NEUDEGG (Born in Banff 1957; lawyer; marketing director of Canadian Mountain Holidays [CMH].)

"I remember the day my buddy Gerald Costigan talked me into skiing the big chair: we were six years old. We were the youngest to ski it alone at that time, might be still.

"I can't forget my last run of 1966. I was skiing with my Dad, Bob Geber and Rudy Erbsland. The lift was going to close for the season in 15 minutes and I broke my leg.

"Steve Becker, who would later become a member of our National Team, made one of the strangest and funniest runs I ever saw. He was having a good run in a slalom course that came off the Lone Pine. He had less than a third of the course to go when he lost control and somersaulted. He was wearing wooden skis and long straps for bindings. The only thing that gave was his feet in his laced up boots, which came right out. Following the flip he landed on his feet and ran the remaining gates in his stocking feet.

"Most of my memories are from my childhood. Once again it was with Gerald Costigan. We decided to look into the old tank that sat on the lower corner of Memorial and the Gulley. We were seven years old and pretty small. After getting into the barrel we found we couldn't get out. It was starting to get dark when Gerald somehow pushed me out and I went for help. Help was in the form of Byron Tarchuk who was only a few years older than we were. Anyway, he had a ladder and we got Costigan out. Exploring the mountain was always fun, especially when we were kids.

"Remember the flashy Schneider ski pants? I got a pair when I was 13 years old. Like most Banff kids I entered the Norquay Challenge skiing the big chair 27 times in one day, for 35,000 vertical feet. The temperature was really low, about − 25°. I neglected to zip the fly closed. I didn't notice it until the day was over. That's when I found out I froze my 'dink'. You remember things like that!

"When I was in my mid-teens I remember the thrill of the World Cup races at Norquay in 1972. For some reason I remember Marielle Goitschel wearing the first Lange Competition boots, and she left the two top buckles open. I think she won the Giant Slalom."

WORLD CUP NORQUAY 1972 (Ladies' and Men's GS and Slalom.)
Ladies' GS (1) Anne-Marie Proell, Austria. (2) Wiltrud Drexel, Austria.
(3) Monika Kaserer, Austria.
Ladies' Slalom (1) Britt Lafforgue, France. (2) Barbara Cochran, USA.

(3) Florence Steurer, France.

Men's GS (1) Erik Haker, Norway. (2) Sepp Heckelmiller, West Germany.
(3) Helmut Schmaizi, Italy.

Men's Slalom (1) Andrzel Bachleda, Poland. (2) Jean-Noel Augert, France.
(3)Gustavo Thoeni, Italy.

GEORGE ENCIL ABOUT HANNES SCHNEIDER (October, 1949)

"I picked up my good friend Hannes Schneider, the man who developed the Arlberg technique of skiing, in Calgary yesterday. We are going big game hunting in the Brazeau forest reserve. I am trying to get him to come back for the North American races next year to set a slalom course. I first knew Hannes from our Austrian homes in St. Anton."

BOB FREEZE (Bob Freeze and Norm Rault, while students at the University of Alberta, and assisted by non-skiing Professor Maury Van Vliet, were instrumental in starting the International Intercollegiate Ski Meet that ran in Banff for twenty-six years. At present Bob operates an amateur sport training center on the outskirts of Calgary.)

"I suppose one Norquay thought that stays with me was the first college meet of 1947. We had just completed the lengthy climb to the top of the downhill and we were all standing around doing up our jackets, except the guy in front of me who was opening his up. He was the first runner and I was the second. He pushed off and schussed the gulley with his jacket flapping madly, had a controlled fall going over the cliff and still won the race by more than ten seconds. His name was Jack Davis, skiing for Montana State. Later on in the Western Canadian Championship quite a few would schuss the course, but on that day the rest of us just stood with our mouths wide open and prepared to ski our original line.

"I didn't learn to ski until I was seventeen. I can thank a Norquay skier for my first racing lessons. Stan Ward of Banff and I were fellow students at the University of Alberta. We seemed to have quite a few free periods in the afternoon which would take us to the banks of the Saskatchewan River where we would ski gates until dark. He was an excellent coach.

"When I was President of the Calgary Ski Club I had another excellent Banff skier, Gerry Monod (Johnny Monod's brother), not long from Europe, give lessons to our club. He was so smooth, he just made moguls disappear on a slope. And the man from Banff who made our collegiate ski meet possible, Stan Peyto, had such a good understanding of Nordic and Alpine events. I believe Don Becker and other members of the Banff Ski Runners always assisted him.

"In 1972, at the last Intercollegiate Meet, which was actually the twenty-sixth meet, we reunited the first team of 1947. There was Bob Sutherland, Bob Turner, Bill Armstrong, Clarence Haakenstad, Norm Rault and myself, Bob Freeze. Stan Peyto was there to complete our memories of that first meet."

THE INTERNATIONAL INTERCOLLEGIATE SKI MEET

The first meet in 1947 only attracted four schools. They were the University of British Columbia, University of Manitoba, Montana State College and the University of Alberta. The first downhill was run the year before the chair lift was built. The climb to the top and the descent were especially hard on the Manitoba boys; they never returned. Alberta won the first meet: Bob Freeze won the Giant Slalom. In the future, Geordie Morrison of Banff who skied for the University of Alberta would become a member of Canada's National Ski Team, as did another Canadian Olympic skier, Irvin Servold, from Camrose.

During the twenty-five years it was held, the best from Dartmouth to Washington State, University of British Columbia to Denver University, from Ontario to Nevada, performed here. The University of Washington always had the best Nordic skiers, and many of the Alpine skiers on the American teams were Canadians, as they could get scholarships not available in Canadian schools. The only expenses a school incurred were for travelling. Once a team was in Alberta the Government picked up the bill. But the Government dropped their backing in 1972 and so ended North America's finest intercollegiate ski meet.

FRANK GOURLAY (Skied Norquay when he was ten years old in 1931. A member of the Junior Team, along with his brother Hugh (Bud), in the late 1930s. A member of the first Ski Patrol after the war and President of the Banff Ski Runners.)

"My first memories seem to be going up Stoney Squaw and skiing down the old trail. The old trail wasn't the Gulley. It crossed the road, which wasn't completed in quite a few places when I first went up to Norquay. When I first went up, there was a road of sorts, but they called it a sleigh road. I believe some people did drive their car up before the snow came. I'm not sure if I remember it, or if I read it somewhere, but Cliff White and Allan Mather drove a car up to the cabin in the fall of 1929. That was five or six years before the road was officially open.

"My Dad would give me $1 for the weekend. I would spend $0.50 on Saturday, and $0.50 on Sunday. I could buy a bowl of soup, a hamburger, a hot chocolate and a chocolate bar, and then do the same thing the next day. There was no tow, so you didn't have to spend money on that.

"I remember climbing up for a downhill; we had about eight inches of new snow. We were tramping. I think Bruno Engler set the course. I was really tramping the line I wanted to take on my run, so when Bruno wasn't looking I moved the gate to where I wanted to go. But on the way down going over the Cliff I shot off through the deep snow and I think I came last.

"Well, I was born in 1921, so I guess some things I remember best have to be like yesterday. I still ski Norquay just about everyday. I ski with Leo Berchtold, Emo Yurasek, Karl Jost and sometimes a couple of old guys will come up from Calgary and ski with us. We call it the 'Crack of Noon Club.' I think Karl gave it that name.

"I do remember our Junior Ski Club in the late 30s. There was Rob Crosby, my brother Bud, Gordie Hoggard, Don Lewthwaite, Gerald Locke, and Norm Knight would coach us. At about that time we built a starter's cabin up on the downhill. I think Dick Pike helped and I believe Rob Crosby was there too."

ROB CROSBY

"I worked on the cabin at the top of the downhill with Frank and Bud Gourlay. We made it from timbers that were available in the area, but we did carry an old stove up in pieces. It never did work well.

"Frank Gourlay and I have skied together for at least 65 years. We still ski together in Bruno Engler's Annual Veterans and Masters Race on Norquay."

CALGARY HIGH SCHOOL SLALOM CHAMPIONSHIP, NORQUAY January 19, 1947.)

WESTERN CANADA, winning team: Norm Russell, Ron Johnson, Doug Hand, Sid Wells, Bill Johnson, Don Parsons, Jerry Campbell, George Williams, Sandy Fraser.

CENTRAL, 2nd place: Joe Irwin, John Bouck, Omer Patrick, Bill MacWilliams, Doug Hamilton, Dick Lyne, Leonard Ramsay, Dave Collins.

CRESCENT, 3rd place: Roy Henderson, Ron Brandreth, Don Martin, Doug Worthington, Willie Ogden, Bill Lamshen, Dick Epton, Stan Earl, Bruce Feeborn.

Western took the first three placings in this race.

Jim Davies skier, heli-pilot. It was lonely on a single chair.

SEPP RENNER (Sepp and Barbara Renner operate Mt. Assiniboine Lodge. Sepp arrived in Banff in 1968 from his native Switzerland where he was a top junior racer. After instructing at Norquay he became a guide for Hans Gmoser and his helicopter skiing operation, Canadian Mountain Holidays (CMH) in the Bugaboos. He joined Leo Grillmair, Rudi Gertsch and Kiwi Gallagher who were the first guides to work for Gmoser.)

"I schussed the Lone Pine with Rudi Gertsch in the spring of 1968. It was a good run, but the parking lot was at the bottom of the hill in those days and I shot right into it and broke a tooth. One of my first acts on Norquay.

"At that time Heinz Vifian had the school; Bob Meggs was there, Johnny Pristov, Norbert Wiegele, and on weekends there was Rudi Erbsland, Bob Geber and Ted Clark. That winter, 1968/69, was so

Ed Aman skier, heli-pilot. Ed and Jim Davies went into the flying business when they purchased a Piper J3 in October of 1959.

bad. It turned cold right after Christmas and stayed that way all of January. I don't think we gave a lesson for the whole month. But Heinz still paid us."

ED AMAN (Austrian skier who after listening to the flying feats of Al Gaetz as told by Lizzie Rummel, got the flying bug. Later Ed was to become a bush pilot and a helicopter pilot for CMH.)

"Upon arriving in Banff (1954), I worked at Norquay on the lift with Pete Jacobs. He was the engineer that built the lift for George Encil. I'm not sure why I remember this, but we were changing the grease which was too heavy for cold weather operation. Maybe it was because I was too cold too! I know why I remember when Jim Davies and I teamed up. We bought a Piper Cub to make our fortune in a mountain flying service."

EDDIE HUNTER

"At jumping events in the late forties, each jumper was introduced by the sound of a horn. I blew my trumpet at Norquay, giving the sound of a 'charge.' If nothing else it certainly got everyone's attention. It was the only public appearance I was ever allowed. My parents were glad to see the horn leave the house."

SENATOR DONALD CAMERON (Director of the Banff Centre, in a wire to Prime Minister Pearson, 1965.)

"The present Park policy is unjust, unconstitutional and contrary to the basic rights of Canadian citizens, and not in the interests of an expanding tourist industry."

DAVID ILES (Skiing with Jack, his two-year-old son.)

"A half day off the big chair is like a full day at any other area. For my son the area encourages him as he can always find a friend here."

David Iles and Jack. Always a friend near-by, 1999.

CRAG & CANYON NEWS ITEMS 1968:

WALTER PERREN passed away in Banff, December 1967; born January 13,1914 in Zermatt, Switzerland. His mountain rescue operation in Banff National Park was considered to be one of the finest in the world. (January 3, 1968.)

Rob Bosinger, Karen Percy and national team coach Bruce Henry, 1988.

LEO BERCHTOLD (Swiss native living in Banff, 1968.)

Leo Berchtold, as President of the Banff Ski Runners is prepared to take the club into the Twenty-second Annual Intercollegiate Ski Meet, assisted by club members, Fred Wonnacott, Howard Morter, Brian Skrine and Jim Webb.

Eddie Cote and coach Bruce with the Rut Runner program, 2000.

KLAUS GEBER (1968)

Four-year-old Klaus Geber skis big chair with Dad.

CANADIAN WINS US COMBINED TITLE (1968)

Scotty Henderson wins American title: 1st in Downhill, 2nd in GS and 4th in

Slalom.
Brother Wayne finished 4th in Downhill, 7th in GS and 7th in Slalom.

NANCY GREENE (1968)
Nancy Greene wins her second consecutive World Cup Crown.

NORQUAY SOLD (1968)
34-year-old Bill Herron purchased Mt. Norquay in the summer of 1968. Howard Srigley continues as manager.

BRUCE HENRY (Bruce, a Banff native, thought the world was all skates and pucks until his good friend Ted Langridge introduced him to a ski hill (Norquay). It was an instant romance. He went on to personal ski victories plus an impressive coaching career. He coached Canada's National Men's Team for 13 years and the Ladies' Team for 2 years. He was with the men's team when they were known as the 'Crazy Canucks,' through the Boyd and friends period, and then with the ladies headed by Kate Pace's World Championship Downhill victory in Japan, 1993.)

"My all-time ski heroes: although we are the same age, Paul Peyto is still my hero. His amazing victories in Nordic and Alpine skiing rate with the best showings by any Canadian skier at that time. Rob Boyd is a hero, and deserves more credit than he has received as a member of Canada's National Team. Other heros, Phil and Peter Monod and Scotty Henderson.

"My ladies heros, Nancy Greene and the amazing Kate Pace. I find it difficult to explain the nerve it took for Kate Pace to win that World Championship of 1993 in Japan. Kate had a broken wrist that had hampered her training, to say nothing of the race. A cumbersome cast covered her wrist and she held onto a shortened ski pole. Imagine how that would affect your balance! She had to modify her style, plus she had a late starting number. Her mental focus and racing ability produced a victory of great depth. When interviewed after the race she was asked if she was surprised at her result. She said, 'No, I knew where my name would be on the board.' It was one of the finest victories I have ever seen.

"Her remark reminded me of a comment made by Nancy Greene when she was winning World Cup races back in the 60s. I also use it as a coaching 'prod' with young racers. It was at the end of the racing season when Nancy and Marielle Goitschel were about to start a race that would decide the overall winner for that year. Goitschel said to Greene, 'May the best gal win.' Nancy replied under her breath, 'Yes I will.' And she did.

"Not all my Norquay memories are of racing, but I guess you could call this one racing too. It was in my younger days, following a summer day of putting bumper cards on cars. Art Ganes and I, in an old 1941 Ford panel truck would race our boss, Walter Fisher down the mountain, he in a new VW beetle. He didn't have a chance. It's all a matter of a strong will to win, or perhaps it's just the thought of a cold beer in town."

CRAG & CANYON (NORQUAY, MARCH 1962)
PAUL PEYTO TAKES ALBERTA SKI TITLE.
Paul Peyto won the Alberta juvenile 4-way combined ski title when he scored 395

points out of a possible 400. He also took the Alpine combined with 196.2 points out of a possible 200.

EILEEN RANKIN (Bob Rankin's Mother. Bob was one of the finest skiers to ever ski the slopes of the Rockies. Mrs. Rankin responded to Norquay's call in 1998 when they first asked skiers to supply stories about the mountain.)

"Robert (Bob) Rankin, my son, worked as a ski patroller during the eighties, and also won the Mountain Smoker five years in a row managing to get 24 runs in a three hour period, a record. As a result of one of his wins he won the prize of a week of heli-skiing with Mike Wiegele at Blue River. He was so impressed with the operation he stayed on as a guide.

"Bob has also doubled in movies for Leslie Nielsen, Paul Gross and Arnold Schwarzenegger. As I write this Bob is preparing to leave for northern Norway to ski for Warren Miller."

ROBERT (BOB) CHRISTIE (Bob has skied Norquay for 50 years. His enthusiasm for the sport appears to be growing with each passing year.)

"My first visit to Banff was in the spring of 1944 when I was training in the RCAF at High River, Alberta. I came back to Calgary in 1950 and started skiing at Norquay. As my four children grew up we became a skiing family in the 1960s and 70s.

"My wife Vina and I have participated in Bruno's races for many years. We have managed to collect 16 medals, and one combined medal for a competing couple, in April 1990.

"On Friday, February 9, 1973, my youngest son Tom, at the age of eleven entered the Norquay Challenge, skiing 27 runs for 35 000 vertical feet. So the next day I managed 31 runs for 40 300 vertical. I went on to better that in 1985 by skiing 35 runs in one day.

"As I write this, April 22, 1998, I am on a committee of the Alberta Stock Exchange that is hosting the 31st International Stock Exchange Ski Race (known as Interbourse) at Mt. Norquay in 1999. I took the first North American Team to Davos, Switzerland, in 1981. Mike Irwin took over as Captain in 1998 and will head the Alberta Team into the 1999 competition."

INTERBOURSE HISTORY

The first Interbourse race was held in France in 1969. At that time there were only three European exchanges taking part. In 1999 there are at least 30 exchanges participating worldwide, with approximately 700 participants. It is held at the finest ski resorts and has evolved into the world's largest international confer-

Canadian Interbourse Team, 1999. Left to right; Andrew Abbott, Dave Lickreish, David Doig, Mike Irwin, Bob Christie and Cam Bailey. Peter Doig is missing from this photo.

Norquay parking lot, 1940.

Norquay parking lot, 2000.

ence for securities traders. Canada didn't compete until 1982, when the Alberta Stock Exchange went to Courchevel, France. Alberta has been the only North American exchange to win this event, which they did in 1996 and 1998.

In 1999, at Norquay, Vienna was victorious. Alberta placed second.

LLOYD HARMON (Youngest son of Byron Harmon, historical photographer of the Banff area. This is the author's account of a visit to see Mr. Harmon in February of 1999, on Vancouver Island.)

It was a trip I was anxious to make. There were so many people living on the West Coast that had once been residents of Banff. My list included Bob Dawson, Dave and Amy Spence, Walter and Eva Fisher, John Watts, Dean Fry, Cliff White Jr. and Lloyd Harmon, plus several Wardens, Andy Anderson and Joe Halsenson among them. While talking with Lloyd Harmon and his wife Beth, I noticed the name of Peter Vadja on their bulletin board. Peter and his wife Betty lived only a few minutes away, that was a pleasant surprise. Peter had arrived in Banff from Switzerland in 1938: I felt he would have memories of Norquay.

I had seen several photographs taken by Lloyd Harmon. One that comes to my mind was a powder shot of two skiers heading just a few degrees away from the camera. The skiers were Rupe Edwards and Peter Vadja. Lloyd photographed all the known ski areas of the 1930s, Assiniboine, Skoki, Sunshine, Norquay and all the terrain covered to get to these areas. Most of the photographs in the program for the 1940 Dominion Championship were taken by Lloyd Harmon, all top quality, shot on 4 X 5 format. I asked him about other images I had seen, each showing good action and composition. It was about this time he said, 'I never did like photography.' I felt like saying, 'come on you don't mean that, you can't mean that!' He said, 'No really, I guess I thought I had to, my Dad wanted me to do photography, all the equipment and the darkroom was there, but I didn't enjoy it.' I felt like I had contacted the wrong person. He did mention a film he had made on his Dad's 35mm movie camera. He made a short film on skiing at Mt. Assiniboine, which he sent down to Larry Crosby. He thought it ended up with Paramount Pictures. He didn't think too much of the film, it was just skiers jumping off cornices, but he was paid $500, the first money he had ever made in photography. For a long time he kept a picture of that cheque pinned to his wall.

He talked about all his friends that he photographed at that time, Bobby Bryant, Bill Wellman, Rupe Edwards, Norm Knight, Ted Paris, Victor Kutschera, the Atkin sisters and others. He even mentioned how much he enjoyed skiing, tennis and the way they would raise a little hell in the 30s. I would call it more than a little hell when they discovered the pile of wood that was gathered on top of Tunnel Mountain. It was only a few days before the King and Queen of England were due to visit Banff. The wood was to be lit upon their arrival to extend a warm greeting, but of course that didn't happen because Lloyd and his buddies lit it a few days early. He said, 'I can still hear the Wardens' cars racing up Tunnel mountain road. My friends had to escape to town, but our house was on Tunnel and I got home quickly.'

All the stories he was telling me seemed so unreal or at least much different than the ones I was expecting to hear. I started to wonder if the Carl Rungius painting looking down on us was real?

I saw Lloyd and his wife Beth, in June of 1999. They came back to Banff for 'Back to Banff Days.' Yes, the Rungius is real and so are Lloyd Harmon's photographs.

IMO VON NEUDEGG (Arrived in Banff from Austria in the early 1950s. Has been a ski instructor, worked for Walter Fisher at Norquay, followed by administration work for Banff National Park and the Banff Centre.)

"I was President of the Banff Ski Runners in 1955 when we started the first children's 'Learn to Ski' program. Bob Geber assisted me with that and it was later taken over by the Kinsmen Club. At about the same time I worked with the German jump designer, Heine Klopher. The government had brought him over to update the Norquay jump and I translated all of his plans.

"During the 50s Norquay was still owned by George Encil and managed by Walter Fisher. George thought of himself as a skier. He liked everything about skiing, starting with the lessons he had received from Hannes Schneider in St. Anton, Austria. Unfortunately George thought he was a better skier than he actually was. This led to a bad fall in the Bowl, and a bad fracture of his leg. I believe this accident prompted his thoughts of selling Norquay. Walter Fisher who bought Norquay was not a skier. I don't believe he and his wife really felt comfortable here. He had thought about installing a counter gate at the big chair because he thought there were more skiers going up than had actually bought tickets.

"George Encil was Jewish, but he donated a stained glass window to the Catholic church. It was called, 'Lady of the Snow,' which refers to Canada, but the skier is Hannes Schneider and if you look down at the bottom you will see a 'Star of David,' so George also got his imprint there.

"You asked if I had met Walter Perren. I was on the mountain when Herman Fuhrer was caught in an avalanche. Perren was there and he took charge of the rescue. I helped with the search party. I remember thinking at the time, 'This is being done the way the book says it should proceed.' Of course later I realized Perren had written the book, and it was done as the book said. He was a wonderful man. He spoke French as well as his Swiss German: he got along very well with people."

PETER COOPER (*Calgary Albertan* Ski Column January 17, 1958)
"Department of Northern Affairs to maintain all roads to isolated tourist developments. It is also expected Mt. Norquay will be able to extend their skiing into the Forty Mile Creek water shed area." This came from a letter written to his superior, by Harry Dempster who was the Superintendent of the Park at that time. Mr. Dempster was trying to explain this information had not come from his office.

WALTER FISHER Made a press release to Peter Cooper of the *Calgary Albertan* in January of 1958. The statement was apparently untrue. Fisher was trying to get the Government to do what the news item stated. He at the time was managing Sunshine and Norquay for Encil. He refused to open Sunshine until Parks maintained the road.

ROBINSONS

If the family of John Norquay decided to withdraw their family name from the mountain, which skiing family of Banff would be asked to donate theirs? This is a touchy slope to contemplate, so many could qualify. There would be the Cliff White family, the Hendersons, Crosbys, Beckers, Peytos, Percys, Parises, the Grandi family, etc. I don't know how you would decide. A leading contender would have to be the Robinson family. Along with Carmen and Doug, are their six children, Wendy, Jill, Lorraine, Rayto,

Jordy Burks and Rayto Robinson, happy Ski Runners, 1975.

Stephanie and Paul. To say this is a skiing family is like saying Banff is beautiful. Tranquil Carmen, a superb mother and ski instructor, inspired so much more than a few words can tell. As for Doug, it might actually be easier to tell what he hasn't done. He did coach the Alberta Junior Ski Team to its first National title in 1962 and repeated in 1963. He was Chief of Race for the Ladies' and Men's Giant Slalom and Slalom World Cup races in 1972, held at Norquay. He was responsible for the challenging Downhill of the 1988 Olympics, contending with its variable snow conditions and extreme wind. He had worked with young skiers in the Nancy Greene League. Before that in 1953, after leaving Shell Oil in Calgary, he biked from Vancouver, B. C. to New York City, sailed to Europe where he continued his ride, before spending the winter in Switzerland working for Carl Molitor, plus finding time to compete in some of Europe's top races. He returned to Canada in 1954, and a few years later left Calgary to become a resident of Banff where he and Carmen raised their family. Doug's mechanical and woodworking talents are endless. His ability to improve the designs of chairlifts and gondolas, plus a knack for getting stubborn machinery to work is known in most ski areas in the Rockies.

At present, in 1999, Doug Robinson and his sons Rayto and Paul are building a house on Vancouver Island, a house that started as standing timber near his home in Golden, B.C. They dropped the timber, milled the lumber and transported it to Victoria with the aid of a friendly retired truck driver, Lloyd Shibley. The Robinson crew had previously built an impressive lodge for

Doug Robinson with some of his junior stars in 1962. Left to right: Wayne Henderson, Shelagh Pike, Scotty Henderson, Garry McGregor, Doug, Bill Wonnacott and George Paris.

Rudi Gertsch and his helicopter skiing operation out of Golden, B. C.

The words of a Banff Rotary Club director in 1970 when Doug Robinson was chosen Sportsman of the Year, give further proof to this man's talent and personality. Peter Millen, hosting the dinner on that evening said, "Banff would not be on the sport scene with the strength it is today if it weren't for Doug's contributions. He has a magic way with kids. His understanding and his own fine example have influenced lives on and off the ski hill."

Carmen Robinson died after her second bout with cancer in 1985. She was 52 years old. Doug married Marijka Patterson in 1988. She had lost her husband, Lief Norman Patterson, and son Tor, along with a young friend of Tor's, Jeremy Saardinen, while climbing Mt. Chancellor in an early season avalanche in 1976.

Wendy Robinson, 1982.

DOUG AND WENDY ROBINSON (I caught father and daughter at Doug and Marijka's home near Golden, B.C. as they reflected on their Norquay memories.)

Wendy: "Norquay is my favourite area, I feel like I have always skied there. Every weekend we would go up to Norquay, no matter how cold it was. Mom would bundle us up and away we would go. If it was too cold to ski we would sit in the lodge and drink hot chocolate. One thing I always liked was the music they had playing on the hill. It was mostly yodelling music, but it just said Norquay to me."

Doug: "That sound system I believe was installed by the Jacobs brothers. It was Pete Jacobs who built the first lift for George Encil. It was great sound which you could hear on some evenings right down in Banff."

Wendy: "I remember when the World Cup was held there and there was so much snow they got all the Banff kids out of school to try and tramp it."

Doug: "There was a lot of snow. I was Chief of Race and I remember the Italian coach wanted the race cancelled because one of his racers had caught a tip on a twig in practice. It was the first race I worked on where the results were coming out as the last racer finished. Chief of Timing was Mike Venner, assisted by Gordon Littke and Stan Peyto. Computers came in from Calgary."

Wendy: "I went into shock on Norquay and I wasn't even the one hurt. I was riding up the lift with my friend Christie Waterworth. She caught a tip at the top and fell off. Brian Skrine checked her out and said, 'I think she's dead.' I reacted so much I had to take the lift down. Christie must have been unconscious, but she was okay."

Doug: "I was living in Calgary when I first skied Norquay. I taught skiing here before I moved to Banff. Later Walter Fisher asked me to come in when he was having trouble with the Wishbone T-Bar. He asked me to stay on. Later I managed the area and told him I could convert the chair lift into a gondola operation which would be better for the summer trade, then back again for the winter, which I did and it worked well."

Wendy: "I remember my little brother Paul when he was really small. Sometimes he would get a free meal by cleaning off the tables in the lodge. Then he discovered another income. His hands were so small he could get them into the candy machine and grab a chocolate bar. They cost 25 cents, but he would tell people he could get them one for 15 cents."

Doug: "After we were married Carmen instructed there on weekends. On one occasion, when she was eight months pregnant, she took this guy out for a lesson and he couldn't keep up with her. I think he quit skiing."

Wendy: "Norquay is also one of my favourite summer hikes. I go up the North American and come down close to the Lone Pine."

VEIJO TIESMAKI (Veijo, along with his brother Hannu (called Joe in Canada), arrived from Finland in 1933. Veijo, an outstanding skier, worked at Norquay in the early years. He married Betty Rae from Banff.)

"It must have been 1937 or 1938, we carried timbers from the lower slopes to the top of the men's downhill to build a starters' cabin. We also carried a French door, which was used for a window, plus an oil drum Sid Graves gave us to use for a stove. This wasn't done in a day, but some of the people I remember helping were the Gourlay brothers, Frank and Bud, Percy Kennedy, Don Lewthwaite, Gord Hoggard, Rob Crosby, Dick Pike; so many helped. When we finished a day at Norquay we always raced the Gulley to town. It was on one of those runs Percy Kennedy hit a tree and broke both legs.

"For a while Dick Pike and myself managed the lodge that was built in 1940. We thought we were going to make a fortune, what a laugh that was, but we did have many real laughs. Later I worked for George Encil when he decided to build the chair lift in1948. He was a character. One day I remember him picking up discarded nails that were all bent. He said to the foreman, Ray Wardell, 'Have zee boys straighten zeese out and we can use zem again.' Ray took them and threw them into the cement mixer and called it reinforced cement. But George was a good fellow to work for and he liked being around skiers. He liked art too. I believe he had two or three Carl Rungius paintings, beautiful animals. Ted MacAulay did surveying for the lift and assisted Pete Jacobs later in the construction. Pete was a smart guy; he always had different ways to do things. I believe he did very well later when he designed a helicopter model. I'm not sure if it was a trainer or an amusement park ride. George met Pete Jacobs when he was in the Canadian Air Force during World War Two. They were both stationed in Lethbridge. Speaking of flying, I went along with Al Gaetz when he flew supplies into Mt. Assiniboine. He had a Tiger Moth and then a Taylor Craft. I remember him landing one day in extremely flat light. We shot across the landing area and started going up a slope. We were lucky, there was no damage done but it was a strange feeling, I wasn't sure if we were on the ground, or in the air.

"Dick Pike had lost one eye during the war. When we were running the Norquay lodge he would have me play ping-pong for hours; he was trying to build up his depth perception, which you lose when you only have one eye. Then we would have him drive the truck up to a marker. We would do this for hours and it worked, he ended up getting a pilot's license, even owned his own plane which he used in his work after he had moved to Oregon."

BETTY TIESMAKI

"I bought a pair of ski boots from George Encil. He had ordered them from Europe but they were too narrow for him. The first time I wore them into the lodge I slipped at the door and slid right across the room on my back. I was so embarrassed."

Author's note: Veijo passed away in the summer of 1999. Dick Pike sent the following thoughts to Betty, and Veijo's son Brett, for a remembrance service for family and friends.

DICK PIKE (A native of Banff. He and his sister Dolly were prominent skiers in the Rockies. Dolly went on to instruct at Sun Valley before returning to marry Jack Hayes of Banff. Dick went to Oregon where he operated a successful construction business.)

"After I was discharged from the Navy in 1945, Veijo and I made a deal with Jim Morrison, who had the master lease on Norquay Lodge. We were to run the lodge and the rope tow for the winter of 1946/47. We thought we would make a killing. Little did we know.

"We lived at the lodge. The sanitary facilities were the old reliable outdoor variety and I remember one morning - temperature about minus 20 degrees - Veijo had to make the trip. He headed out with a broom and a lit blowtorch. The broom was to clear off the frosty seat and the blowtorch to warm the thing up. About half way there a large doe blocked his path and trip, which had a certain amount of urgency to it. He started yelling at the deer, but she didn't move and suddenly charged right at him. He was making like Zorro with a broom and a hot blowtorch, while yelling at me to do something. I was laughing so hard it took me a while to react. Finally the deer took off and so did Veijo, making record time over the remaining distance.

"During our time at Norquay Lodge we had a red Dodge truck which we used to haul supplies from town, including water. We usually made our trip down early in the morning, never anyone on the road, and that crazy Finn would drive like Mario Andretti skidding around all the corners.

"On busy weekends the floor of the lodge was pretty well covered with melted snow. After all the skiers had left, Veijo and I had to mop it up. When we were finished, around ten o'clock, we would pull out a couple of easy chairs, load our sound system with classical music, and relax with a Calgary Ale. We worked our butts off, didn't make much money but had a good time.

"Veijo was my best friend for over 60 years. He was a man to 'Ride the River With.' He was the brother I never had."

Author's note: Apparently it was always difficult to make money in the lodge. Veijo and Dick found that out. With their fun-loving attitude it didn't appear to be a big problem. They must have experienced skiers bringing their lunch and only buying a coffee to go with it. Walter Fisher certainly did when he took over managing the area in 1953. As they were experienced business people, Walter and his wife Eva tried to do something about it, but they too were unsuccessful.

The following figures are from the Park Superintendent's office. They also were concerned, as they would collect 5% on the profits, if and when any were made. This included the lodge and the upper Tea House when it was open.

Year ending November 30, 1950........Net operating loss, $5,502.63
Year ending November 30, 1951........Net operating loss, $9,729.29
Year ending April 30,1952.............Net operating loss, $13,707.08

UNKNOWN J2 RACER 1999 (This self evaluation sheet was found on the floor of the Norquay day lodge during the winter of 1999. There is no name, certain remarks indicate it is a male racer.)

At the top of the single piece of paper was sketched a small podium with the three levels; the center and highest position is for the winner. Here a small figure is drawn with caption, 'Hopefully Me.' This is followed by goals the skier wants to achieve.

GOALS
1   GO TO CANADIANS.
2   GET A FULL SPONSORSHIP BY DYNASTAR.
3   GO TO WHISTLER CUP AGAIN.
4   IMPROVE ON SLALOM RESULTS, SUCH AS TOP TEN IN J2.
5   PRACTICE ON MY POSITIVE OUT LOOK TOWARDS SLALOM.
     SUCH AS ALWAYS TELL MYSELF I CAN DO IT, I WILL DO THIS
     EVERY WEEK.
HOW AM I GOING TO ACHIEVE THEM?
1   I will be positive about my slalom training, such as getting out of the lodge
     first.
2   To not get mad when I have a bad run in slalom and G.S. and I will achieve
     this by thinking of 'chicks' instead of the run.
WHAT'S IN IT FOR ME?
1   You get CHICKS when you do good.
2   You some times get money and most important you have FUN."

(If the author of this sheet would like it returned please contact the author of this book. It is in good shape, only stepped on once, I think.)

HENDERSON BROTHERS, WONNACOTT NAMED TO NATIONAL SKI TEAM.
(*Crag & Canyon* May 23, 1962.)
Scott and Wayne Henderson and Bill Wonnacott have been named to Canada's National Ski Team. The three Banff boys will compete in Europe next season.

STUTZ, PATTERSON, BARNES ON ALBERTA TEAM.
(*Crag & Canyon* May 1999.)
Luke Patterson and Paul Stutz, young Banff racers, have been named to the Alberta Ski Team. They will join Cameron Barnes of Canmore, also named to the team. The three 16-year-old racers will start training with the team immediately.

MARY ALICE STEWART AND DOLLY IVERSON (The family history of Mary Alice is older than Banff National Park. The marriage of her grandmother, Mary Jane Boyd, to James Irvine Brewster took place before the railway reached Banff. Dolly Iverson has lived all but a few of her 94 years in the Banff area.)

Mary: "I seem to remember the road as much as anything. Sid Graves would drive us kids up here in his old Texaco gas truck. We would stand on the platform around the tank. It was cold, but even worse was the truck of Sam Evans, if you could call it a truck. It was really just a platform with a steering wheel sticking up. Sam sat on a box to drive it. Some said he would drag his feet to stop it. I know he was big enough to do it. He was the first man I ever saw wearing blue jeans skiing, but he wore them all the time. Dolly, do you remember the ski clothes we had made by 'Ping' the little tailor that lived in the alley behind the Dominion Cafe?"

Dolly: "Yes, and he made me a Hudson Bay coat, they were all the style. They didn't ski much when I was a kid. I would wear snowshoes, because I lived up on the Great Divide where the snow was fifteen feet deep. My dad worked for the Alberta Box Company. They would cut timber up there that was used to make ammunition boxes for the First World War. I was his barn boss. I looked after eight horses when I was ten years old. I know they did some ski jumping from Tunnel Mountain in those days, but that was before Norquay."

Mary: "I remember coming up here with my sister Ralphene and Barb Whyte to watch the Swiss ski team in 1937. A couple of them stayed at my house, they were so cute. Dolly, you can't see the new ski area from here, but they have two big lifts down towards the Forty Mile Creek area and they have closed the North American run down."

Dolly: "What are they doing over there in that hole, they seem to be skiing on one ski?"

Mary: "Oh, they're snowboarding."

ELEANOR LUXTON (Author and Banff school teacher, daughter of Norman Luxton, adventurer and publisher.)

"A Boston resident, Owen 'Bugs' Bryant, who came here very often in the 20s thought the young skiers of Banff should have a cabin. He encouraged Gus Johnson to cut timbers along the edge of the avalanche area and piled them near the proposed site. That was apparently three or four years before the cabin was built." (The logs were stolen or taken by the logging operation before the cabin was built.)

ROBERT CROSBY (Rob has one of the longest histories of skiing on Mt. Norquay. He was winning races in the 1930s, and still is in the late 90s.)

"When the Dominions were held here in 1937 it greatly increased the interest in skiing. I remember our equipment was inferior to that of the Swiss team that arrived that year. Shortly after we ordered a Swiss ski that was called the Walter Praeger. They were made of hickory, had steel edges and cable bindings that would apply good heel pressure. But they cost $22.

"Our early downhill races had few, if any control gates. You could come down the mountain any way you wanted. It was a lot like powder skiing.

"Yes, I had rides on Graves' Texaco truck and Sam Evans' model-T deck with a steering wheel and a kitchen chair. Sam lived here for a few years. He was from a

wealthy American family and was one of Banff's famous characters. I remember we were at Sunshine, it was about ten o'clock at night when Sam said, 'I think I'll go to Assiniboine.' And off he went, twenty-plus miles to Mt. Assiniboine. Sam came back just a few years ago; he still flies his own plane. He landed here to protest the closing of our airfield. Yes he was fined, but that was Sam Evans.

"What I remember with the fondest memories of Norquay is the junior ski team I skied with, and our trips to Jasper in a car supplied by Jim Brewster. There was Don Lewthwaite, Gordie Hoggard (both killed in the war), the Gourlays, Frank and Bud, and Gerry Locke."

EVE CROSBY

"I remember the accident on the jump when Sandy Thompson broke his back. He went off on a funny angle and landed on an uneven slope. There were doctors from

all over the country that offered to operate on him, but his mother was Christian Science and refused the help. I believe he died about two years after the accident."

Eve and Rob Crosby. Always in the medals, generally gold.

NORTH AMERICAN DOWNHILL (The lower section of this run was closed in 1990. The owners at that time, Sulphur Mountain and Brewsters, exchanged it for slopes in the Forty Mile Creek area.)

NORTH AMERICAN RUN (The person who wrote this was probably a staff member. It was found with Norquay papers from the 1960s. That person had strong feelings for the run, and as stated, they went from the greatest joys, to the depths of terror.)

"To the right, a funnel through which a mountain laden with snow sometimes pours its tempestuous white fury. Above, the crags of a bare rocky peak. To the left, the dark evergreens dividing one white slope from the other. Below, 6824 feet of white, dropping through 2149 vertical feet, giving an average slope of 20 percent which will often change to 40 percent.

"A downhill course which shakes the hardest of steel nerves, the North American can be the greatest of joys, or the depth of terror. With a long sweep of some carefully controlled turns, one descends from the pinnacle into the fir-lined, narrow winding S turn, which has often seen the best racers lost in the green fringes.

"After shooting through this green-lined column, one turns sharply to the right, across a short traverse, and plunges into a horror of bumps known as the Rock

Garden. Across this, legs work like pistons, trying to avoid the challenge of the mountain. For a brief second the slope levels, then drops again into the upper Hogs Back, a series of round waves that deceive. The necessary pre-jumps, if missed, can lead to the ever-waiting evergreens on both sides of these humps.

"Then a brief flat into what appears to be a wall of trees: this is the End of theWorld, and it can be. To the left an abyss of white opens up to clutch the unwary in the grip of the Widow Maker. If legs remain strong the skier has no worries, for all that is left is the lower Hogs Back, which takes one short plunge into the Gulley. From terror to timid, the Gulley is a passive run which will end in about a kilometer at the Timberline Hotel.

Roy Andersen (#2) talking with General John Rockingham following his victory in an army Biathlon, 1963.

"The run can have a similiar feeling to that of a water slide before you hit the water, or perhaps that of being thrown in a laundry chute for a hasty descent to the basement. But when raced in control or skied in powder, it is a run to be remembered for a lifetime."

This run was open to skiers and racers. It was cut for the North American Championship of 1950. The first winner on this course was Zeno Colo of Italy. In 1952 Bob Dawson won the second North American. He beat Colo's time. I found this description of the run unsigned. I made some minor additions. The writer had also said that the record for the run was held by Fritz Frey, a native of Switzerland who lived here for many years.

ROY ANDERSEN (Photographer, ski instructor, public relations manager at Norquay in the 1960s. Chairman of Ski Jumping and Nordic Combined, 1988 Olympics.)

"I had a different reason for going to Norquay than most people, at least on my first trip which was in 1957. I came in from Calgary just to see the jumps. My interest at that time was strictly Nordic skiing. I was born in Norway where jumping and cross-country were generally our introduction to skiing. When I arrived Norquay had a 60 and 80 meter jump; the judges' towers were to be built two years after that.

"Later when I was in the military I had an interesting contact with some people who played a major role at Norquay. I was instructing biathlon in the army. We used the same training area that Banff National Park used for training wardens at Cuthead, up the Cascade. Some of these wardens would be on the ski patrol, which the government supplied for the ski areas at that time. Two of the people who came in to instruct us on avalanche control and rescue, Walter Perren and Bruno Engler, were also very active at Norquay. We couldn't have had better people.

"I coached the western army team that competed at Norquay in 1974. General G. Brown was in command. He and his men had played a major part in preparing the Norquay slopes for the World Cup races that had been held two years earlier. He, along with General John Rockingham, was an enthusiastic supporter of skiing.

"I have so many memories of Norquay. I was introduced to alpine skiing there. I

No longer do you have to ski like mad to the Cascade Beer Hall to beat the dinner closing time.

Youth must be served, Jeff Gall and Dave Tremblay, 1999.

To the Victor
go the Spoils
and What Spoils!
MOLSON'S
EXPORT ALES

loved skiing Norquay, still do. I enjoyed working for Walter and Eva Fisher in the summer of 1967 as a promotion manager. I left that same summer, as my Canadian Centennial project was to get my flying license. Doug Robinson was managing the area at that time. Catharine Whyte encouraged Doug and myself to buy Norquay. The Fisher asking price was, I believe, $650 000. The deal fell through. Doug also left at about that time. One other day I remember at Norquay; I was skiing for Eddie Hunter who was shooting a promotional ski film. He asked me to do a minor jump off a ridge on the upper Lone Pine. He thought, and I thought, I would go about twenty feet. He was directly below me, hand-holding a 16-mm camera. I took off with greater speed than planned and headed right for Ed. Even looking through the camera he realized things didn't look right. He managed to move a bit and I swear I did a turn in mid air: I went by Ed still four feet in the air. If we had hit, the best scenario would have been the passing of my left ski on his right shoulder and my right ski on his left shoulder. The worst outcome would have happened if he had been using a tripod and I had landed on it. I would have been shish-kebobed in 3-D!"

DICK MOORE (Calgary oilman. Terrorized Norquay and the town of Banff with many Calgary friends in mid-century.)

"In my early trips to Banff I had to find a ride each weekend, not too many people had cars. My best chances came from Stu Miller, Bob Hall and Bill Trigg. In 1951 or '52, Dean Fry got a new Mercury convertible, but he wouldn't let us in his car with our skis on. Arrival in Banff was followed by checking into a reasonable room; reasonable in price only. A King Eddie or Mount Royal room with sink. It was actually less spartan than four walls at the Brewster Annex where Warden Louise ran a very tight ship.

"In time our skiing improved to the point where we would ski 25 to 35 runs off the chair, or to the time when we heard the English voice from the lodge say, 'Buses are now loading for town.' We didn't take the bus, but we waited for that fine announcement before skiing the Gulley on our way to the Pub, in the bowels of the Cascade Hotel. There, the fastest waiter in the west, Les 'Paly' Zarkos, would slalom his way around the tables with trays of 10-cent beer high above his head. This après-ski evening would encourage bonding, romance, laughter and courage for the Cascade Dance Hall, where we would all end up dancing to the swinging tones of 'Hutch' on piano, Louie Trono on trombone, and the mad clarinet polka of 'Cazalli,' which, in four or five minutes would kill the effects of three hours of drinking, except for those who passed out.

"I remember 'Ping' ski pants, 'back alley' design. The ultimate in style was the gray and black striped morning trouser material. The style in skiing was changing from the 'Arlberg' to the Emile Allais 'French Method,' but I stuck with the Early Alberta Technique.

"I can think of so many great people from that time. Peter Matthews and John Watts were always there. Characters at Norquay were Mark 'Red' Crozier and Louis 'Louie' Luvisotto, Ross Maxwell, John Holland, Peter Van Wagner, Benny Judah (who married Jim Vanderbeek), Franz Gabl, Ian 'Zeno' Nielson. Oil people from Standard Oil (later called Amoco): Ian McCartney, Tom Hewitt, Bob Adair. Socony Oil people (became Mobil Oil): John Townlry, Dave Gossling. Jeanie Barnes, Norm Russell, Terry Hawitt, Al Bahan, brothers Terry and Jay Kellam, Duke and Eric Lovett, Bob, Dave and Howard Freeze, Jack and Dick Bruce, Bill and Merlin Trigg, Stu and Gerry Miller, FranWatts.

"So many great people and great times: without Norquay I wouldn't have met many of them."

JERRY AND ANNE JOHNSTON (Jerry is Executive Director of The Canadian Association of Disabled Skiing. Anne is his guiding spirit and right hand, also a former ski instructor. The following is a morning with Anne and Jerry at their Kimberley, B. C. home.)

Jerry: "My first recollection of Norquay is from a Banff Elementary school Friday afternoon program. Lois Woodworth and Peter Johnson gave us ski lessons, I was probably 11 or 12 years old."

Anne: "I came much later, I was a Calgary gal. I don't know why I was riding down the mountain on the lift, but as I was leaving the top this monstrous guy jumped on the single chair with me and rode down. I was terrified, I thought I was going to fall off. Later I was to learn this was a minor bit of action for the flamboyant 'Red' Crozier."

Jerry: "I was on the Ski Patrol in 1954/55. I worked for the Park Wardens in the

Ironleg Triathlon 6 March, 1988. Bike from the valley 6.5 kilometers, climb 1150 vertical feet and return on skis. Best time Andy Tout, 37.5 mins.

summer and we ran the patrol in the winter. I became a certified instructor in 1956. I instructed for Johnny Monod in 1958/59, then Fritz Frey in 1959/60. I had seen Anne skiing on the hill; she looked pretty good. This one day when I was sending classes around I told her to go with a group up the big chair. I was suprised when she refused to go. It was fortunate I didn't insist because it turned out to be Anne's twin sister Jeannie Whiteside who never did learn to ski."

Anne: "I remember the way Jim Davies could control a toboggan when he was on the patrol. People at Yosemite, California witnessed another bit of skiing by Jim. I was teaching there when he dropped in. The snow conditions were rotten. California concrete, hardly anyone tried to ski in it but Jim just bounced his way through it like it was perfect powder. He was the center attraction that day."

Jerry: "When I was with the government, Bob Powell and I built a new warm-up cabin at the top of the lift, with one minor mistake. We made the door opening 30 inches. When they sent the door up we discovered the plans had read '3 ft. 0 inches.'"

Anne: "There was this day, a Tuesday, the mountain was empty. It was when they still had a line of trees down the middle of the Lone Pine. This character came from behind one of those trees and hit me, but good. We were the only ones on the hill. I chewed him out fifty different ways. He apolgized fifty different ways every time we met after that.

"We went East last summer (July 1998) to Mt. Tremblant for the 60th anniversary of ski instruction in that area. Did we have a good time or what!"

Jerry: "They had a demonstration of skiing, complete with original equipment and clothes, through the years. Some were the original people. They had made a huge bank of snow in the spring and covered it with sawdust. On July the first they spread it out and had enough for a good run. Peter Duncan gave the commentary on the skiers, 450 people attended, it was great."

RUDI ERBSLAND (Banff business man and ski instructor. Came to Canada in 1954 from Germany.)

"Now I have three generations skiing Mt. Norquay. When my daughter Frances was a baby she would sleep in a small crib in the Ski Patrol hut; somebody had to be there anyway. If she woke up they would put out a yellow flag I could see from anywhere on the mountain. When she was old enough to ski I could leave her without fear as she knew everyone, and they knew her. Now my grandchildren ski here.

"For a while I instructed at Norquay. I taught Carrie Hunter for several weeks. Her husband, Eddie, filmed her progress and showed it on his weekly Channel 4 TV ski show. My business really picked up.

"I went with Rudi Gertsch to Norquay on New Year's Eve. He had always jumped in the dark at New Year's in Switzerland. I guess it's a symbolic leap into the unknown coming year. I believe Howard Srigley was there too. It's a strange feeling jumping in the dark.

"When I was instructing with Heinz Vifian's Ski School we celebrated New Year's in the upper Tea House. It was a nice start to a New Year looking down on the town. I also burnt holes in many clothes while skiing the New Year's torch parade from the top of Norquay."

MARCEL FERRARIS (Marcel and his wife-to-be both worked on the Norquay patrol in the early 1950s. Marge, from Calgary, was a volunteer on week-ends.)

"When I arrived from Switzerland and saw the Big Chair at Norquay I freaked out, I had never seen anything that steep. When I was on the patrol we would start tramping the North American slope early in the moring even if it didn't need it, because George Encil could see that area from town. If he didn't see us tramping by 8:30 a.m. he would phone up to see where we were. In the early 50s I was on patrol with Jack Pugh and Jimmy Innes.

"What else do I remember? I remember the Cascade beer hall would close for dinner, what a rush! Some skiers put thermogene in their boots to keep the feet warm. The first stretch pants. Louie Louis splicing the rope tow. Digging Bill Trigg and Merlin, along with Fran and John Watts, out of a good-sized avalanche. Skiers were different in the 50s; they were all characters. Waiting 45 minutes in a lift line was no problem; they shared their lunch and moved on. Oh yes, I remember Marge saying, 'You can't go on thinking you're a king in the winter and becoming a 'bum' in the summer. You will have to get a job and become a Canadian citizen.' We were married in 1955; we still ski together."

LAST DAYS OF NORQUAY FOR THE WINTER OF 1998/99

The final two days of skiing for the spring of 1999 had very little in common. On the 8th of April the lodge was packed with relatives and friends of Ian Wilson who had passed away after a short battle with cancer.

It was a perfect setting for friends to give their spoken and silent thoughts to a young man who had shared his life with them in these mountains. Friends vainly trying to give the right amount of light to their memories, which pale in comparison to the stronger images of his family standing before them. The Rockies looking down on the lodge, sensing they should hold the last rays of sun for fear this day will end too suddenly.

Ian Wilson and his wife Trudy owned the "Coyote" resturant in Banff. A demanding job which both managed while providing time and love to their three children. Everyone felt the pain for Trudy, and teenage Laurel. I felt they were wishing the pain wasn't as great with the young boys, Malcolm and Reid, but that's all it was, a wish. A different grief was with Ian's mother, Margaret who was there with her sister, Jackie.

Ian's friends shared the good times once more, this time without their friend who inspired them. Ian always carried the biggest pack, more than his share of the load.

LOUIS COCHAND
Second, 1936 Quebec Kandahar

This autographed photo of Louis Cochand is owned by a very proud Sean Booth of Canmore. The 83 year old Quebec skier lived in Banff for a couple of years in the early 1990s.

The last thing he would want to do is leave the load for someone else. He had no choice this time. He had already made the right decision when he married Trudy. I'm sure he knew his family would continue on the same mountain slopes sharing the quality of life he loved.

COMMENTS FROM NORQUAY STAFF ON THE LAST DAY OF THE SEASON, APRIL 9, 1999

The final day of skiing and work for the staff carried mixed emotions, the sadness of leaving friends and the joy of looking ahead to summer and new experiences.

Wandering through the main lodge on this final day of operation, as the season ends, the staff appears to carry an extra charge. Some are thinking of the big wind-up party to follow later in the day. Some feel a little down because they will be saying goodbye to many of their friends, friends they possibly may never see again. I asked several staff if they had saved any money this winter? This generally drew a big laugh. Most spent their money on equipment, rent and booze, not necessarily in that order. One saved for education, another bought a return air ticket to Australia. One Aussie said they get taxed at a higher rate in Canada, but another told me they get it back when they leave. Another important factor in Canada vs. Australia, a case of beer in Aussieland is about $25, in Canada around $16. Of the 28 staff members asked this question only three had not spent their money as quickly as they had received it. The main reaction was, "We didn't come here to save money, if you want to save money, you do that with summer jobs." Other information given, tips are best for those working around food or the bar. Tips are better for Level IV ski instructors than Level I or II. People taking their first lessons don't think of tipping. Europeans very rarely tip. Two young ladies volunteered information on what had been a great winter for them. Speaking of the staff, one said, "Norquay is the most awesome place to work, because it is so small everyone is like a big family. So all the lifties, maintenance people, the ski school and snowboard school all know one another on a first name basis, they all go out together and everyone takes care of one another." The other, a smiling gal from Australia: "I've never been so poor in my entire life, but it doesn't matter, I have snowboarded, met some terrific people." How will you get home to Australia? "The next twelve months I will work my butt off and get home whenever I get home." You have enjoyed working in Canada? "Yes, I want to live here, definitely, for sure."

The main living conditions seemed to be crowded; if you lived in a three-bedroom suite there would be five or six living there. This didn't appear to be a big concern. Just about everyone was there to have fun and share the winter with friends. One fellow, who was saving some money for school, admitted he probably had the lamest nightlife in Banff, but he was given a free lift pass and the skiing was great.

It didn't matter if they came from Newfoundland, Nova Scotia, Vancouver Island or Australia; they wanted to ski or ride and have a good time, and come back next year.

HEATHER STEWART, a happy gal just completing four years of instructing at Norquay, enjoys the fun in teaching kids, but needs to teach adults once in awhile just to explain the dynamics of skiing. **DOUG SAVAGE**, volunteer ski patrol, loves powder off the big chair. Likes the feeling of control at Norquay. **LINDA DEM-INCHUK**, has been a ski host for eight years. This year she wanted a change so she got her Level I ticket and instructed on weekends. Linda has a full time job in Calgary. She had a terrific winter. Most of the staff seemed to be 'Aussies' or 'Quebecker's.' I did meet smiling **KARA RITZ** from Winnipeg, and her friend **VERONIQUE** from Trois Rivières, Quebec. Ran into lift manager **SEAN BOOTH** with his wife **JOANIE**, with an army of friends enjoying the last day of skiing.

When asked about his staff he said, 'You can't beat the kids from Saskatchewan and Newfoundland." Two happy instructors, **TRACY ELLIOT** and **PAUL DESIGNES** had a good year teaching many British skiers. They said the 'Brits' really go wild when they get on real snow, they're so used to skiing on dry slopes, which are basically plastic.

I ran into smiling **PAT COTÉ**, area manager. He too had a certain sense of sadness overshadowed by a great sense of accomplishment. He was referring to the winter in general with no major accidents, no liability situations, and no staff injuries, but lots of

Standing in their laced leather boots with trophies, (L to R) Dennis Smith, (unknown American racer,) Ian Neilson and Jim Davies, top Banff skiers in the mid 1950s.

snow and people. This season would be his 21st season as a ski area manager, 17 years at his Glen Mountain area in Quebec and now 4 at Mt. Norquay. In a short while he would thank all the staff at a wind-up party and invite them back to recharge the spirit of Norquay for another year.

JIM DAVIES (Helicopter pilot, artist, skier. Jim pioneered heli-skiing with Hans Gmoser in the Bugaboos. Outstanding record as a heli-pilot for skiing and in mountain rescue. As a junior racer he was one of the best. If he had pursued racing he would definitely have been National Team material.)

"When I was a kid growing up in Banff it was Norquay every weekend. I skied a lot with Ian Neilson and George Capel. The only time we would stop was when we got too cold, then we would go in for a hot chocolate. We were so lucky to live only ten or fifteen minutes from this ski area. The school would take us to Norquay for a PT class. Later on in high school, on fresh snow days, we would skip school classes and head for Norquay. Muriel Gratz, our principle, would know where we were, but when she phoned up to the hill, Red Crozier would always say, 'I haven't seen them.' Every weekend the Ski Runners would hold races, thanks to people like Cyril Paris, Alice Neilson, and Mr. Wonnacott. The timing system was the dropping of a flag for the start. Your score would be the average taken from three stopwatches at the finish line. After the race we would line up to get our ribbons, depending on where you finished. They are good memories. We skied all the time, as young kids we would jump after dark off the old 'Learns Jump,' up by the cemetery. There was a dim street light nearby, which didn't help very much.

"Doug Robinson coached our junior team when we went to Vancouver for the Western Finals. The Banff team was unknown to the coastal area. They didn't give us much of a chance as they had Rod Hebron who was about to join the Olympic Team. They had different thoughts when we left. I had won three gold for GS, Slalom and Combined. I would have won the Downhill, but I had to stop with spectators on the course; I ended up second, one-tenth of a second behind. Not only that, Doug foreran a course and had the fastest time.

"I was lucky to ski in a 'Timex' watch commercial on Norquay. They tied a watch on the tip of my ski and let it bounce around on the slope as I skied down to an announcer who took it off and held it up to the camera to show it was still ticking. I received cash and residuals; money needed for my art school classes.

"I worked a couple of summers putting people on and off the lift. Some would panic, they would be holding on to the center post so tight when they arrived at the top you had to literally pull them off. I had to put a bag over the head of one lady before she would consider taking the chair down.

"Good times, with good friends. Just to name a few, John Derrick, Jay and Terry Kellam, Chester Bell, Tom Morrison, Dave Scatchered."

INEZ PEYTO (Married to ski pioneer Stan Peyto. Mother to Paul, Gordy, Judy and Jimmy Peyto, all outstanding skiers. Inez lived several years in Exshaw before moving to Banff in 1939.)

"The Norquay road; Oh My! I thought, would I have to take this road whenever I want to go skiing. I think it had more turns in the late 30s, didn't it? I got used to it of course and when the kids started skiing nothing was going to stop us from going to Norquay. I had a friend who one day said, 'Can't your kids beat those Becker kids?' Once the boys started competitive skiing Stan and I were heavily involved. We worked races with some great people, Ruth and Don Becker, Fred Wonnacott, Jimmy Masterson, Jean Kelly, Hilda Kelly, and Betty and Peter Cooper from Calgary. Fred always

Red Crozier, Norquays first liftie, always a smile, always a remark. Circa 1950

brought a big thermos of hot chocolate for the kids and something to keep the adults going. It was always fun, my boys won many races and so did the Becker family."

ELAINE MAXWELL (Born in Banff, ski instructor, and managed Sunshine six years for Cliff White. Married Ross Maxwell.)

"Ross schussed the bowl one day. When he came into the lodge George Encil asked him, 'How did you do you do zat?' Ross said 'The conditions were perfect, it was no problem.' Apparently George said, 'I think I'll do zat tomorrow.' I'm not sure if he actually tried it, because his skiing ability didn't compare with Ross', who was still one of the best downhill racers in Canada. But the next day the patrol, Jack Pugh, I think, took George off the mountain with a broken leg.

"Red Crozier and Louie Louis were always playing tricks on Walter Fisher. One day they were so mad at him they turned his VW Beetle upside-down.

"Norquay started as a party place. My Dad, Jack Brown, helped build the first cabin. People would volunteer, work a few hours and generally end up partying. They were depression years, people were looking for things to lighten their lives.

"Teaching with the Kinsmen classes at Norquay was a good time. I think the kids paid almost nothing, maybe a dollar for the whole winter. They did run them at Sunshine for awhile, but that was awful. Going up on the buses some of the kids would get sick and many of them were poorly dressed. At Norquay they were close to home and they didn't have to have money to stay for a full day."

CRAG & CANYON (January 1966.)
Banff Ski Runners, Marilyn Kelly, Paul Peyto and Brian Becker have been named to the National Team hopefuls. Greg Henderson has been invited to try out. Stan Peyto will be Chief of Race in this year's Intercollegiate Meet.

ROB TOOKE (Banff Born. First skied Norquay in 1965 at the age of four. Rob is co-owner of the "Rude Boys" snowboard shop. He and his wife Kate are about to introduce their two children, Georgia and Jacob to Norquay.)

"Norquay was my baby sitter. We always skied to town. It was a real kick coming across the railway tracks into Banff, our metal ski edges would complete the circuit between the tracks and set off the automatic warning system. The Norquay Challenge was cool. On the day I tried it I was the first up the mountain, I skied until noon, took a half-hour lunch break and completed my 27 runs by three o'clock. I still had enough energy to ski home. I guess I was 12 years old, I couldn't do that today.

"My dad, Glen Tooke would help with races on the mountain. He was also a photographer. He found out, quickly, if he wanted to get a picture of me in a race he would have to sign up for the first three gates as that was about as far I generally got in a race. Annually our ski shop sponsors a snowboard competition called the 'Banned Beaver.' Our logo for this was a takeoff on the Parks Resident's sticker for cars. In place of the 'R' for resident we had a 'R' for Rude; this didn't harmonize with their thinking so we had to change it.

"I believe snowboarders and skiers are melding together. I know a lot more are running the hills together. The styling of clothes is also coming together, but favoring the snowboarder, it has more practical features. I do believe skiing will hold its own and maybe even make a bit of a comeback in four or five years. The 'punk' era of snowboarding has passed."

PETER COOPER (Writing in a ski column, Calgary Albertan, March 1959.)
Two Banff Skiers best in Tournament.

Juvenile Paul Peyto and Midget Marcel Fisher took top honours at Mt. Norquay on the weekend. Peyto won the Juvenile slalom, downhill, and cross country, and placed 2nd in jumping. Fisher won the Midget downhill, cross country, and slalom, and was 4th in the jumping.

PETER COOPER (Ski column, *Calgary Albertan*, 1959)
Banff Ski Runners and Calgary Ski Club hold end of season races. Both clubs running the same courses for individual club trophies.

Jim Davies of Banff raced for the Calgary Club as he was a student there at the time. He won the slalom in 1:32.00, Pat Duffy was second, 1:38.00. In the Banff race, Scott Henderson was first with a time of 1:26.00, followed by Brother Wayne in 1:27.08. Lynne Becker of Banff had the girls' fastest time, 1:51.04, followed by Bev Steele. Calgary ladies winner was Pat Clark, 1:55.06, second went to Betty Kent, 1:58.08. In the downhill Jim Davies won followed by Duffy. In the Banff race, Scott Henderson won the downhill with second going to Bill Wonnacott, followed by Wayne Henderson. In another few years all three Banff racers would be on Canada's National Team.

BRIAN SKRINE (International Ski Federation (F.I.S) Technical Delegate, 35 years on the racing scene for young Albertans, World Cup races and disabled skiers.)
"I became involved in racing when my son Michael started skiing. I had taken him and a few other Banff skiers to Red Deer for a race and was frustrated on that trip because of the problems we had with our bindings on the icy course. They were a combination of a Marker toe and a cable with a front throw. It was impossible to get enough pressure against the 'toe,' as there was so much vibration on the ice it kept releasing. From that point on I tried to learn about equipment, waxing and the technique of racing gates, combined with the knowledge of organizing races from the F.I.S. point of view.

"I have worked on mountains in every type of weather imaginable, but never alone, there was always someone next to you working just as hard and they too were donating their time. I admire the young racers who give their all to perform well, their ability to concentrate, to memorize a slalom course. I believe that training helps them in their future professions after skiing. I admire and enjoy working with disabled skiers, who have the greatest outlook on life and the sport; they are so positive.

"Jerry Johnston and his wife Anne did a wonderful job in developing the disabled program, which I believe they have been doing for over 35 years. Skiing and snowboarding does so much for the mental and physical health of people. I can't understand the anti-social environmentalists that want to close down ski areas in the Park. One thing I have noticed with that group is not many, if any, have children."

ROB DeMONTIGNY (From Vancouver Island, employed in Banff 1999.)

"My memory of Norquay is not a good one. I was on top about to hit the powder. Before taking my first run, in bounds, I decided to put my pack behind a tree that was just out of bounds. The Ski Patrol came along just as I was storing my pack with the news 'We're taking your lift ticket away.' That was it."

(There must be a moral to that one. The line between right and wrong can be very narrow.)

HELEN AND ELLWOOD THOMPSON (Enthusiastic skiers and veteran racers. They farm in the Innisfail area of Alberta.)

Du Maurier 1966.

Ellwood: "I skied with Thomas Grandi the other day. I would give the farm to be able to ski like that. My friends don't believe me when I tell them I ski with National Team coaches, Ray Seguin and Bruce Henry."

Helen: "We train every Friday with Ray Seguin's Rut Runner program, and have done that for seven years. We didn't start skiing until we were 35."

Ellwood: "We have spent the bulk of our lives working alone, in a field or yard, not around the public very much. Now we are awe-struck to be taken in by the people in the Rut Runners and the staff at Mt. Norquay. Our skiing is still improving, but we race in Bruno's Veterans and Masters Race: we have even won medals. We are used to grass-roots type people, people who make deals on a handshake. That's what we feel here, and someone knows how to run that tractor out there, the grooming is excellent."

PAT DUFFY (Could possibly make the list as one of the top 25 characters ever to ski the slopes of Norquay. In the early years of the single chair when the serious skiers lined up for the first run of the day, Duffy never missed a 9:00 a.m. call -- with a 'barb' for his friends.)

"In the Ladies' Slalom of the 1965 DuMaurier International, held on the Lone Pine, we had to cope with dry snow that wasn't going to hold up to training sessions and two runs in competition. The feasibility of watering the slope was looked into. The race committee, George Kent, John Pendergast (Chief of Race), and I (Chief of Course), along with the host club, Banff Ski Runners, decided we had no choice but to go for that option. It had never been done before, or since. So we got Haliburton Oilfield Services to come up with pumps and water the hill. The result was excellent, although we had to use a fertilizer to soften the surface. (The National coaches were the forerunners and they had a helluva time staying on the hill, let alone the course!) By the way, the Canadian Army Infantry, under General John Rockingham, foot tramped everything we needed for racing and training."

CRAG & CANYON (February 16, 1966. Same race? This DuMaurier was 1966. In the paper the F.I.S. member from Switzerland, Mr. Gertsch, thanked the Chief of

Race, Joe Irwin, not John Pendergast, as Pat Duffy remembers.)

Nancy Greene of Rossland wins DuMaurier, winning both runs in the Ladies' Slalom for a total time of 1:04.06, more than three seconds ahead of second place Heidi Zimmerman of Austria. Christl Haas of Austria, was 3rd and Canadian Karen Dokka, 4th. In the Men's Giant Slalom, Kurt Huggler of Switzerland was the winner. Scott Henderson of Banff was 5th. Canadian Peter Duncan was 9th with a fall.

Author's note: This was the start for Nancy Greene who went on to win World Cup honours in 1967 and 1968, including a gold and silver at the 1968 Olympics.

Nancy Greene and the national team trained in Banff in 1966. Nancy won the Du Maurier International slalom at Norquay in February of 1966; she was more than three seconds ahead of second place Austrian Heidi Zimmerman.

GEORGE PARIS 1999 (The skiing history of the Paris family is the history of skiing in Banff. George Paris in 1894 was possibly Banff's first skier. In the 1920s Cyril Paris was instrumental in developing Norquay and young skiers. In the 1930s Ted and Herb Paris (twins) were at the top of Banff's ski scene. Ted was one of Canada's first stars in slalom and downhill. In 1962 George Paris was a member of the Alberta Junior team that won the national title. Today George and Irene ski with their children, Caitlin and Kelsie Paris, on the slopes their grandparents pioneered over seventy years ago.)

"My mother took me to Norquay when I was three or four years old, along with other mothers and children. It was the thing to do. My Dad was still in the service during World War II. I remember what a struggle that was, when I was big enough to ride the rope tow. It was so heavy to hold, half way up my hands would give out, so I would try to put my arms around it. Because the rope was always twisting, it would grab my jacket and I would literally be tied up by the time I reached the top. If I got that far, I would drag through the safety gate and stop the tow. Hopefully someone would come along to untie me.

"As a competitive skier my fondest memories would be of my double win at the Brewster Memorial in 1959 and 1960, then our Alberta Team victory in 1962. It was the first time Alberta had won a Canadian Championship. I trained with Scottie and Wayne Henderson on the National Team at Nelson in 1964, but I had broken an ankle the year before which hadn't healed properly. That was the end of my competitive skiing.

"Norquay is still home to me, the memories of skiing with my older sister Zona; we would ski the Gulley and hope we could get a ride into town. It was all good stuff."

Author's note: George Paris mentioned Nelson. For a couple of years Canada's National Team attended classes and trained at Notre Dame College in Nelson, B. C. He would have been with the Henderson brothers, Nancy Greene, and Peter Duncan. The coach at that time was Dave Jacobs.

WERNER ZULLIG (Banff cafe owner, Swiss born. Long time skier now starting over again as a snowboarder on the slopes of Norquay.)

"I was having trouble mastering the board with adults so I decided to go with kids. I mean 4- and 5-year-old kids. I talked with them and tried to mimic their actions on the snowboard. Kids learn in a natural way. I figured it would work for me. I humbled myself and it worked. I can't wait for next winter to start."

CYRIL PARIS (Pioneer skier of the Rockies in the 1920s, reviewing his early days of skiing.)

"When skis were equipped with brass edges in the late 30s I was advised not to buy them as they would surely cut one's legs to pieces."

JANICE PEERS (Former Jasper resident now living in Banff.)

"Norquay! I love it. It's just a cycle in my dryer away. It's the way I remember the old Whistler area in Jasper."

JIM CHRISTOU (Banff born, 1940. In his younger years had worked summers at Mt. Norquay. Passed along this information in the spring of 1999 on a visit to Banff from his home on the West Coast.)

"The first paying customer on the chair when it opened in 1948 was not a skier, not even a Canadian, but an American from New York City. He was a bit of a character who loved the Banff area. Upon his retirement from United Artist Film Producers, he would spend his winters in the Mount Royal Hotel, same room each year. His name was Leo Adler."

Stephanie Townsend and Brian Becker, outstanding young Banff skiers and national team members in the late 1960s.

NORQUAY GONDOLA Promotional manager, Doug Robinson, announced major change to Norquay chair. Area is now known as Banff Cablecar Lift on Norquay. The Gondola will operate in the summer and change back to a double chair for winter skiing. The year was 1966.

NORQUAY TICKETS 1967/68.
Special season pass for Banff residents: all lifts $60. (Others paid $100.) Day ticket was $5.50.
The owner was Walter Fisher. Howard Srigley became new manager of lifts, October 1967.

Skiing in the Lowell Thomas F.I.S. Classic at Park City, Utah in 1968; **STEPHANIE TOWNSEND** was 1st in the Slalom and 5th in the Giant Slalom. **MARILYN KELLY** was 3rd in the Giant Slalom.
DANNY WILSON noses out **PAT ADAMS** in Alberta Junior 'C' slalom. **JACKIE WILSON**, 2nd in women's slalom. **JENNY GOURLAY** won Midget girls. **GERALD COSTIGAN** 2nd in Midget boys. The year was 1968.

BONNIE WIEGELE (Longtime Banff resident, instructor and racer. Married to Mike Wiegele, owner of Mike Wiegele Heli-skiing at Blue River, B. C. Daughter Michelle.)
"I love the Excalibur run from the Mystic Pathfinder Quad. It is fabulous for my training. The vertical I can get there in one day is greater than any other place I might ski, and that includes heli-skiing.
"I am not sure why I remember two embarrassing situations experienced by my daughter Michelle when she was younger, but I do. Embarrassment reserved for 10-year-old daughters. She was about to start a slalom as racer number one when she realized her dad, Mike, was the forerunner. Her faithful dog Denver supplied the second embarrassment. Once again she was about to start a race when Denver spotted her from the finish area. On his run to see her he suddenly stopped near the top and deposited a 'steamer' right in the middle of gate 5. Just some of the hardships experienced by young racers."

JOAN WILSON (Member of Canada's National Ski Team in 1973/4. At that time she was the only skier from Nova Scotia to make it to the Alpine squad.)
"We had a small reunion of ex-national team members at Norquay. This was a few years after we had retired, you might say we were not in top shape, but no one was ready to admit it. There was Steve Podborski, Ken Read, Phil and Peter Monod, Keith Humphrey, Vania Henning, John Hilland; I'm probably missing someone. We skied the Big Chair like we would have in our prime. No one wanted to be the first to stop, the competitive spirit was still with us, but not the legs. I don't know how they felt the next day, but I know I really paid for it. But it was worth it."

BERN SMITH (Local watercolour artist. He had worked on the construction of the upper Tea House in the year 1952.)
"It was my first job in Banff. I worked with Ross Maxwell and Peter Van Wagner at the top of the lift. We were breaking stones for the new Tea House. To the tourist

coming that way we probably looked like criminals on a chain gang, but we set them right when we told them we were a team of archaeologists studying an ancient society of skiers. In time I started to believe it myself."

SUSAN CLARK (A Canmore resident skiing Norquay.)

"I love the Big Chair and the challenge of trying to calm myself down before starting my run."

CLARKE LeFAIVRE (Norquay Ski School Director.)

MAUREEN LeFAIVRE (Children's Program Coordinator.)

Author's note: Before talking to Maureen and Clarke I looked at 44 survey sheets that had been completed by parents and individuals who had been involved in lessons. I believe there was only one that was negative. Parents were

Norquay Ski school in morning huddle 1999.

very pleased. I read comments that said, "The instructors Kelly and Kim were a positive influence on my 4-year-old son." "My daughter loved Stephen," and "Neil Marsh, the instructor had great enthusiasm, patience and he made it fun for my son's group. He has developed a relationship with the kids that extends past the one-hour session. Great job!" The one negative said, "I don't know what happened with my son and the teachers, but I think the teachers need to work on their methods with reluctant skiers or those having a bad day."

The survey also covered Ladies' Day, with comments, "I feel I'm ready to tackle bumps and speed (only kidding)." "Thanks for the easy approach to skiing and enjoying the outdoors. Thanks Jason." The sheets continued with other positive comments, so I didn't have to ask Maureen and Clarke many questions about the school.

Norm and MJ Russell had mentioned Maureen's name to me when I spoke with them in Calgary. MJ, Norm's wife, couldn't say enough about the skills Maureen brought to her job when organizing the Weekend Warriors, a group of 6- to 12-year-old children they take to Norquay each week. Clarke explained to me that they also have a 12- to 16-year-old group. From this group he likes to encourage those who don't want to race, but may become part-time or full-time instructors. It's a step program implemented by the Canadian Ski Instructors Alliance. Some have already come back to teach in the program where they were once students.

The stage for the Norquay Ski School with this pleasant couple, and their group of young instructors, headed by Sean DeKoning, looked like it lacked nothing. Then it got even better when the day-care door opened and two happy children, Brodie and MacKenzie, came running to Maureen and Clarke with a cry to their parents, "It's time to go skiing!"

IAN NORQUAY (A member of the Norquay family, explaining the origin of the family name.)

"Norquay is a Canadian surname. It is pronounced 'Norkway'. The family forefathers emigrated from the Orkney Islands and settled in 1791 in the Red River Valley of Manitoba. Our many ancestors, the Honourable John Norquay (Premier of Manitoba, 1878-1887) included, all answered to 'Norkway'. There is no confusion amongst us as to what our name should sound like.

There is no reason to confuse this Canadian surname with names of towns in some other country."

LEO BERCHTOLD (Born in Zurich, Switzerland. Arrived in Banff 1955. For forty years he was an active instructor, coach and F.I.S. race official. He is a past President of the Banff Ski Runners. He worked with Stan Peyto and Doug Robinson on the International Intercollegiate Ski Meet, the most successful 4-way college competition in North America, which ran for 26 years.)

"I have many wonderful memories of skiing on Norquay and some not too good, but I am still skiing at 69 and looking for many more good years.

"I worked on the Norquay Ski Patrol for a couple of years after arriving here in 1955. I instructed with the Johnny Monod Ski School and during one of those classes I met my wife to-be, Marion. Some of the instructors I worked with: Ted Clark, Jerry Johnston, and Heinz Vifian. One day when I was coaching the Monod boys, who were excellent racers and later to become members of Canada's National Ski Team, an unknown skier ran into me. It was an awful hit. When I fell I landed on my ski pole which penetrated my kidney. I required an operation, which kept me off skis for about a year.

"In 1972 I was Chief of Course for the World Cup Slalom. It was the first World Cup held in Canada. Excitement ran high as we had all the top skiers, ladies and men, who had just returned from the Olympics in Japan. Also arriving the night before was three feet of snow, the last thing you want to see before a race, but we had the Army and kids from the Banff school who helped us get it all tramped out and the race went off as planned. The racers were having such a good time skiing the powder I don't believe they cared that much.

"The most unusual accident I saw on Norquay happened when Jerry Johnston, coming off the traverse towards the Lone Pine, ran into a ram. Both were suprised but not hurt.

"I love skiing. I am still working in town but I can make it up to Norquay during lunch hour for a few runs, generally with Frank Gourlay. I have another friend that comes up from Calgary, Ethan Compton, who is 82 years old and has had two hip operations. He still skis a lot and enters Bruno Engler's Veterans and Masters Race each year. I think skiing aids the health of everyone, no matter what their age might be. I know even after my few runs during the lunch break I feel recharged and ready to go back to work."

LEO BERCHTOLD (Leo won Bruno's first Veteran's race in 1967.)

Skiing in the 35 to 45 year class, 37-year-old Leo Berchtold won the overall

Regular and disabled skiers excelled in the Norquay Interski of 1987.

Veteran's Trophy. It was Canada's Centennial year. Also racing that day were Cliff White, Rod Adams, John Monod and Stan Peyto. The initial race was held at Sunshine and then moved to Mt. Norquay, where it is still run.

JIM "Bucky" BUCKINGHAM (Mountain Manager at Norquay in the 1980s. Was there to consult and plan the large expansion that took place in 1990.)

Jim 'Bucky' Buckingham, mountain planner. 1999

"I arrived at Norquay in 1983. It was a small area with limited skiing for the beginner and expert skier, with even less for the intermediate skier. Snowboarding was yet to arrive on the scene. They had started making snow in 1978, however it covered a small area and the system probably produced more problems than pleasure. Danny Cox started the system for making snow and was there to improve it during the expansion of 1989-90, when Brewsters joined the people from Sulphur Mountain for a seven million dollar expansion. This included a new lodge, two lifts on new slopes and the upgrading of the snowmaking system. Before the improvement of the snowmaking system, there were problems with the water lines. They would freeze up when the temperature hit minus 20. To clear the pipes from Forty Mile Creek of 40-foot ice cubes on a 40-degree slope, was a great challenge. Who said, 'running water doesn't freeze?'

"Before the expansion of 1990, Norquay was in a critical situation as far as management was concerned, but the good things about the slopes remained true, which we proved in the running of the Interski Competition in 1987, the year before the 1988 Calgary Winter Olympics.

"Interski brings together the leading countries of the ski world to display their

Fri and Gloria Rodley enjoy a Calgary Ski Club social event with Betty and George Kent, 1958.

system of skiing. The programs displayed by each country demand flow and timing. In order to do this I had to replace a hand tow with a larger tow that would keep the teams moving without delay.

"I was working with Norm Crearar, who decided to bring in a Mueller portable spring-box platter lift, which the Whistler, B. C. area used for their summer camps. Footings for this lift had to be prepared in the autumn and the lift was assembled for a test, then taken down and a helicopter stored the towers a short distance from the slope. In January, before Interski was to start, we removed the handle tow and flew in the platter lift, which was installed in less than three days. It performed as planned. The Interski ran without problems. When it ended at noon on the Saturday, crews jumped in to make the final switch. They worked until 9:30 p.m. that evening, plus a little more time for grooming and the slope was ready for the start of ski classes on Sunday.

"I consider myself an environmentalist, as do most people I know in the ski business. The difference between my outlook and that of the 'environmental groups' that hate ski areas with a passion, is that I don't believe that ski areas that are planned, in size and design, are a threat to the environment. When I do consulting work for ski areas I keep in mind preservation and restoration. If skiing were to cease tomorrow, I could clear the area and in twenty years you would be tested to find traces of that ski area."

JAKE AND NOAH MAISONET (Jake 8, Noah 5, have skied their whole life at Norquay, except for two days when Jake tried a snowboard.)

Jake: "Norquay is the best ski place I have ever been. I'm happy to live so close to it in Banff."

Noah: "I like Norquay because I get to go skiing. I went up the Big Chair with Mom, but I couldn't keep up with her. It was steep and powdery."

Jake: "And I like the chips and hot chocolate."

Noah: "What's that you're holding Grampa? It's a microphone … Oh!"

JOHNNY MONOD (From his ski column in the *Crag & Canyon*, January 1972.)

Jim Hunter and Reto Barrington are skiing Europe on the World Cup Circuit. In the New Year's Slalom at Mt. Norquay, Keith Humphrey was 1:14.04, John Hilland, 1:16.08, Rick Merriam 1:19.04. Ladies' Slalom: Jackie Wilson, BSR 1:25.01, Pat Gordon 1:28.01, Vainta Haining 1:32.02. The Kinsmen Ski School has to be the best. It costs $1 a week. This year 169 kids have signed up. Competing in this year's Intercollegiate Ski Meet are teams from Denver University, University of British Columbia, Brigham Young, Montana State, University of Montana, Pacific Lutheran, Ricks College, Selkirk College, University of Idaho, University of

Saskatchewan, University of Calgary, University of Western Ontario, Laurentian University and University of Alberta.

The snow is so deep this year Erwin Tontch is skiing with a snorkel.

I believe Karl Schranz is the greatest downhiller of all times. Schranz said, "I go free skiing after a race is over, I don't think of gates, I just relax and help regain my balance, which is skiing itself."

CALGARY HERALD 1940 (A special page of ads in the *Calgary Herald*, February 1940, promoting the Dominion Championship at Norquay.)

Special train to Banff $2.10 return. ($2.25 with Banff transfer to Norquay.)

An ad by Russell Sport Shop: SKIS from $1.95. SKI BOOTS $2.95 and SKI POLES $0.95.

Also on this page the R.C.M.P gave traffic times for the Norquay road. You go up between 8:45 a.m. and 9:30 a.m., down from 10:00 a.m. to 10:20 a.m. These times alternated throughout the day. They even gave driving tips. "No attempt

Doug Robinson and Norm Russell with the Canadian Junior Championship Trophy won by Alberta in 1962.

should be made to 'make it on high.' Gears should be shifted to second early to avoid wheel spinning. Second gear should be used as a brake for most of the descent."

THE RUSSELLS, MJ AND NORM (Russells pioneered the ski shop business in Calgary. They supplied equipment to the hardy city folks that were willing to risk their lives in the Rockies on the weekends of the late 1930s. True warriors of children's ski programs, for over 30 years they have taken children to Mt. Norquay each weekend for a program known as 'Weekend Warriors.')

NORM: "My Dad ran ski buses from the store which was in downtown Calgary. The year was 1939. We continued with the Calgary store, while running the ski shop at Mt. Norquay. We ran the store at Norquay for a couple of years before reaching an agreement with Walter Fisher which would see us build a new shop, with offices upstairs for him as well as a ticket office for the ski lift. The building was to revert to him in ten years, however Bill Herron bought him out in 1968 and Herron purchased the last two years on our lease.

"The most popular items at our Norquay store were small things like glasses, gloves, mitts, socks and ski boot laces. Mrs. Fisher was always after us to bring items like Bogner ski pants and fancy sweaters, which we finally did, but they didn't sell. Most people thought they would cost more in Banff, which wasn't true. Still they would wait to buy them in Calgary.

"When Norquay built a rope-tow in 1941, I was 11 years old. We would go up the lift and straight down to repeat the ride up. My Dad noticed what it was costing him. He finally said, 'Can't you make a turn or two on the way down?'"

MJ : "We have been running buses from Calgary to Mt. Norquay for over thirty years. They are children's programs for recreational skiing. It is not a racing program. The objective is to ski well and safely. Throughout the years we have had many students come back to assist in the program. The Norquay Ski School, headed by Clarke LeFaivre, gives the lessons. Maureen LeFaivre, Clarke's wife, is a real 'Cracker Jack' at organizing our group, which is known as the Weekend Warriors. She knew the names of all the kids in no time; she has really made a difference.

"Each weekend we take three buses with about 130 children, to Norquay. Another 50 will probably drive up with their parents, including some from Canmore and Banff. Three years ago we had 12 snowboarders, last year 20, and now 36 this year. It doesn't matter what they are on, as long as they do it well and enjoy the outdoors."

RALPHENE (HARVEY) LOCKE (The lineage of Ralphene Locke and her sister Mary Alice Stewart comes from Banff's earliest families. Their grandmother, Mary Jane Boyd, married James Irvine Brewster. She was the niece of the Reverend George MacDougall who founded Morley's first church in 1862.)

"I remember the road before it was completed to the original ski cabin. It stopped below the Green Spot quite close to the Gulley area. There was a parking area from which we had to climb a fair distance. My dad, Ralph Harvey, was involved with the Ski Runners and the development of Norquay. I remember the opening of the new lodge in 1940. They had a special party up there for the Banff people. They had music and we danced; we just thought it was the most glamorous place."

GERALD (COCKY) LOCKE (Was a member of the famous Banff Ski Runners Junior Racing Team of the late 1930s. The following information is from the *Globe and Mail*, "Lives Lived," by Alanna Mitchell, 1996.)

"Dentist, accomplished skier, raiser of French cattle and Belgian horses, holder of strident opinions, born June 8, 1923, died of cancer in Okotoks, age 73.

"Gerald Lorne Locke was about 17 when he became the first man to schuss the Memorial Bowl, the toughest ski hill at Norquay in Banff National Park. That was in the days before ski lifts, when if you wanted to ski a steep one, you had to walk up first.

"He trained himself by steps and when the day came he strapped on his 230 centimeter skis with bear-trap bindings and soft boots. A crowd gathered at the bottom to catch the thrills. And Cocky Locke, as he was known then and forever after, came barrelling faultlessly straight down that mountain. His life was always like that; living on the edge and winning."

Author's note: The article went on to relate more colourful moments in his career. At one time he had three 1976 Cadillac Eldorados, not being able to part with any of them. He was known to simply send patients home who were late for a dentist appointment. On the up side, other dentists would send their wives to him to get the best dentistry going. He resented paying taxes and loathed the Liberals until the day he died. Ralphene and he were divorced in 1978. They had two children, Christie and Harvey. Harvey Locke is Vice-President of the Canadian Parks and Wilderness Society, a locally based lobby group that's often led the fight to stop commercial development in Banff National Park. Apparently Harvey Locke's approach to the Park isn't severe. He has accepted alpine skiing as an acceptable activity within Canada's National Parks, providing the resorts aren't allowed to expand beyond their existing boundaries, while other evironmental groups want the resorts shut down.

Currently, Harvey Locke has accepted a posting with an American group in Boston. He is on a minimum three-year contract with the Kendall Foundation, a Massachusetts environmental research and advocacy group to study issues and formulate policy.

SULPHUR POOLS AT BANFF

Did the Sulphur water of the past have greater medicinal qualities than the water of 1999? Check this testimonial from a Hot Springs visitor in the 1920s:

"I had to be carried up to the springs, I could not bear even the motion of a carriage. I had not walked for two years, and every movement was an agony. In three weeks after coming here, I walked down to Banff and in five, I ran a foot race. Praise the Lord."

RUSTY KIRBY (Rusty's first words, similiar to the opening line spoken by hundreds of people living in Banff: "When I arrived in 1976 I planned on staying one year.")

"I didn't take to skiing right away. On my first effort I was poorly dressed, I ended up a soaking mess. A few years later Pamela Knott tried to get me back to Norquay. I tried again but it just didn't click. I was a total klutz. A few more years passed. Because my husband worked for Brewsters during the years when Brewsters had an interest in Norquay, we received passes at lower rates. So here I go again. One day I was watching the young Alpine Racers. I started talking to one of the parent volunteers, Dave Wills, who gave me advice that changed my skiing career. No, I didn't join the Alpine Racers. He asked me what my favourite drink was. I told him tequila. He said, 'Okay, put your hands out in front of you like you were carrying a tray of margaritas. The idea is to get this tray to the bottom of the hill without spilling a drop'. After taking my poles away, he told me, 'Keep your upper body pointing straight down hill, swivel your lower body and let your legs do the work of turning.' I was amazed. Suddenly all my lessons fell into place.

"My husband agreed, he said, 'You look great, now you'll never want to leave Banff.' You're right, I laughed, I have 17 years of skiing to catch up on!"

MAGDLENA KORNDORFER (Magdlena worked 20 years at Norquay; in length second only to Klara Huser's 24.)

"I worked at Norquay from 1959 to 1979 selling lift tickets. But for several summers I looked after the Tea House at the top of the lift. I worked for four owners, George Encil, Walter Fisher, Bill Herron and Art Haenni. I didn't really ski. When I thought of it in the early years, Mr. Fisher said to me, 'What if you break a leg or an arm, how will you sell tickets?'

Beth Cairns: "It warms my heart to feel the original spirit is still here." 2000

BETH CAIRNS (Started skiing at the age of three in

Quebec. Came west to look at the Rockies 18 years ago, still looking. She carries vitality and charm combined with excellent skiing skills onto any slope she skis. Beth is a member of the "Ski Stop" Gang.)

"I love every minute I'm here. I believe those old photographs in the lodge put a nice perspective on what it was and what it is. It warms my heart to feel that original nal spirit is still here flying around. You don't get that at other resorts."

Dave Irwin interviewing Karen Percy at Sunshine World Cup Downhill, 1985.

Dave's dad in the Norquay Dominions of 1940.

DAVE IRWIN (A member of the Crazy Canucks, what else can you say! One day in the winter of 1999, I spoke with several people at the Norquay lodge, starting with two members of the Crazy Canucks, Dave Irwin and Ken Read. Both were on the Canadian Downhill Team of the 70s, when more Canadians occupied the podium than ever before or since.)

Dave: "Norquay! To Banff locals it's everything. You can come and ski for an hour or three, or follow my good friend Ratso here, and take every afternoon off and come skiing.

"The first time I saw Norquay was the first time I raced in World Cup competition. The year was 1972 and I believe I started with the same number in the slalom. By that time the ruts were so deep it was a four-foot drop between the gates. My dad, Bill Irwin, raced here in the 1940 Dominions. He was a member of the Amber ski club from Princeton, B.C. Dad would have been 21 at that time, now I'm skiing with my 9-year-old son, Dean, who likes the gnarly features off the Big Chair and the North American."

Dean: "Gnarly? I like it because it's steep and has moguls."

KEN READ (Outstanding downhill racer. First Canadian to win a World Cup Downhill (France, 1975). During his career on the World Cup, Ken won 5 gold medals.)

"Norquay for me goes back to '68, that would be the first time I skied here, but my thoughts go back even further because my mother competed at Norquay in the 1948 Dominions. In my younger years when she told me how she raced downhill in the Bowl, I had trouble trying to understand how she ever survived. Of course in those days she had to climb to the start. Now, I ski with my 7-year-old son Erik, and tell him how I skied the downhill, just the way my mother had told me years before. He looks at me and says, 'You did what?' reacting pretty much the same way I did to my mother over 30 years ago.

"My first big race was a Pontiac Cup here in 1969. The Pontiac Cup focused on Canadians, but for that particular race a group of Americans, 'The Aspen Wildcats,' had come up. It was my first exposure to international racing. The next was when I was a forerunner in the World Cup Slalom that was here in 1972. It was a great thrill, and even more so when I became a member of the team a couple of years later, and all that went with racing on the World Cup circuit."

In 1983 Ken Read retired from competitive skiing.

Author's note: As I was about to end my talk with Ken I asked him what his greatest strength was in downhill racing.

KEN READ: "My strength in downhill skiing was gliding on high speed turns, being able to carry that speed through. Along the way I was fortunate to have some crucial coaching. Starting in my young years with Mike Wiegele, who said to me, 'The season starts with the day the ski area opens and it ends the day the ski area closes and you take every advantage in between,' to coach Othmar Setzer, who introduced discipline, to coach Butch Bootrey, who introduced principle, to Scott

The Crazy Canucks: Dave Murray, Ken Read, Steve Podborski and Dave Irwin. 1975.

Henderson who introduced work ethic, to Heinz Kappler, who introduced some of the subtle skills at the top level - being able to communicate. The best money anyone can invest in a racing program is in coaching."

GREG HANN (National Alpine team member 1976-79. Second oldest of the skiing Hanns of Banff, Andy, Greg, Kevin, and Brian. Their Dad is Bob Hann, chief guide of the Abominable Ski Shop world. Their uncle, Dennis Smith, was a member of Canada's National Alpine Ski Team. I caught up with Greg at Norquay on the day he was competing in the 'SMED International Corporate Challenge,' along with Ken Read, Dave Irwin, Wendy Lumby, Chris McCready, John Hilland, Bill Irwin, Felix Belczyk, Jim Hunter, Jim 'Bearcat' Murray, Lee Lee Morrison, Susan Auch, Bruce Henry, Lynda Robbins, and Jim Peplinski, all leaders of the various corporate teams. Not all were members of Canada's National Ski team, but all were sport celebrities.)

"What do I remember of my early Norquay? I was four years old so I don't remember much. I would, however, like to thank Thomas and Kika for all they're doing for Norquay. And those old photos on the wall taken by Bruno, they make me feel good. Of course skiing with and against the Monod brothers, Phil, Peter and Nicky, my brothers Andy, Kevin and me pretty well match them in age. The team I'm leading in this corporate race is called 'The Wood Worms'. Do we sound fast or what!"

CHRIS McCREADY (Member of Canada's National Alpine team in the late 1970s. On this day she, as one of our skiing Legends, was leading a team in the 'SMED Corporate Challenge.')

"Funny, I should remember this, but when we were training at Norquay the coaches wanted the guys to go off the big jumps. What were they, the 'A' and 'B' jumps, 70 and 90 meters? They would only let the girls go off the smaller 'C' jump. Probably just as well. I might have broken my leg again. Four times is enough. Well, I had better run, my team is to be in the gate at 2:10."

LYNDA ROBBINS (Member of Canada's National Alpine team, 1981-83. A Toronto girl now living in Calgary with her husband Ken Read and their skiing boys, Erik, Kevin and Jeffrey, members of the Banff Quickie program. On this day Lynda was leading a corporate team against Ken.)

"Norquay, for the family, is ideal. For me personally, I like to take the Big Chair for some of that upper powder. I had better run, I have to beat my husband."

WENDY LUMBY (Made it to Canada's National Team when she was 15. Competed for seven years and retired following the 1988 Olympics.)

"The family would come to Norquay on week-ends. We would park our camper in this area. At night my sister and I would go out and jump the little 'C' jump that was at the end of the parking lot. I skied the big chair when I was three, as fast as

Alberta Team training in France 1982, Wendy Lumby, Kendall Hunter and coach Glen Thomsen.

I could go. It really was a fun time: it was a blast. I really miss those years. I'm coaching now, so I go to other hills, but I would like to come here more often."

MALCOLM CULLEN (Malcolm and Sheila Cullen dedicated their skills to helping young skiers for over thirty years, mostly on the slopes of Norquay.)

"My thinking for young skiers has always been to have them learn to ski well and enjoy the sport. There will come a time when they will decide if they want to go into racing, become an instructor or just ski for their own pleasure.

"Sheila and I have worked with different programs through the years. I started in Banff with some of the active young skiers from Banff and Calgary. Some of the names that come to mind from a four-way competition we had in 1959: big point getter was Paul Peyto in the Juvenile class, Marcel Fisher in the Midget group, both of Banff. Doug McManus, Hux Johnson, Ricky Cooper and Derek McManus from Calgary were on the podium, as was Bill Keys, Toby Keys, Gordon Peyto and Mike McKenzie. It was so long ago I must be forgetting many of those kids, but they are memories we both enjoy.

"There were weekends at Norquay when we had 192 kids in racing programs. At one point in the 1960s I had 52 coaches to organize into programs.

"We have worked with other programs through the years, including several with the Calgary Skimeisters. I split with them when they decided to focus on a more elite racing program. They also wanted to move their training site to Fortress. We worked with Norm Russell and his wife MJ, who had similiar thoughts to ours when it came to teaching children. They too preferred Norquay.

"Unfortunately I remember a day at Norquay when one of our young girl skiers was killed. She had gone up the Memorial slope to bring down some gates from a slalom course and was hit by another young skier who had come over the Cliff at a high speed and ran into her. She was ten years old.

"Just before I became President of the Calgary Ski Club in 1959/60, we ran a Standard race at Norquay for the adult members of the club. It was a challenging run. It started on the wide opening of the North American, just below the upper 'S' turn. It cut across the slope to Rick's Cut Back, down to the Cliff and took that sudden drop down the Memorial slope. To get a Gold Award you had to be under 45 seconds, Silver 1:25 minutes, and 2:00 minutes for the Bronze. It wasn't heavy with gates; the slope pretty well controlled your run. It was a fun event for our club."

STEVE ORCHIN (Long time instructor, all-around good skier and innovator of ski programs for visitors to the Rockies.)

"I really had to push myself to master the ride down the Pine when I first came here. I was a Champ off the Cascade chair, but a Chump off the Big Chair. Later when I was teaching, Johnny Pristov showed my how to take a good snowplower off the top. It meant a lot to some skiers at that stage in their skiing. It was a trip of courage rather than a skiing accomplishment, but once they made that run it put them at another level as a skier, at least they told their friends back home it did.

"After I spent a winter in Europe, I came home to set up a touring program with John Heinz. The idea was to take people out for a full day at any one of the three areas; we called it 'Mountain Madness.' Later, when Hans Gmoser had the ski school at the Banff Springs, this would be in the mid-70s, we discussed a program that would prepare some of the people that were going into his heli-skiing just for a day. It also acted as a screening process for some that weren't ready for heli-skiing.

We called that program 'Powder, Bumps and Bushes.' It was about that time, or shortly after, that 'Club Ski' was set up by Andre Schwartz and Ladd Snowsell: it is still running today.

"I have so many good memories of this mountain. The torchlight parade was always, if you'll excuse the expression, a 'highlight.' You could tell the veterans that showed up for it; they always had their oldest burnt-out clothes on. My good friend Bobby Crone kept getting lost on these runs, so the next year they put him in front and we all got lost. I always remember that view looking down on the town at night; it's so serene."

"You spoke to me before Ed, but I wanted to set something straight. The old 'Rusticana' house of the mid-1970s had a bad name it didn't deserve. I heard someone say the occupants of that house had a total income of several thousands of dollars, all from U.I.C. (unemployment insurance). That wasn't true, we all had jobs, either at ski areas or in town. That included Jerry Tucker, Mike Miskow, Larry Williams, Ian Wilson, Bobby Crone, John Heinz, myself and others. There was room for seven to live at a time. There were always enough around for a party."

KATHY MAITRE (Canadian Mountain Holidays (CMH) employee, wife of Steve Orchin.)

"Don't tell anyone, we used to take the trays from the cafeteria and slide down the Gulley."

PAUL STUTZ (Born in Banff, skied Norquay since the early 50s. Father of Paul Stutz, National Juvenile Champ 1998, and named to the Alberta Ski Team in 1999.)

"Norquay? It's the most challenging mountain in Canada, and reminds me too of my Dad who helped clear some of these slopes back in the 30s. I remember the old rope tows that ruined your gloves and pulled the sleeves right out of your jacket.

"This is a special place: it's a social place. We would spend our winters here, and then there were those spring days you never forget. It was almost like a private club we would let the rest of the country come to, once in a while."

THOMAS GRANDI AND MIKE NECESANEK (Two young boys who grew up in Banff. Thomas at present a member of Canada's National Alpine Team; Mike a racing coach. The two were near the Spirit Chair working with young racers when I talked to them.)

Thomas Grandi with his sisters Vania and Astrid. Thomas was the first Canadian male to reach a World Cup podium in a technical discipline, 1998.

Thomas: "My Dad and Mike Wiegele started the Quikies back in the mid 70s. I guess I was three or four. I remember skiing the Big Chair when I was three. Actually I don't remember it that much. I thought I took my skis off and walked down, but they tell me I skied it. My sister Astrid told me I was two and a half when I skied it, so there you go, let's say I was pretty young. I do remember jumping from the old 'C' jump with Andrew Sheppard. Every time I went over my hat would fall off and each time Andrew would pick it up when he came over. Of course I remember breaking my leg going down the Gulley on a GT Racer, I was 12 then.

"This year on the World Cup circuit was disappointing for me. I didn't prepare myself 100 per cent. I am looking ahead with confidence for the year 2000 and the 2002 Olympics at Salt Lake City."

Mike: "Yes, I skied with the Quikies. They were fun times. The little runs we would have to make before classes would start. The one we called the 'Holy Jump.' (It was short for Holy Shit!) That was back in the days when you could tuck in a run and the patrol didn't get on you. Then there was lunchtime, when we had our lunch up in the old Tea House: it was all fun. Excuse me Ed, I have to go to work."

LICHTINELD FAMILY (I was passing by this family, parents and two children, when I heard one of them make a complimentary remark about lunch. Not a common comment at ski areas. I apologize if the spelling of their name is incorrect. My small recorder picked up a wind sound just when the gentleman gave me the spelling of his name.)

"Yes, we did enjoy our lunch. We thought it was very good value for the cost. We're from the States, Chicago. We have skied in many areas of the western States. I guess we would consider Vail our home area. Today we came to Norquay to get tuned up for the week and test our equipment. It's close to town just in case we're not ready for a full day. But we are enjoying it very much."

PHILIP LECCESE (Retired Banff resident, very good skier.)

"I remember the old Norquay with pleasant thoughts and I still enjoy it today. I will ski the Big Chair with friends, but I'm not really a fan of the upper moguls. I enjoy cruising with George Raham and going into Bruno's Veterans and Masters Race. This year I was in the running for a medal, but I misjudged a gate they had changed on the second course. I have several friends I like to ski with on Norquay, and I enjoy it very much now that it's spring."

MOUNT ROYAL HOTEL destroyed by fire March 1967.

LOUISE VIEN (Originally from Montreal. Raced and trained on Norquay for many years, including time with the Alberta Team. Should be living in the area when this goes into print.)

"Norquay is a big home for ski racers, an extended family that is still here. You come here and you catch up with old friends you haven't skied with for fifteen years. I skied with the Norquay team. We would train on the Memorial slope off that speedy little rope tow. Next to us would be the Sunshine Club, Lake Louise, the Banff Ski Runners, everyone trained here.

"I still lived in the east when they held the World Cup here in 1972. But there is a spinoff story from that race. The winner of the Slalom was Andrzel Bachleda from Poland who also had a brother on the team. Their coach was Piotr Gelen. After they returned to Poland, Gelen was being forced to join the Communist Party that had overtaken his country. Rather than do that he came back to Canada. Because of his limited English he got a job coaching our juvenile team and he worked up to a zone team and coached us when we came west for a Shell Cup race in 1977. That was his first time back since he was here as the coach of the Polish team. He would tell us these stories and it was so exciting, because I remember watching the World Cup Race on TV. Today he is coaching Melanie Turgeon on Canada's National Team."

WORLD CUP SLALOM 1972 (Norquay)
(1) Andrzel Bachleda (Poland)   (2) Jean-Noel Augert (France)   (3) Gustavo Thoeni (Italy).

MIKE BAKER (Mike and her two daughters were skiing at Norquay. Her husband Ken, who has instructed and skied in the Rockies for forty years, couldn't leave the ranch near Sundre because it was 'calfing time.')
"I did instruct here part time, in the mid 80s. That was with Edgar Margreiter's Ski School. Mostly I have just listened to Ken telling wild tales about Norquay, some were pretty hard to believe. Ken even remembers Jerry Johnston when he had hair. Did you know Ken was that old?"
Little Jocelyn Baker started to talk about Paul Peyto, a neighbour of hers near Rocky Mountain House. Her story was about him having a ranch and selling Jack Russell puppies. She didn't know he was a native son of Banff and one of our best all around skiers in the sixties.

VIRGINIA HEMINGSON (Well known artist of the Bow Valley.)
"Perhaps a strange memory for Norquay, but I believe we had some of the greatest dances ever held in Banff. I don't think the old lodge ever held more people than it did during those summer dances. They were held from 1964 to 1967, generally on Friday and Saturday in the summer, and only Saturday in the winter. I know it was crowded, because I sold tickets. I never did get to dance. Strange, the same thing happened in the winter. I was always so busy around the lodge, in the kitchen and changing records for the on-hill sound system, I never did have time to learn to ski."

EMIL YURASEK (Ski Instructor, musician, long time resident of Banff.)
"I instructed with Heinz Vifian at Norquay along with Bob and George Geber. The dances at Norquay, oh yes! I was a member of the 'Playboys' along with Harold Naffin, Dennis LaRachel and Ernie Smith. We played to good crowds. One night the 'Safaris' who were on tour dropped in and we jammed most of the night. Their big number at the time was 'Wipeout.' It was good stuff and good times. I still ski Norquay, the slopes, the grooming, I still hear music when I ski here."

BETTY (HOGGARD) PURCELL (Born in Banff, 1919. Her brother Gordy Hoggard was an outstanding racer before the war. He was killed in World War II in an air raid over Essen, Germany.)
"George Encil and his mother stayed in one of my mother's cabins when they first came to Banff. In fact my son George who was born the same year they put the chair on Norquay, was named after George Encil.
"I didn't ski much, but I remember my brother winning a race that was run off Tunnel Mountain at Carnival time. He didn't have a proper binding, just leather toe straps, but he got into the toboggan slide that came down into town and he held it to the finish line."

The Banff racing team of 1947. (Back row L to R) Bob Dawson, Irene Clarke, Lois Woodworth, Eddie Hunter, (centre) Gordie Morrison, Ila LaCasse, Yvonne Legace, Barb Whyte, Ted Robley, (front) Bill O'Brian and Donny Hayes.

BARBARA WHYTE (Excellent skier and winner of several club championships at the Banff Springs Golf Club. Has lived in Banff 77 years.)

"I remember climbing up the Gulley and Ike Mills shooting by with his sleigh and dog team. I remember the 10-cent hamburgers, they tasted so good, nothing like today's hamburgers.

"Myself and some other kids would watch where Norm Knight and Ted Paris would hide their wax under a bear skin that hung on the wall of the old original cabin. When they left we would rub some of it on our skis and put it back. I remember George Encil sent Gordy Hoggard and Jerry Everell down to North Conway to take lessons from Hannes Schneider and his Arlberg style of skiing. Remember that darn ab-stem, once you started doing it, it was so hard to make a turn without starting with one.

"I sued Walter Fisher once. The lift dripped oil on my new Bogner ski suit and he wouldn't pay to have it cleaned. Finally he cried so much I said 'forget it.' Then he gave me a season pass. Another time I was skiing with Kay Monod on the Memorial rope tow. They had just put a new rope on, which really twisted. It twisted so much I couldn't get my arm free. I was hurt enough they put me in the hospital, but George Encil brought me flowers and candies.

"We had the best years. It's a wonderful place to live. You meet people here from all over the world, artists, musicians, and business people, people you would never meet living in any other city or town. And we looked after the Park. These darn environmentalists today, they won't even let me feed the deer. When they come looking in my window how can you refuse them."

LOWELL THOMAS

Pioneer radio and TV newscaster; celebrated his 85th birthday at Norquay and Sunshine, April 1977, skiing with another pioneer of skiing and documentary ski films, Dick Durrance of the 1936 American Olympic Team. Lowell Thomas received his first formal ski lesson from Erling Strom, of Assiniboine fame, in 1932. That was at Lake Placid, N.Y. He was probably best known for the 46 years he spent as a TV anchorman.

Because of skiing he had met Ivor and Phyllis Petrak in Stowe, Vermont. Because of film productions he had worked with Milton and Eva Fruchtman. Both couples now live in Banff and were on hand to help Thomas celebrate his legendary life of travel, writing and reporting.

BANFF 1948

The year the first chair was built on Norquay. The chair was constructed during the summer, and opened in December of 1948.

The population of Banff was 2300 in 1948. The snowfall up to the opening of the lift had been 11 inches; 6 in November and 5 in December. The total for the next four months was only 35 inches, with 21 of that being in February. So much for the good old heavy snow years people talk about. In the next fifteen years the total snowfall would go over 100 inches only twice. The highest was 108.5 inches in 1951 and that included 14 inches in September. The record snowfall for Banff was in 1972, the year the World Cup Slalom and Giant Slalom were held on Norquay. That year we had 175 inches.

In 1948, Banff had only three hotels open in the winter, the King Edward, Mount Royal and the Cascade. It would be another 21 years before the Banff Springs opened for winter operation.

ROCKY MOUNTAIN SKI ZONE CHAMPIONSHIP, 1947

This was being held for the first time since the start of the Second World War. Earl Pletch won the jumping. Eddie Hunter won the Slalom, Gordie Morrison was second. The Downhill was won by Gordie Cowan of Vancouver, B. C.

At the time these races were held there were only rope tows servicing the lower slopes. For the downhill races in the Bowl you still had to climb the better part of an hour.

Jack Davis, Montana skier competing in the first University Meet of 1947. Jack schussed the Bowl with jacket and mouth wide open.

Norquay was still the major ski area in the Park. Sunshine had a lodge for skiers, most of whom stayed for a week. Weekends would probably have less than one hundred skiers. Lake Louise at that time was "Temple" skiing, with even fewer skiers. Norquay would have about three hundred skiers. If there were a special jumping event on, it would draw at least 5000 spectators.

EDMONTON SKIERS START TO SHINE

In 1948 Edmonton defeated Calgary in their annual inter-city competition. Top Edmonton male skiers were Bart Foster and Clarence Haakenstad. Top woman, Norma Howard. Best Calgary skiers at that time: Tom Morrison, Stew Rosamund, Bruce McGavin. In the ladies there was Shirley McKeen, Jeannie Barnes and Gerrie Bailey.

DOWNHILL SKIING, 1948

The downhill Bowl had been schussed the year before in the Intercollegiate Ski Meet by Montana's Davis. In 1948 at the Dominion Championship eleven competitors beat the time set by that college skier; they all schussed the Bowl. The winner was Peter Johnson of Westmount, Quebec. Junior Men's Downhill was won by Remi Cloutier, Ste. Agathe, Quebec. Lucille Wheeler, Ste. Jovite, Quebec won the Junior Ladies'. Dorothy Burden of Montreal won the Senior Women's Downhill. Peter Johnson also won the Slalom followed by John Frazee of Vancouver. Ila LaCasse of Lake Louise won the Ladies' Slalom. Open Slalom, Eleanor Boyle of Banff. Men's, Leon Goodman of Sun Valley, Idaho.

BRAD WHITE (Grandson of Cliff White, ski pioneer who led the first families to Norquay in the late 1920s. Sitting with his wife Donna and daughter Virginia in that same area 70 years later.)

"Well, Dad bought Sunshine when I was a year old, but I skied here a lot. I started racing in the Nancy Greene League. When I was older I remember chasing Danny Wilson down the Bowl. We would cut through the trees over to the inrun of the big jumps and without stopping we would hit either the 'A' or 'B,' what were they 90 and 70 meters? There was another little jump they built next to them for Geländesprung competitions. I recall that because I beat my big brother in one of those events. Roy Andersen tried to get us to jump with regular jumping skis, but I

Dale Dorian and Mike Necesanek coaching young racers, 1981.

felt better on downhill skis.

"Now my five-year-old daughter is skiing in the Nancy Greene League. Virginia, how did it go today? 'I was racing against my friend Sydney, she beat me once and I beated her twice.' I ski Saturday and snowboard on Sunday."

DALE DORION (Grew up in Banff, raced on the Alberta Team and coached in Alberta racing programs. Owner of The Viewpoint book store in Banff's Town Centre Mall; for copies of this book phone 762-0405.)

"I can't help but think of the old North American run. Through the S turns down the Hogs Back, then the End of the World, through the Widow Maker and into the Gulley. It was a fabulous run. I enjoyed racing and coaching. In racing I was up against Peter and Phillip Monod and Greg Hann; it was a hot time for Banff racers. Today my son Danny and his friend Nicholas Christou have biked up to Norquay. We'll ski tomorrow."

Danny, did your Dad teach you to ski?

"No, I taught myself."

WAYNE CHURCH (Banff business man skiing with his son while his parents watch their grandson.)

Grandparents: "It's such a pleasure to watch little Ben ski that Big Chair. I skied it when I was younger, but my body doesn't want to do it now."

Ben: "I ski with the Quikies. I would rather ski than snowboard."

Wayne: "Good boy! That just saved me at least three hundred dollars."

FRANK TURNER (Calgarian at Norquay with his wife and son. His boy is competing in the J3 Provincial races.)

"For my days of fast skiing I enjoyed the old North American, it was an incredible run. Right now I'm waxing my boy's skis to see if he can get a little more speed." How was your first run Jeffrey?

"It was okay, but it could have been better. Near the finish on a little pitch I jammed on a lower gate. I have to remember to 'setup' and stay on my downhill ski."

ANDY TESSIER (Banff businessman skiing with his eight-year-old son Nick (on snowboard) and Karli Abelseth. Both these children have pioneering grandfathers. Nick's grandfather is Rob Crosby, from the Banff Junior Ski Team of the late 1930s. Karli's grandfather is Bob 'Steam' Watt, skier and official of the Banff Ski Runners.)

"We are having a great day, good skiing, the children are meeting a lot of their friends and so am I; that's what Norquay is, it's a great social area. No, we didn't do the chair today, I think Nick is waiting to do that with his Grandfather Rob."

Nick: "Hey! I'm on a board not skis."

KARLI AND STEVE BUTCHART (Both working in the Lone Pine Bar.)

Steve: "This is my third year at Norquay, my second in the Lone Pine bar. I love the area, the staff here is closer than any other ski area. I would like to get a job on the outside crew in the summer, as this bar is closed then."

Karli: "You asked about the tips. Tips here are good, the locals tip better than the visitors. Of course for the 'Brits,' it's something new for them and the Europeans. I believe they have it added on to their bill so they don't have to think about it. I love it here, you look out those big windows and there it is, practically the whole mountain. I look the other way and there is my husband Steve working at the bar."

OCTOBER SKIING

The earliest start for skiing on Norquay happened in 1966. It must have been October the 13th or 14th, a snowfall of a couple of feet plus, hit the area. The staff on hand didn't want it to slide; they wanted to have it packed into a good base, so they called their friends for a great treat. About two hundred showed up for the best Norquay opening ever.

SCOTT HENDERSON

Also in 1966, Scott was awarded the John Semmelink Award as Canada's Top Skier. Semmelink had been killed in 1959 while training with the National Team in West Germany. Doug Robinson, who had coached Scott Henderson said he was the best male skier to come out of Banff. Scott went on to coach our National Team that was also our best: the Crazy Canucks.

JIM McCONKEY

Outstanding powder skier, racer, instructor. Was the Banff Springs Golf Club Champion in 1952. Publicity manager of Norquay lodge in 1951 and 1952. Franz Gabl, who has experienced everything from war on the Russian front to a Downhill Silver medal in the 1948 Olympics, says of Jim McConkey, "He is one of the most 'Gung-ho' men I have ever met." Jim currently lives on Denman Island, B. C.

I can't think of another life on skis that would compare with the skiing life of Jim McConkey. For longevity, energy, pleasure and ability, it has to be Jim. But, it almost didn't happen that way.

In 1948, close to his 22nd birthday, Jim was working with a film crew on the Columbia Icefields. The film, *Shadow of Time* produced by George Encil, was telling the story of an airplane crash in the mountains and a rescue group that came in looking for survivors. All of a sudden it turned into a live rescue unit when Jim McConkey fell into a crevasse. That would have been the end of his life if he hadn't landed on a large piece of ice that had wedged itself 85 feet from the surface of the glacier. Beyond that a rescue would have been impossible. It was still a very dangerous rescue. It was fortunate the crew included Toni Matt, a world class skier and mountaineer. Going that deep into a tomb of ice put two lives in jeopardy. Jim was found unconcious and upside-down. His body temperature at that time must have been pretty low. Matt completed the rescue and Jim survived with only a broken collarbone.

Jim stayed on in Banff for a couple of years. He was an instructor, but George

The dynamic Jim McConkey, 1964.

Encil saw his infectious personality as his strength, especially when it came to promoting Mt. Norquay in the winter and summer. Jim was an excellent golfer. Encil saw this as a plus when he could entertain a special guest on the Banff Springs Golf course. Jim probably would have stayed on at Norquay, but he had married a southern girl who wanted to be closer to her family. Jim was to spend ten years at Alta, Utah, one year at Park City, four years at Todd Mtn. B. C. before moving to Whistler, B. C. where he lived until he retired in 1994.

Jim had worked on the construction of the lift with Ted MacAulay and Ross Moore. He skied in other films produced by George Encil with Harvey Clifford, Herb Schneider, Jerry Everell, Vic Allan, 'Hap' Smith and Art Krowchuck. In 1951 and 1952, he was the publicity manager of Norquay.

To give a full account of Jim McConkey's life would be another book.

GOVERNMENT CORRESPONDENCE, October 31, 1950. (Part of a letter from Parks Controller J. Smart, Ottawa, to Mr. C. E. S. Smith, Director of Immigration, Ottawa.)

"…Mr. George Encil of Banff, who is operator of the skiing organization located on Mt. Norquay, has recently arranged for the employment of a European by the name of Franz Gabl. It would appear that Mr. Encil is endeavouring to arrange to have the entry of Mr. Gabl to this country put on a permanent basis and he asked me if I would take the matter up with you and see how the application stands.

"I might say that in so far as the National Parks administration is concerned, we are anxious to see this type of recreation carried on under the very best arrangements, as it is an attraction to our National Parks. Mr. Encil has made a very large investment in the plant he now operates and it is an attractive acquisition to Banff Park in the promotion of winter sport. It also is an operation of considerable importance during the summer season, taking many thousands of visitors to viewpoints on Mount Norquay."

The Story of Franz Gabl

Franz Gabl the first Austrian downhill hero, silver medalist 1948 Olympics.

FRANZ GABL (Austrian Racer, Silver medalist in the 1948 Olympic Downhill.)

Franz Gabl added much to the Norquay ski scene when he arrived in 1951. His friendly personality combined with his skiing skills made him a popular figure and an inspiration to the young skiers.

Franz liked to jump. I believe he was the first to cut from the Bowl to the 'A' and 'B' jumps of that time. He would get good air with what seemed to be a pumping motion from his legs, but always with perfect balance over his skis.

Franz Gabl coached the Canadian Ladies' Team at the 1952 Olympics. John Southam of Calgary, always a supporter of western Canadian skiing, paid Franz's expenses to coach the ladies in Norway. These were years when the Canadian Amateur Ski Association donated very little to the expenses of skiers and coaches. The races in Voss, Norway, were the first races for the ladies against the strong European teams. They made a very good showing; they were the only team that placed their four racers in the first sixteen. Joanne Hewson was 8th, Lucile Wheeler, 9th, Rosemary Schultz, 14th, and Rhoda Eaves, 16th. Gordie Morrison of Banff was on the Men's Olympic Team in 1952.

Franz Gabl coached the Men's Olympic Team in 1956 at Cortina d'Ampezzo, Italy. That was the year the amazing Austrian skier, Toni Sailer, won three gold medals. For the Canadians, it was another story. Franz was coaching the team at St. Anton, his hometown. He had only three men, Andre Bertrand of Quebec and the Tommy brothers, Andy and Art. While training on the 'Galzig' Art Tommy broke his leg. Andy did the same thing the next day, almost in the same spot. Meanwhile, the ladies' team won Canada's first Olympic medal. It was a bronze for Lucille Wheeler. Besides all the wonderful things Franz Gabl did on skis, he holds the memory of driving a sightseeing bus for Brewster's as one of his most pleasant experiences - a job given to him by Rod Adams.

Franz Gabl lives in Bellingham, Washington. He still races in senior races. He recently came to Norquay to run in Bruno's Veterans and Masters Race. Franz has written a book about his wartime years on the Russian front. The title is Franzl. (How a mountain boy survived four years of combat on the Russian front to become Austria's first Olympic medal winner in skiing.) He is currently writing of his life in Canada and the United States. Most of what is printed here was sent to me by Franz Gabl, in the summer of 1999.

CHARLIE JOHNSON AND CHUCK NOWLIN (Two members of Calgary's Senior Ski Club. They had Banff and Norquay connections several years ago.)

Chuck: "I worked for the government back in 1954. Jimmy Mitchell and myself surveyed the center line for the new 90-meter jump. John Watts was the draftsman up in the government office. I had actually quit skiing for about twenty years, then Charlie here told me how good Norquay was now so I started again. I am President of the Calgary Senior Ski Club: we have over 800 members."

Charlie: "As a Brewster driver in 1953 and 1954, I remember driving some of the movie people that were in production in the Banff area. There was a wrap-party we were invited to with Marilyn Monroe and Robert Mitchum; that was pretty wild. The Big Chair! I haven't skied it for many years but I'm thinking of trying it again, but right now we are both happy cruising from the Mystic Pathfinder."

KARL JOST (Came to Canada in 1953; born in Ligist, Austria. A very technical skier with non-technical jokes. Instructed, coached and was an examiner for the Canadian Ski Alliance.)

"As an unpleasant memory of Norquay, I remember the day the outrun of the big jumps looked so good we decided to ski it. Waiting at the bottom was the ski patrol, and they took our passes away. I think it was 1954 or '55. Frank Gourlay might have been on patrol, I'm not sure. I remember Rudi Gertsch climbing the mountain above the Tea House and then jumping over it, clearing the ramp and the little hut below. He was mad, but what a skier.

"Years ago we had a summer ski race, the good speakers against the bad speakers. We who came from Europe were the bad speakers. The Canadians were the good speakers. We beat them in the ski race. To get even they wanted to play soccer; I guess they didn't know we had all played it as children, so we won that too.

"Now we're all one team. We call it the 'Crack of Noon Club.' We're not so fast, but we make it up to Norquay by noon. When most come in for lunch we go out and ski like mad for a couple of hours. The lunch people come back and we go in for a beer. Some members? There is Frank Gourlay, Emil Yurasek, Ross Gilmour and anyone else who can fit into our timing pattern and drink beer.

"Another memory, the year I foreran a college meet. It was so cold I froze my kneecaps. I believe Pat MacKenzie also foreran. At the bottom of the course her face was all frozen in little spots. I think that might have been the year one of the racers was killed on the North American."

CRAG & CANYON, February 1962. SKIER KILLED ON NORQUAY.

A young Calgary skier lost his life on Mt. Norquay Saturday when he went out of control on the North American run and crashed into a tree.

Dave Borgal, 20, UAC student, competing in a race was killed instantly when he ran into a tree in the 'S' section of the downhill course.

Borgal's fatal accident was the second in this particular area of Norquay. On March 10, 1957, a Vancouver skier, Ronald Tonnesson, while training on the downhill hit a tree in the upper 'S' turn: he died in the Mineral Springs Hospital the following day.

MALCOLM CARMICHAEL (Banff photographer and skier)

"I worked at the Banff Springs in the late 1970s and early 80s and skied Norquay. To get pumped for the mountain we would watch the World Cup downhill races on TV in the lodge. There was always a Canadian on the podium in those years. After watching the race we would turn into Ken Read, Podborski, or whoever, and just terrorize the mountain. They were great years.

"I didn't see it, but they say Bob Rankin and Dave Irwin skiing in the 'Mountain Madness' Race, did a cross-over in the air while bombing down the 'Widowmaker,' apparently there were a lot of people there who saw it."

STEPHANIE ROBINSON (Youngest member of the famous Robinsons.)

"Norquay, every weekend we got up, put our ski gear on and headed to Norquay. There were no questions asked, we did it automatically.

"I remember Chris Kent. Whenever I was behind him on the old Memorial rope tow, I was young and I could hardly hold on to that rope anyway, but when we neared the top he would bounce the rope and send me flying. I would cry and he just laughed.

"And the old washrooms, they were the dugouts, no flushing. I just hated them, there was always a line-up. I would hold it as long as I could before going in there. And I remember the Nancy Greene races and all the badges we would have down the sleeve of our jackets."

MIKE WIEGELE (Outstanding skier and coach. Owner of Mike Wiegele Heli-skiing, Blue River, B. C. Austrian born; came to Canada in 1959.)

"Norquay makes a man of the boy."

"The Canadian Consulate in Vienna showed me a variety of pictures, I was to chose the one where I wanted to go. I chose Banff with Cascade as a backdrop. And it was true, it's just as beautiful today as it was 40 years ago. I met my wife

Norquay makes a man of the boy, Mike Wiegele, 1969.

Bonnie at Norquay. My daughter Michelle grew up skiing and racing on this mountain; my dog 'Denver' came to watch the races. I'm so glad to see how Norquay is run today. Kika and Peter have to be proud. And young Thomas Grandi racing in the International World Cup Races, should he need a break, can always come back to Norquay to tune up. It is a perfect mountain for training. I know Bonnie who still races against some of the world's best skiers in her age group prefers training at Norquay.

"I think Norquay has proven we can work and play in the Park. For myself, whether I'm skiing here or heli-skiing, any time I meet animals I respect them and they respect me. I don't understand some of these groups that think we threaten the animals. We want to preserve the mountains and wildlife possibly more than they do."

LOUIS TRONO (Musician, writer, entertainer, Banff's "Signature Citizen." Born six miles from Banff at Bankhead in 1909.)

"In the days when they were building the first Norquay cabin in 1928 I did a little skiing and helped with the cabin a bit, but most of all I remember playing my banjo with the White brothers Cliff and Jack, who played guitar. We christened that cabin with some fine parties. Later I did some part time work on the road to Norquay. They paid even less than musicians were paid in those days."

Bonnie Wiegele, one of North America's top senior racers, 2000.

RAY SEGUIN AND BONNIE WIEGELE (Ray and Bonnie had just come into the lodge for lunch. Ray had completed a morning class with his Rut Runners, a racing program he has been operating for twenty years. Bonnie mixes her training with Ray and the Banff Mountain Ski Academy. She is training for major senior races in the States.)

Bonnie: "Slalom racing is a whole new sport if you compare it to running gates before the break-away gates. It took me a couple of years. I kept getting closer and closer to the gates, but I had trouble hitting them."

Ray: "Slalom racing is now a full contact sport. Every time you turn you hit a gate."

Bonnie: "On a turn you're angled like this, so you just ski through the pole or hit it with your arm and upper body; it took me a long time to get it."

Ray: "I started the Rut Runners hoping I could get skiers who hadn't raced to love it as much as I did. I found out there were many, of all ages, who wanted to learn and were willing to work at it. Norquay is ideal for training regardless of what program you're in. The lifts are short enough to keep a good flow going between runs. It's ideal for a coach and the racers. I'm speaking of runs off the Spirit and Mystic chairs. As for the Big Chair, I remember my first trip up there as I stood looking down at the lodge between my tips."

Bonnie: "I remember that too. When I was teaching part time I would drive down from Edmonton every weekend in my 1950 Ford with a big hole in the floorboards.

You could see the road passing below. I would check into the Otonobee Lodge for $1.50 a night, and check the crowd in the Beer Parlour. In the morning I would hope I didn't have a class so I could ski the big chair with the guys. There was George Geber, Al Jacobitz and Rudi Erbsland; they were really nice to me because I was enthusiastic but some said it was because I wore the tighest red Bogners on the hill. That might be true because I noticed Mike Wiegele's tight black Bogners. Come Sunday evening I would look at the road back to Edmonton through the hole in my floorboard. Monday morning I would be back teaching synchronized swimming."

Ray Seguin getting his Rut Runners out of their ruts. (L to R) Ellen Brenner, Ray, Deanne Monod, (horizontal) Kathryn Cooke, 2000.

Ray: "Those guys you mentioned Bonnie, are still around. Just like many of the Calgary and Edmonton people who raced, the Rooneys, Irwins, Reads, so many, they're coming back with their children. Nikki Hansen, here at Norquay, has started a new Nancy Greene program and there are quite a few other racing programs on the mountain. Lots of kids and they're not all in racing programs, many just want to be taught good skiing and the pleasures of the mountain. In my Rut Runners I have people well into their sixties and older. You can improve your skiing no matter how old you are. How long are you going to race Bonnie?"

Bonnie: "I'll race as long as you keep coaching Ray."

Jim Uffelmann and Dave Spence racing for the sun, 1982.

JIM UFFELMANN (Skier, racer, who found out twenty years ago the Rockies have better powder and parties than Waterloo, Ontario.)

"I can thank Ray Seguin for improving my gate racing. I worked in Lake Louise for a couple of years, but I would come to Banff for the 'Race for the Sun' races that were run here each week. I got tired of following the Hann brothers, Greg and Kevin, and Dave Spence. The coaching by Ray helped me and I started

Jim (right) congratulating Spence who wins the trip to Hawaii, 1982.

winning some good prizes. I don't know how many times I ended up second.

"I remember one year they arranged a bus to take us up to Ron 'Ratso' Hallam's for a post-race party that followed the pre-race party and the race party. I have a picture somewhere, we're all lined up in front of his house. Another year when we had the post-race party in the old lodge, things got a little wild. They had a DJ and the place was rocking, people dancing on people on tables. Someone was up on the shoulders of another person trying to turn the wagonwheel chandelier. I'm up there boogie-ing away, the place is just in a frenzy. Well, this wheel swinging over my head mesmerizes me, so it was clear to me I just had to jump up and swing on it.

Unfortunately the weight capacity of the chandelier didn't meet mine and it came thundering down. As I rolled down with the wheel, Paul Sylvestre, who was the DJ had the music peaking when I hit the floor. All of a sudden you hear this zzzzzzip as the needle races across the record and then comparative silence as Paul comes on in well modulated tones... 'Welcome to the end of the party'"

Author's Question: "What about snowboarding Jim, are they taking over?"

Jim: "No, eventually snowboarders will realize skiing is a lot of fun and they'll come back. They'll say 'Hey, this thing is really awkward, why am I killing myself?' I'm tired of rolling around on my butt... Then we'll have more skiers than ever."

RYAN BAKER AND CRAIG BURLEY (After I finished talking to Jim Uffelmann, I noticed Ryan and Craig, two snowboarders, sitting at a neigbouring table. They couldn't help but overhear Jim's lively account of skiing.)

Author: "What did you think of Jim's remarks about snowboarding?"

Ryan: "I just heard him say snowboarders will get tired of rolling around on their butts. The thing is everyone has to learn the sport. Actually when you learn snowboarding it becomes just as versatile, we can actually ride powder a lot faster. I think it will even out, those who want to ski will ski and those who want to snowboard will do snowboarding. I should add I teach snowboarding here for Monod Sport."

Craig: "I didn't hear what the skier said. I come here for the Snowboard Park."

Question: "Do they keep skiers out of the Park?"

Craig: "No, skiers can ride it: it took them a while to get on to it, but it also took snowboarders a couple of years to get on to the Halfpipe. Now we respect one another. It's pretty cool."

ANNE AND JERRY GOULET (Jerry and his skiing buddies of the mid-70s terrorized Norquay with a 'Take No Prisoners' attitude. We're looking at a level of skiing understood by only a few. Their drive to be the first and fastest in the powder and the last on the hill was the only way they knew how to ski.)

Jerry: "It probably started in my first winter of 1972/73. I was not long from the east when a fellow by the name of Dave Carter told me the only way to ski the Lone Pine is non-stop. At that time, coming from Quebec, it was a challenge for me. But skiing with Ian Wilson, Graham MacDonald, Mike Miskow, my brother Mike along with many locals, I quickly got up to speed. We just didn't stop. I can remember passing a fellow who had crashed. He was standing, but looking rather dazed, but I kept going. On my next run he was still there, so I stopped. He had been looking, unsuccessfully, for a ski in pretty deep snow. I don't know how we spotted it, but a good distance from where he had fallen there was his ski up in a pine tree, several

Hang gliding off the Big Chair. Dave Howell made a dramatic evening flight down to the Timberline Hotel, before Parks said 'No More flying,' 1974.

feet above the slope. That was a fall hard to figure."

Anne: "We were living in Canmore at the time, but I was working in Banff. This morning, Jerry was driving me to Banff and he was heading up to Norquay for a fall of fresh snow. When we hit the Norquay turn-off, west of town, he asked me if I would mind walking to Banff from there; it would get him to Norquay and the powder a little earlier. I couldn't believe what I had heard, because I was seven months pregnant."

Jerry: "When our daughter Dominique was about eight months old, and still too young to be taken into the nursery at Norquay, I would ski with her on my back in a Jerry Pack. I was still high on the Bowl when I stopped to talk to Gary Schultz. As I pulled my shoulders around to complete the turn, Dominique squirted out like a newborn and started sliding down the slope. Schultz stood there with his mouth wide open as I skied below my daughter and scooped her up. No damage done. But Gary Schultz couldn't contain the event. By the time I got home Anne had the full story."

Anne: "My good friends Mona and Mia were going to introduce Petri and myself to the Lone Pine. The snow was so heavy and I got so wet, it seemed like it took hours to come down. On top of that, there was a photographer up there taking pictures of our run. I still live in fear that those pictures will show up someday. I just didn't ski well enough to handle conditions like that."

Jerry: "We had one run that was good for our group, but there was another fellow on the mountain at the time that wanted to follow us. Unfortunately, the one that he wanted to try was the run off the Bowl in a traverse to the top of the jumps and then down the 'B' jump. I won't mention his name, I think he might still be mad at me. Anyway, I told him it was just a matter of 'guts.' It was really a smooth ride. You tuck during the inrun to make sure you have enough speed to clear the brow of the landing hill and from there you just enjoy the ride.

"Well, he stood above the jump for the longest time while Ian Wilson and myself waited below for his run. Finally he started down, but no sooner had he started than he seemed to be trying to grab the air behind him. He had changed his mind but it was too late. From down below all we could see was the base of his skis coming over the jump, then he hit the brow, which broke both skis and knocked all the wind from his sliding body that stopped not far from where we were standing. To add to his problem we couldn't stop laughing. I don't believe he ever tried it again.

"My worst moments on the mountain came when I started hang-gliding. My parents had just arrived for a visit when Anne suggested she take them to Norquay to watch me do a little flying. I impressed everyone by crashing on the Lone Pine.

"Dave Howell was a good flyer. It was just about dark when he with two flares on his glider took off from the top and landed at the Timberline Hotel.

"I really thought I might kill myself at the sport. I had heard of so many doing just that. Bill Taylor was one of the best flyers around. I heard he was killed while flying in B. C. I decided to get rid of my glider. I gave it to a kid by the name of Tony Black. He ended up being a paraplegic.

"I remember much more, like the masquerade race at Norquay. The torchlight parade down the North American. I still enjoy a run from the big curl off the top."

LYNN AND DOUG GODFREY (Lynn and Doug Godfrey are excellent skiers and owners of the "Mountain Magic" sports shop in Banff.)

Doug: "Lynn and I arrived from New Brunswick in 1971. We were coming to Banff for one winter, that was 28 years ago. At that time we had an old car that didn't want to travel too far from town. Norquay was a safe distance, especially for that winter of 1971/72 when Banff experienced a record snowfall.

"Norquay was, and is, a demanding mountain. You learn to ski it or you don't survive. I watched some of the guys that skied the mountain with so much energy. They challenged the mountain on every run. In time Lynn and I did the same thing, but it took a while."

Lynn: "I remember falling practically all the way down the Lone Pine. Dennis Deltor reconized the polka-dot suit I was wearing and he threw himself in front of me. That was my first winter; it could have been my last.

"Later, when I was improving, but still having problems, Mike Miskow mentioned I had problems in getting my shoulders around. His solution was to ski right under the chair lift, from top to bottom. That's where he took me and it worked, but did I ever work on that run."

Doug: "In 1976 after we had started a sport shop, the image of those hot skiers was still with me. There were the local guys that had always skied the mountain that way from the day the lift opened 25 years before we arrived; Gerry Locke, Ross Maxwell, the Henderson brothers, Jim Davies, Ian Neilson, Rudi Gertsch, Sepp

Renner, the list goes on. Anyway, we decided to hold a race that would challenge these skiers in what they like to do best, shred the mountain. It was to be called 'Mountain Smoker.' The concept was easy: ski the big chair as many times as you can in three hours. All you needed was speed and endurance. Its name grew from an earlier wild man of the mountains. In the 1950s a common phrase was to 'crash and burn.' This race idea grew from one of those runs.

"On March 17, 1956, a strange face appeared at Mt. Norquay. No one knew who this skier was - he called himself Billy Binder. On his first ride up the chair he told the lift operator, Red Crozier, that he was going to 'smoke' the hill. As far as is known Billy made only one turn off the chair and headed straight down the North American. He hit terminal velocity in the middle of the 'Widow-Maker' and disintegrated in flames. The only thing found was a single burned boot. In memory of Billy 'Smoker' Binder, the 'Mountain Magic' sport shop held its first annual 'Mountain Smoker.' To honour Billy Smoker, the race was held on March 17. In true Smoker fashion, the winner appeared without fan-fare, and smoked everyone. That winner, Roland Fuhrmann, was a suprise only to the older crowd who didn't know him. Roland was a 14-year-old Junior High student. He skied 18 runs in 3 hours. Bob Hemming followed in second spot and Jerry Goulet in third place."

Doug: "The 'Mountain Smoker' isn't running today. In time we had a little concern about the safety of the skiers. In the beginning we had a variety of starts, including a LeMans, which became a little frantic. We didn't want the skiers to be fighting one another so much for position or desperately charging the lift when there was no chance they could get on properly. In time, for safety reasons, we dropped the race. But I still have thoughts of reviving it, it was such a test.

"Of course I remember a couple of friends from those days who are no longer with us, Noldie Keach, Norm Murray and my close friend Ian Wilson."

No one SMOKED the mountain like these three: (L to R) Bob Rankin, Dave Bammer Raham and Roland Fuhrmann, 1974.

MOUNTAIN SMOKER (A grueling three hour downhill run from the Big Chair. Originated by Doug and Lynn Godfrey in 1976.)

The first Smoker was won by 14-year-old Roland Fuhrmann -- a surprise win in that such a young skier could win such a demanding three-hour race. He ran 18 runs in the three hours.

Philip Monod, a former member of Canada's National Team, won the next Smoker. He skied 20 times in the three hours. Mark Mills of Calgary was second followed by freestyle skier Larry Bakstad, an employee of Norquay.

In the fourth running of the 'Smoker' Bob Rankin appeared on the scene. Bob was an outstanding free-skier, working on the Norquay Ski Patrol at that time in 1979. The previous year Keith Humphrey, an ex-National Team member had skied 21 runs in winning the event. Bob Rankin won the fourth running of the 'Smoker' with 23 runs. Bakstad was second with 22 runs.

From that point on Bob Rankin won all the 'Smokers' until it was stopped a few years later for liability reasons. Bob Rankin is presently a mountain guide with Mike Wiegele's Heli-skiing operation at Blue River, B. C. Dave 'Bammer' Raham had placed second on a couple of occasions working his way up to 24 runs in the three hour time period. Raham holds the record of 45 runs, during the lift hours, in one day.

EDNA BROWN AND BARBARA (Edna's daughter)
(I ran into Edna Brown and the other people who appear on this page at the 'Back To Banff Days,' June 1999.)
Edna: "We lived on Deer Street in 1950 when Zeno Colo was here skiing in the North American Championship. I watched his whole run from my house through binoculars. I was glad to see him win, and he didn't have all that modern fancy equipment."
Barbara: "I skied and raced with Lynne Becker, Bev Steele, the Henderson brothers and my brother Bobby. Bobby kept in touch with racing; he helped out with timing on some of the World Cup Races in B. C. when he was with B. C. Telephone. Norquay was always a big part of our young lives."

MARY DEEGAN (Mary went to school here in the 1930s. Her brother Jimmy was a packer into Skoki and a writer.)
"I remember we would tramp up to Norquay and sit outside the old cabin and have our egg and onion sandwich. Then we would ski back to town: a town that was empty. If you saw anyone on Banff Avenue after the early movie ended at the Lux that was unusual."

JIM ROUSE (Jim worked on the construction of the Norquay jump in the 1950s. Heine Klopher, a German jump architect, had come over to design a new jump. Jim made his plans into a reality.)
"The most vivid memory is of an almost fatal day. I was standing at the bottom of the hill watching a truck deposit a load of dirt on the landing area. The procedure was to have the truck loaded below and then pulled up by a Caterpillar winch. Following that the truck would back down to the slope and drop its load. On this occasion the load stuck in the box. When it released the truck bucked up and rolled over right down the length of the jump landing area. The fellow standing next to me said, 'We don't have to rush, that driver must be dead.' Fortunately the driver had jumped out at the top and wasn't seriously hurt."

CRAG & CANYON, March 5, 1950.
Biggest crowd ever takes in jumping event at Norquay. Six to seven thousand watch. Art Devlin of Lake Placid took top honours with jumps of 211 and 220 feet, and perfect form. Combined cross country and jumping was won by Noel Paul of Kimberley. Clarence Servold of Camrose was second.
Credit for the success of the meet was largely due to the efforts of Dave Spence and Ralph McKenzie of the governing body of the Canadian Amateur Ski Association (C.A.S.A.).

Frank Gourlay new holder of Ski Runners Memorial Trophy.

Junior Girls: Lois Woodworth followed by Sally Becker, Yvonne Legace, Barbara Whyte, J. McDonald and Joan Rusk.

Junior Boys: first, Keith Schneider; second, Roy McCowan; third, Bob Neish; fourth, Connie McCowan and F. Johnson, fifth.

GEORGE CAPEL (Grew up in Banff. Started skiing Norquay about the time the lift was built in 1948. Was an excellent racer and instructor. George was the second instructor in Western Canada to receive his Senior Pin from the Ski Instructors Alliance. Bob Dawson was the first.)

"I believe Jim McConkey was the one who really opened the mountain up for me. When he came here in the early 50s, he had already developed a good deep snow technique. It was a big wind-up of the upper body, a power turn that really worked. He said 'crank it up.' After that we skied the mountain where we had never skied before.

"When I was a kid, Friday after school we would always wax our skis for the next day. Depending on the temperature of course, but Red Wonder was a popular wax we would melt and iron on the base of our wooden skis. It was something we took seriously. Also, I remember going out with Stan Peyto in the autumn to cut small trees, which we would paint and use for slalom poles. Stan always checked with the Wardens first to see what we could cut.

"There were some excellent programs for teaching kids to ski. The Kinsmen's program certainly got a lot of kids enjoying skiing, many went on to be good racers. The Nancy Greene League did the same. Young ski programs today seem to be different, at least for racing. Parents don't seem to think they're getting anything for their children unless they spend five or six thousand dollars each year, or more. But the concept is lost: I don't think we're turning out the skiers we did in the past.

"I worked on the patrol for awhile. The toboggans that were designed by Jack Pugh in the 50s were easy to handle. We could come straight down the Lone Pine. The toboggan had a drag-chain system. If we pushed down on the handles the chain would dig into the slope and slow it down. If we would lift up, the toboggan rode on the back area and speed increased. The system was so much better than the metal toboggans put out by the military.

"My best day on the mountain? Well, it would have to be one of my last (I hardly downhill ski any more). The conditions were the best. The snow was about waist deep. I was skiing with Norbert Wiegele and Andre Schwarz and we just kept going until we were exhausted. I figured it would never get any better, so I keep that as an outstanding memory of Norquay; along with all the things my boys have enjoyed on that mountain."

CRAG & CANYON, March 19, 1975
KINSMEN SLALOM ENDS SUCCESSFUL SKI SCHOOL
Another successful Kinsmen Ski School came to a close with the annual school slalom on the slopes of Mt. Norquay. A total of 157 youngsters ranging in age from 7 to16 years received instruction during the past ten weeks from the Jerry Johnston Ski School.

Most improved girl and most improved boy skiers were Carol Plummer and Ken Hansen.

HEATHER AND GERRY PERCY (Mother and father of the skiing Percys, Corinne, Sharol, Karen and Ross. They were at Norquay in early April attending The Ronald McDonald Ski Challenge, a charity race which is hosted by their daughter Karen Percy, double Bronze winner in the 1988 Olympics.)

Heather: "Strange, my first thought is Ross breaking six pairs of skis on that jump over there. But I remember the Brent Marshall Memorial race which everyone would show up for at the end of the racing season."

Gerry: "We moved to Banff in 1976. For two years before that we would drive from Edmonton down here every weekend to go skiing.

"We had good times here. I had an old half-ton truck I would use to give the kids a ride to Norquay. I picked up the Robinsons, the Capels, the Paltingers; they would stick their skis in the mound of snow I kept in the back, then probably pick them all up a few hours later at the ski out.

"Then there was the year we did the clearing on the Wishbone slope and sold the wood as a fundraiser for the Ski Runners.

"You asked about Karen's medals at the '88 Olympics. Yes, we were proud, happy and all that. Especially with it happening in Alberta where family and friends could share that great time. I think it was good for my girls and a lot of Banff and area girls that had skied with Karen. They too felt good because one of them had made the goal they were all trying for."

Ronald McDonald Charity race: (L to R) Felix Belczyk, Lori Graham, Karen Percy Lowe and Brian Stemmle, 1999.

KAREN PERCY LOWE

"I was nine when the family moved to Banff and Norquay quickly became my backyard. The first races I entered would have been the Nancy Greene and the Buster Brown races. Now when we come up here my six-year-old son, Keegan, likes to ski off the slopes through the trees just like we did over twenty years ago.

"This Ronald McDonald Challenge is fun: it seems like we always have good weather for it. I'm not sure how much we will raise this year, but it will be close to $100 000. With the help of National Team members, Lori Graham, Brian Stemmle and Felix Belczyk, I'm sure we'll make it."

CRAG & CANYON 1980
BANFF GIRLS WIN AT NORQUAY.
13 year-old Karen Percy placed first on both Saturday and Sunday in the southern zone race hosted

Karen Percy in a quiet moment between medals in the 1988 Olympics.

by the Banff Ski Runners. 16 year-old Corinne Percy placed second on Saturday. 14 year-old Kendall Hunter placed second on Sunday. 149 young skiers turned out for the race.

CALGARY SUN, February 23, 1988
KAREN DOES IT AGAIN
That headline sat next to a full page picture of Karen Percy who sat on the shoulders of 'Jungle' Jim Hunter shortly after she had won her second Bronze medal at the 1988 Winter Olympics. Waving a red bouquet of flowers and a smile as wide as Canada, Karen had just placed 3rd in the Super Giant Slalom. She had earlier placed 3rd in the Downhill, and was only 1/100 of a second away from winning another Bronze in the Combined.

DON AND ARDENE HOWE (Banff business man. Worked at Norquay in the 1970s.)
"I started working at Norquay in 1971. That was where I met my wife Ardene, she was working in the gift shop.
"The project in the fall of that year was to install the Cascade Chair. Bill Herron was the owner and the engineer on that job. My immediate boss was Dean Christou. The equipment we had on the job was really something. An old Ellis-Chalmers tractor did everything, including the installation of towers. Backing it up was a 1947 Dodge Power Wagon and a 1952 Jeep.
"Probably the day most vivid in my memory happened when we were blasting stumps from the North American. I was taking a fifty-pound pack of dynamite up the mountain. We would go as far as tower nine on the lift. The lift would stop there. To get off I would swing the chair over to the tower. While I was doing that someone started the lift up and I almost fell forty feet with the load of dynamite. I was left hanging from the chair. Finally, my co-worker Vern, standing on the tower, grabbed my foot and pulled me to safety. If I had fallen the dynamite wouldn't have exploded without the caps, but the forty-foot drop would have probably done me in. It affected Vern so much he went straight down the mountain, punched the time-clock and quit.
"I was there when we had the record snow fall. The town was just stymied; everyone was skiing to work. At Norquay it was even heavier. I was trying to get the Cascade chair cleared. The snow had slid all around the top station and covered the return-wheel. I started climbing up to dig it out and just as I was coming to tower four Jim Davies, from his helicopter, dropped a bomb into the upper snow pack. Everything just went wild; it was like the whole mountain was coming down and such a dry snow. I held on to tower four while the snow funneled around me, the vacuum was terrific and my ears crackled and popped. Over on the next slope trees were thrown in the air with many landing up in other trees. Later in the spring I had to take a chain saw to cut many of them out, in fact that area, because of the avalanche, became a new run. Of course the skiing that year was the greatest, but you had to ski with a snorkel, the snow would go right over your head and you couldn't breathe without one."
Ardene: "I remember that winter of heavy snow. My dad was a schoolteacher and I remember he went to school on his cross-country skis.

"My sisters and I all skied Norquay in the Kinsmen Ski School. Dad would line the three of us up, get our boots all done up and walk us down to the old bus depot to get the bus for Norquay. It doesn't happen much any more where you can go out and have fun with twenty friends."

CRAG & CANYON, January 31, 1979
First for Greg Hann in Red Deer race. In second place Jim Read, followed by Chris Kent.

BANFFITES (A Sunday afternoon I came across a group of locals, some serious skiers and some still trying to get serious.)
Ross Pringle: "I grew up trying to hold on to the Memorial rope tow. I was generally a couple of feet off the ground and it cost a dozen pair of gloves each year."
Sharon Pringle: "This mountain never scared me, I grew up in the mountains around Boston Bar, B. C. Do I ski the Big Chair? No, that's one of my future projects."
Tommy Soukas: "Did I scare myself here? Yes, one time I did. I went up the Big Chair in 1978, but I walked three quarters of the way down; never again - well, I might try again as my millennium project."
Jodi McCaw: "I grew up skiing here. I started when I was around six. I still love it here, it's community and now my kids ski here."
Jack Pedersen: "Yes, I have memories of skiing here when I was a kid. There was the T-Bar that was behind where this lodge is now and we would do slingshots from it. We would get the operator to hold us as long as he could and then let go; we left very quickly. And there was the old 'C' jump just off that slope; we would fool around on it for hours. To get up on the scaffold you had to shimmy around. I remember Nigel Capel slipped going up and got caught upside-down and we had to get his Dad to get him out."

BILL IRWIN (Bill and his brother Mike were members of Canada's National Team in the late 70s and early 80s. His Mom Jeannie, and Dad Joe, were excellent Calgary skiers.)
"Scottie Henderson turned us into downhillers in the 70s, but I got even with him last year, I won our annual 'Crazy Canuck Challenge' at Lake Louise. My brother Mike was here at Norquay earlier in the winter skiing in the Interbourse competition. That's a competition of International Stock Brokers and they have some excellent skiers. Canada has won it twice in recent years. Excuse me Ed, I'm on my way to the nursery to see my little daughter."

Stacy Kohut forerunning the Pontiac Cup races held at Norquay in March, 2000. Stacy is expected to be on the Canadian National Disabled team competing in the 2002 Winter Olympics.

STACY KOHUT (28-year-old

Calgarian now living in Banff. Trains on Norquay for the Paralympics at Salt Lake City in 2002.)

"I had an awful accident seven years ago when I broke my back doing a super-loop on a swing set, but I would have probably never moved to the mountains if that hadn't happened. I won three silver medals at the 1998 Special Olympics in Japan. At present I feel like I may have to quit our National Disabled Ski Team, it's just too expensive for me to continue this life style."

MOUNTAIN MADNESS

The Banff Winter Carnival had run into bad times in the late 1960s. Rowdy behaviour was responsible for the cancellation of the Carnival for a few years. When it came back to life in 1977 something new had to be added. Steve Orchin, John Heintz, and Jerry Tucker came up with the 'Mountain Madness Relay,' an event that has grown in popularity up to this year's 1999 event. A downhill skier runs the first leg from the top of the Big Norquay Chair to the Timberline Hotel, followed by a runner, a classic cross-country skier, a skater on the Bow River and ended with a cross-country skate-skier.

Mystee Hunter (skier) hands off to Juli Grinder (runner) in the initial Mountain Madness relay race. The young High School team went on to victory, 1977.

MOUNTAIN MADNESS 1977

The winning ladies' team of that initial race was a group 14-year-old Banff Junior High students, Mystee Hunter, Maria Hawkins, Carrie Tollstrup, Juli Grinder and Dodi Neidermeyer. The winning men's team, from Calgary, was Matthew Potts, Bob Rooney, Brian Hilland, Jay McKim and Glenn Thompson.

MOUNTAIN MADNESS 1999

The overall winner was a team called 'I Owe my Mom Big' with Jake Howe on downhill, Paul Watson, runner and skater, Marilee Howe, classic skier and Davin MacIntosh was the skate-skier.

The youngest team was the 'Banff Mountain Lions' from the Banff Elementary School. Nine- year-old Nick Christou said his favourite part was crossing the finish line.

CRAG & CANYON 1981

Skier Dies at Norquay.

Dead is Osamu Gotoh, an employee of a fur retail outlet in Banff. According to the Banff RCMP, Gotoh was near the top of the Bowl when he fell on the hard-packed slope. He slid 1000 feet down on his back, taking the occasional tumble as he did so. Towards the bottom of the Bowl he slid over a small embankment and through a snowfence. The patrol had him off the mountain within minutes. When it was decided that his only hope lay in Calgary, a helicopter was used to fly him there.

Author's Note: Mr. Gotoh had been wearing a ski suit made of a shiny, slippery material. It was a popular material for a while, but not for long as any fall immediately put the skier in a helpless sliding position. Friends of Mr. Gotoh had offered an amount of cash to repair the slope where he fell, thinking it might be the fault of the slope. This was not the case and the money was returned following an investigation.

NORQUAY TEAM CAPTURES PRO RACES
Reporter Fraser Martin in Calgary newspaper, April 21, 1977:

Victorious Norquay ski team, Jim Montalbetti, Dave Grierson and Dave Larkin. For the first time in five years, Alberta ski pros took the top two spots at the Fifth Annual Molson Canadian Ski Instructors Alliance (CSIA) Pro Team race at Silver Star ski area. Second place in the Dual Slalom team race was taken by the Banff Springs Hotel Ski School consisting of Peter Hornung, Tetsuo Fuji and Rene Zeller. Forty teams from Western Canada participated.

CRAG & CANYON, May 14, 1975.
TRAGEDY STRIKES BANFF FAMILIES

Last Sunday evening a fatal airplane crash took the lives of four Banff residents, Jim Peyto, 23, Greg Henderson, 24, Dave Howell, 28, and 23-year-old Tom Kelly. According to reports the Cessna 185 returning to Banff from Brooks was attempting to make a forced landing just west of Exshaw when it collided with some high-tension wires and exploded. All were killed instantly.

Peyto, Henderson and Kelly were born and raised in Banff. Dave Howell came from Calgary originally but has lived in Banff for many years. He was married to Marilyn Kelly, Tom Kelly's sister.

Author's note: This was an unbelievable accident. All the boys were so well known in the town and ski community. The Peyto, Henderson and Kelly families were such a large part of this town's ski history. Each family had members on our National Ski Team. Dave Howell was an excellent skier and hang-glider pilot.

RICK MAISONET (Nine-year resident of Banff. Business, acupuncture)
"When I was 12 years old I came to Norquay with a friend from Calgary. Well, I thought he was a friend. He was entered in the Norquay Challenge, where he was going to try and ski 27 runs in one day off the Big Chair. He said, 'You might as well come up the chair.' I said, 'But I haven't skied before!' He said, 'You're athletic, you won't have any trouble!'

"It was awful! I sat down to change direction. About half way down I broke a ski -- they belonged to my friend's sister. While I was sitting on the slope a hot shot sprayed me with snow. As he went by he yelled, 'It's slugs like you that ruin the hill for us good skiers.' I didn't try skiing again for fifteen years. Now I snowboard."

CHRIS GROZDANOV AND VIC SAKIS (Two guys on Norquay in the 60s. Chris is from Toronto. He worked at the Globetrotter bar in the Voyager Hotel.)
Chris: "I was wearing Blue Kneissls. Vic had the top of the line White Stars.

Neither of us had ever skied before. Being young and enthusiastic, we decided to go up the big chair. Naturally it was a mistake. We probably took about an hour, doing kick-turns all the way down, but we did get down. When we got on the lower slopes our confidence returned and we challenged one another to a run in the Gulley. It was a race to the Timberline bar. The loser buys the winner a Harvey Wallbanger and I won the drink because Vic had to go around a moose and ran into a tree half way down the Gulley. Somehow the 'Wallbanger' seemed appropriate."

MYSTEE HUNTER AND MARIA HAWKINS (Two Banff High school students in the late 70s.)

Mystee: "I remember those beautiful spring days. If Maria and I had a free period or two we would combine it with our lunchtime and head up to Norquay. We also entered a High School team in the first 'Mountain Madness' competition in 1977. We were all about 14 years old, and we won it. I had been skiing Norquay for fourteen years at that time; my parents had started me and my sister Kendall on skis when we were one year and a couple of months old."

NICKY AND MATTHEW MONOD (Father and son, second and third generation at Norquay.)

Nicky: "I was about Matthew's age, probably about five, when Mom dropped me off at Norquay. I had on leather boots and the skis were too long: we couldn't control our equipment the way my son can. He skis in the Halfpipe, we could never have done that."

ROGER WITNEY (Skiing photographer, 21 years in Banff.)

"Shortly after arriving from eastern Canada in 1978 I came up to Norquay to watch a freestyle competition. At that time I took a photo of Laura Lee Bowie; she was a ballet champion. It was my first effort at ski photography and I sold it to her for $2. Recently she told me it still stands on her mantel. One of my best days was in March 1991. It wasn't a very good snow year, but we had this lovely surprise dump. Norquay people sent me along with a couple of instructors to shoot some promotional shots off the big chair. It was magic; ask Beth Cairns -- she was there. My worst day was 15 years ago while I was competing in the 'Mountain Madness.' While going through the Widow Maker I lost a ski and everything else. The ski-patroller said it was the best crash he had ever seen. I strained my medial collateral, but it's the good runs and good shots I remember."

NORQUAY 1941 (*Crag & Canyon*)

Mrs. J. Morin, a Parisienne who escaped through Brussels at the time of the German invasion today christened the first rope tow in the Canadian Rockies on the slopes of Mt. Norquay. The tow was called "Pick Me Up." A name that lasted about as long as the bottle of wine that christened it. The date was January 12, 1941.

EDGAR MARGREITER (Ski Instructor at Norquay from 1984 to 1988. Presently owns Bow Valley Realty in Banff.)

"I remember my first winter here, I had just left Mike Wiegele Helicopter skiing. On opening day I couldn't believe it, it was like the best day of heli-skiing; we skied the Big Chair from top to bottom in hip deep powder. Norquay was a small operation at that time, but we all worked well together, the patrol, the lodge and lift people and my ski school. Corinne Percy, Nick Drongelen, Edmar Richards, were a few that worked for me."

The Edgar Margreiter Ski School try early man-made snow on Norquay, 1986.

DIK WALMSLEY (Co-owner of "Ski Stop" with Ron 'Ratso' Hallam.)

"I came here in 1972 following my graduation from Western University. My background was hockey; I had never skied until my first day here at Norquay when I went up the big chair and practically ripped my face off. It was one of the best years of my life. Skiing captivated me and I could never leave the mountains. Now I ski with my wife Viki, and my boys Cooper and Wilson. Cooper is five and he just skied the Big Chair five times non-stop. I'm thankful he never saw my first run from that chair. Through the years I have done it all, 'The Mountain Madness,' 'Race for the Sun,' and today I'm skiing against 'Jungle' Jim Hunter in our Rossignol 'Ski Stop' Challenge."

MIKE KIRBY (Calgarian who has skied Norquay for over forty years. A regular competitor in Bruno's Annual Veterans and Masters Race.)

"Yes, I remember the old days. In the spring they never had an attendant on the lift, you loaded yourself and then you came down in moguls I swear were 10 feet high. And they would shoot us down to the basement of the old lodge if we brought our lunch."

SPENCER THACKRAY (Norquay lodge, March 1999. People were talking about the skiing ability of this little guy, so I spoke to him.)

Hi! Your name is Spencer?
"Yes, my name is Spencer!"
Spencer, what ski are you skiing on?
"Bandige."
Bandage?
"No, Bandige!"
Oh, Bandit?
"Yes, Bandige!"
Is this your sister?
"Yes, that's my sister, she is four!"
And is this your sister too?
"Yes, that's my sister, she is two!"
Spencer, what is your last name?
"Zachary!"
Zachary?
"No, Thackray!"
Do you live in Banff or Canmore?

Laura Lee Bowie in the 1970s, the freestyle years.

"In Canmore. What is that?"

It's a microphone, I am recording your voice and it counts the freckles on your nose.

"Cool!"

How old are you, Spencer?

"I'm six!"

Cool, thanks guys.

RYAN CAPEL (Born in Banff 1962. The Capel family reflects the history of skiing in Banff.)

"My thoughts go back to the jumps we had here at Norquay. We started on the old 'C' jump as kids. We always jumped on downhill skis, except my brother Colin who went on to become a member of our national jumping team. But the day I remember was a jump made by Greg Paltinger: he was an air guy. On this day we had built a kicker on the big 'B' jump and had cut some of the alders down so he could get a run at the jump from away up in the forest. He hit that kicker and just flew with so much air he passed the transition and landed in the ditch on the flat where he just exploded. His skis went one way, his boots and socks came right off and went another way. He just sat there on his ass with bare feet. He had gone further than Steve Collins or any member of our Olympic team who were jumping at that time. It was amazing.

"As a little kid I remember the pool that developed in the spring where the present lodge now sits. We shot down the slope from Stoney Squaw and water-skied across it; of course we were soaking wet when Dad came to pick us up."

JOHN STERCHI (Born in Banff, John is presently a pilot for Air Nova out of Halifax, Nova Scotia.)

"Norquay is still the place I want to ski. I am probably the only holder of a midweek pass living in Halifax. I will have breakfast in Halifax at about 6:30 a.m., fly five and a half hours, drive to Banff from Calgary and with the change in time I can still be at the top of the Big Chair by twelve noon. I will generally stay for a couple of days on each trip."

LYNNE RICHARDSON (Currently Lynne is a physiotherapist with Canada's National Alpine Team and working at a clinic in Banff.)

"As a young racer from Edmonton I remember the spring days and races on Norquay, skiing with Jennifer Percy, Kendall Hunter, Karen and

"I loved racing." Lynne Richardson with racing buddy Kendall Hunter.

Sharol Percy. I loved racing, that's why I am here today taking part in Bruno's Veterans and Masters Race."

ETHAN COMPTON (81-year-old skier competing in Bruno's Veterans and Masters Race, 1999. The Compton family operated a sport store in Calgary.)

"How was my first run? I am reasonably happy with it. It could have been better. I am 81 years old and I took less than 81 seconds. Is that like shooting your age in golf? Let's look at it in that brighter light."

DAVE RAHAM (Dave's skiing ability has defeated Norquay in many ways; he was also employed there for nine years in a variety of jobs.)

"I was always a fan of the steep and bumps and I liked the staff parties. In the 'Mountain Smoker' I generally came second to Bob Rankin, but I do hold the record for the most runs in a single day, which is 45. That would be close to 60,000 vertical feet."

PATTY SCHULTZ (As a young Patty Clark of the Calgary Ski Club in the 50s she was one of their top racers.)

"There is so much to remember. I know in one race they ran out of bamboo poles and they stuck in 2 x 2s for a gate. I skied with great gals, Joanne and Jeannie Campbell and Betty Leper, who married George Kent. I also recall Malcolm and Sheila Cullen starting ski programs for children long before there was the Nancy Greene and other kids' programs. They did so much good work for the kids."

BRUNO ENGLER (As he completed his first run in the 33rd Annual Bruno Engler Veterans and Masters Race.)

"I just found out I feel better on my skis than I do walking, it hurts less. My wife had a good run. Vera is very competitive, she has been an athlete all her life and an ex-Olympian. She competed in the shot put at Rome in 1960 for Czechoslovakia.

The history of skiing right here: (L to R) Pat Duffey, Bruno Engler, Hans Gmoser, Leo Grillmair, 1999.

She is enjoying the new challenge of ski racing."

LEO GRILLMAIR AND ERWIN WIDMER (In conversation during a lunch break at Bruno's Veterans and Masters Race, 1999.)

Erwin: "It was at the Bugaboos in 1969 that I had to teach Dustin Hoffman how to ski, at least enough so he could snowplow down a small slope while Bruno filmed a close-up, which would be a fast cut on someone else skiing for him. Jim Davies flew him in the helicopter up a gentle slope only about 300 meters; it took quite a while to get that one shot."

Leo: "He was good to work with and had a sense of humour. I know he kidded with Bruno when he was trying to film him. You talk about using the helicopter. When Hans Gmoser and I started heli-skiing in the Bugaboo lumber camp with the old 'B' helicopter, which would have been in 1964/65, the guide would go up first. Then each trip Jim Davies would fly two skiers up. If we got the group up in one hour we thought it was fantastic because before it would have taken us five hours. Now if we're not up there in five minutes they bitch like hell. Of course in the first years, I think we charged either $240 or maybe $280 for the week. Now it depends on how much they ski, but it's around $6000."

HANS GMOSER (Now retired from 35 years of ski touring, filming and his world-renowned Canadian Mountain Holiday heli-skiing empire. On this day he was taking part in Bruno Engler's Veterans and Masters Race on Mt. Norquay, 1999.)

"After arriving in Canada my first skiing at Norquay would have been in the winter of 1952/53. I skied quite a bit during that winter, but in 1954 I started tours in the high country. I didn't come back to Norquay until last year, except for in the late 60s or early 70s when I came up to help officiate when my boys, Robson and Conrad, were jumping. When I first came to Norquay the good skiers I remember: there was Ian Neilson, Bob Dawson, George Capel; and Franz Gabl was still here. That first year I came in from Calgary every weekend and tried to kill myself. I probably thought I was a better skier than I was and skied faster than I should have. They were exciting times."

PETER MONOD (Second son of the famous Monod family. Peter was Canada's top slalom skier in the late 1970s. Today he was in the Veteran's Race.)

"I still have nightmares from jumping off the 'A' jump when I was 11 years old. Our coach at that time thought it would be good training. I skied by that area today and looked

Nancy Knechtel, Peter Monod, Virginia Monod., 1999.

down and immediately felt the urge to go to the bathroom. I remember skiing with the Costigan brothers, Norm and Gerald. There was the day Norm got his jacket caught in the rope on the old Memorial rope tow and it lifted him right over the safe-

Peter Monod on course, 1981.

Nicky Monod and Byron Tarchuk, 1999.

ty-gate and wedged him in the little shack on top. They figure he was in there for a couple of runs before they discovered him. Gerald was a great skier and hockey player, he won most of his ski races along with my brother Phil and he scored most of the goals for his hockey team. I remember Gerald competing, I think it might have been in a junior 'C' Championship, the only guy that had a chance of beating Gerald was George Motter. Anyway, George caught a tip and his glasses came shooting off. Gerald was there and being Mr. Nice Guy, picked the spectacles up and handed them to George who couldn't ski without them. This is for the only guy that had a chance of beating him. Because someone had touched his equipment, Motter got a re-run and beat Costigan by a whisker, but that tells you a lot about Gerald Costigan."

DANAZE CHAMBERS (Medical doctor and active skier living in Banff.)
"Further to what Peter Monod was saying about the integrity of the Costigan boy. I believe great young skiers become great people. Those who work hard and focus on succeeding lay their ego on the line. They develop fine qualities along with the respect they have for their fellow skiers. They may not always like the gal or guy they're competing against, but they get along with them because they respect the efforts made by that person. This is a very important lesson for a successful life."

PHIL MONOD (Oldest son of Kay and Johnny Monod. National Team member 1976 to 1978. He was at Bruno's Race competing in the 35 to 45 age group.)

"When I was a kid, maybe nine or ten, a cable fell off the old Poma lift and it almost took my shoulder off. My Dad gave me hell because I got grease on my jacket. Look at this picture, this is my wife Beth snowboarding in the race today wearing a skirt, doesn't that look classic? Today's race? Yes, my little brother Peter beat me in both runs, but not by much. If Nicky could have raced today he would probably have beat Peter. You know when Peter was on the National Team in 1979/80 he was our best slalom racer and Canada didn't send him to the Olympics. But the week following, at the American Nationals in Squaw Valley, California, he raced against Phil Mahre of the US who had won the Olympic GS, and he beat him. Who is the best skier in our family? I think I would say my Dad is."

JAMIE FUKUSHIMA (Project manager for the building of the present Norquay Lodge. At Bruno's Race, competing in the 45 to 55 age group.)

"I had a good first run, believe I was in 5th or 6th position. My second run I would rather not talk about, I lost a ski. Thank you for your compliment on the lodge: I didn't design it, the architect was John Novotny. I built it in 1996, since that time we have had many favourable comments, and I am also happy with the way it is servicing the public."

LARRY BOYD (Larry managed Mt. Assiniboine Lodge in the late 1940s for Erling Strom.)

"My skiing was just about all touring, but I did meet George Encil in 1945, which was a couple of years before he built the lift here at Norquay. He was interested in hunting and I took him on a hunting trip in the Assiniboine area. I think he might have got a goat on that trip. I see Rob Crosby here today, which reminds me of something his brother Doug accomplished. Erling Strom, as you know, was an outstanding climber. I believe he was the lead climber on the first winter ascent of Mt. McKinley in Alaska, the highest peak in North America. He admired anyone who could out-perform him, and Doug's feat did just that. Doug left Banff early one morning and hiked to Assiniboine and climbed up that mountain to the Bowl, an area a couple of hours short of the summit. He slept there and climbed to the summit early next morning. Somewhere around noon he was back at the Assiniboine lodge, where he probably had a cup of tea or soup, then he hiked the 35 miles back to Banff. Erling of course checked the summit of Assiniboine and found Doug Crosby's note indicating his arrival at the peak. All that in two days, impressed even Erling Strom."

PAT DUFFY (Has skied Norquay for over 40 years. In Bruno's Race he was competing in the 65 to 74 age group. He currently lives in Vancouver.)

"Believe it or not, Buzz Lorimer and myself were outside the day lodge in 1957, maybe 1958, and Walter Fisher presented us with a season's pass for skiing in the torch light parade the night before."

BILL SCOTT (Has lived most of his life in Banff. Born 1911.)

"It would be in the early 1930s when the government started a winter work project, which was building the road up Stoney Squaw to Mt. Norquay. Any member of a family could sign up to work a maximum of ten days a month. My Dad, myself and my younger brother all took turns at working there. The pay was 30 cents an hour. No one really enjoyed it; it was cold work, and progress was slow. I recall an elderly gentlemen who couldn't work was hired to keep a fire going."

Coaches Nikki and Marty Hansen direct the Mt. Norquay Avalanche Club, 1999.

MARTY AND NIKKI HANSEN,

March 1999 (Marty is now Head Coach of the Banff Mt. Norquay Avalanche racing club; his wife Nikki is the Director of Racing for Mt. Norquay.)

Marty: "At present I am Head Coach of the Ski Academy assisted by coaches John Evely and Ryan Whetung. We are currently working on a new program called Alpine Adventure. About half of the people in this program will be dedicated to racing while the other half will be interested in a total mountain experience which includes rock and ice climbing, winter camping and so on. Next winter the Ski Academy will have a different approach. A student will be able to take the academic classes and ski with the Academy and our Avalanche program or the Banff Alpine Racers."

Nikki: "We have a new racing program which starts with the Nancy Greene age skier right up to 18 years of age, and it's called 'Avalanche.' I believe it is the first racing club operated by a ski resort, at least in Western Canada. I also work with the local Banff Alpine Racers and the Academy in providing slopes for training. Marty and I are really happy to be back here. Marty started with the Academy and then we spent three years in Australia."

Coach John Evely surrounded by young racers during autumn rollerblade training.

JOHN EVELY (Head Coach of the Banff Alpine Racers for the winter of 1999/2000.)

"I am excited about this coming winter. We have an outstanding group of young people in our program about one third of which come from Banff, a third from Canmore and a third from Calgary. Coaching with me will be a National title holder, Joanna Magee, better known as Jo Jo, and Sven Pouliot. This year, the 13- and 14-year age group that was known as J2, will be called K2. This is the same title the European clubs use for this age group."

JOHN THORNTON (Public safety, Ski Patrol and avalanche forecaster, 1999.)

"Whenever I step into the old ski patrol hut, which was moved in the expansion of 1989/90, I feel a sense of history, especially when I'm making recordings of snow conditions and I see the initials of the Government Wardens who looked after the mountain for so many years. There was Bill Vroom, Keith Everts, John Wackerle, Cliff White Jr., Doug Martin, Don Waters, Scott Ward, Tim Auger and many more. Also looking back at the operation of the mountain I feel the present owners are doing a much better job. A better operation of the mountain and better at bringing skiers and snowboarders to the area."

DAVE MORRISON (President and CEO of Brewsters. Was in partnership with Art Haenni and the Sulphur Mountain Gondola when they operated Mt. Norquay and made the expansion of the ski area in 1989/90, then sold it to the present owners in 1995.)

"I always considered Mt. Norquay to be the area where Banffites went to ski, and it never seemed to get out of that no matter how much you invested up there, it was still Banff's local ski hill and they always resented anyone else being there."

BEATE (A young lady working in the Banff area in 1975.)

"I hitch-hiked from Lake Louise to Banff for a citizen's race at Mt. Norquay. I don't know what they called it, but everyone dressed up in costumes, it was wild and great fun."

CALGARY HERALD (A photo in the Calgary paper of Jim Morrison, manager of the new Norquay clubhouse, with a pair of old skis close to eight feet in length.)

"The pioneer skis unearthed last December from the ruins of a construction cabin near Castle Mountain in the Canadian Rockies. The find establishes the date of the first skiing in the Rockies as about 1887. The skis have a place of honour over the great stone fireplace in the clubhouse."

Author's Note: This is a little confusing. The paper, although not dated, I believe to be 1940 when the new lodge was built. But that lodge never had a fireplace. If the reporter was correct in saying the skis are placed over the fireplace, that would have been earlier in the cabin that burnt down in January 1938, which had a fireplace. That would mean the skis were destroyed in that fire. If the paper was older than I had thought it was and if the reporter, when he referred to the new clubhouse, was actually talking about the original clubhouse of 1928-29, the end result is the same. The skis were destroyed in the fire. If it was a 1940 paper and the skis were placed on a wall, not over a fireplace, then the skis must still exist.

TED CLARK (Arrived in Banff in 1957 from Ottawa. Ski School Director and father of National Ski Team member, Marcia Clarke.)

"I always enjoyed Norquay and the ski out to the Timberline Hotel was a perfect way to end a day of skiing. I am disappointed the way we treat, or rather don't treat, our skiers and sports people of the past. They should be our role models for our present young athletes. I'm thinking of people like Gordie Morrison who made our National Team, but still manged to get a PhD in engineering. I'm not just talking skiing, look at Jack MacAulay and the hockey legacy he has given us. I guess what I'm saying is we should at least have a sport museum to honour the many achievments of Banff athletes."

KLARA HUSER (Started working at Norquay in the summer of 1970. She had a variety of positions including managing the area and looking after special events.)

"I can't believe I was at Norquay for 24 years. Mr. Bill Herron hired me about a year after he and his wife Carol took over Norquay from Mr. and Mrs. Fisher. It was exciting to work right in the middle of a ski area. Of course we had the summer operation as well. At that time the summer lift consisted of three gondolas in a group, then we changed it to two gondolas with a chair in front and behind. With the Herrons it was a family operation and I was treated like family. I could always talk to Mr. Herron if I had business or personal problems. Later when the two big companies took over Norquay the operation took on a corporate attitude: they didn't have the same interest in their staff. I did enjoy working with Mr. Whittick when he came to manage the area. He was very good with people. I learned so much working with the various owners. They wanted to have the confidence in me to do what had to be done and preferred that I do it, and explain it to them later. That was true with Herrons, Mr. Haenni of Sulphur Mountain and the Brewster people when they arrived in 1989/90. I left Norquay for health reasons just before Kika Grandi and Peter White purchased it in 1995. The 24 years at Norquay for me had been wonderful years."

DON AND JO HAYES (Don and Jo grew up in Banff, both skied. Don was one of Banff's top racers in the late 1940s and early 50s. They lived in Jasper many years working for Brewsters, where Don continued to support ski programs. He also spent several years as a director of Travel Alberta for the provincial government in Edmonton.)

Don: "My earliest memories would be before the road was completed. I know we had to climb beyond the end of the road, and ski down on the old ski-out that crossed the road four or five times. For awhile we would take our sleigh up and after skiing we would tie our skis to the sleigh and ride down to town. I also remember the night, in 1938, when I heard on the radio that the Banff ski cabin was on fire. I was impressed because I think it was the first time I heard Banff mentioned on the news."

Jo: "I worked in the lodge that would have been built in 1940. I was a waitress along with Pat McLeod and we worked for Margaret Morrison. It was a weekend job as I was still in school. Also, I was into knitting. I made a Norwegian sweater for Don, plus racing sweaters for some of the kids that were racing at that time."

PAULA ASHBY (Paula, from Ontario, had been on the Ski Patrol for only a short time in March of 1999.)

"I think Norquay has a positive environment. The staff working here is just great, they all seem to click. The people coming here seem to be a nice mix of skiers and snowboarders. I believe Norquay has the best Snowboard Park. Yes, I will be back next winter."

CHRIS KENT (Chris is an Alberta racer who raced seven years on Canada's National Team. Born in Calgary, 1964.)

"My first reflection on Norquay would be 'long, steep and the "B" jump' plus all the training we did on the Memorial slope. Before that I remember coming to Norquay to watch my first World Cup Race, which was in 1972. I remember one of the best was here, Karl Schranz, and they didn't let him race because he was apparently receiving money from his suppliers. But that was a different time. Now you look at the Olympic controversy and all those Olympic officals that were 'on the take.' The best year I remember with the National Team would have been 1980. I won my first race that started the year, in New Zealand. We then went to Val D'Isère in December for our best team showing. Ken Read was 2nd, Steve Podborski 3rd, I was 4th, Dave Irwin 5th and Dave Murray was 7th."

SCOTT HENDERSON (The Henderson family moved to Banff when Scotty was two years old in 1945. He and his brother Wayne made the National Team in 1962. Following his time as a racer Scott coached the National Team, specializing in downhill: it was the birth of the 'Crazy Canucks,' a proud era in Canadian international ski competition. Scott, along with his wife Barb, formerly a member of the US National Team, are independant sport representatives, living in Colorado.)

Scotty Henderson 1999 while attending Ken Read's annual Lake Louise charity race to raise money for Cystic Fibrosis.

"My thoughts go back to skiing the Gulley early in the season when we were told we shouldn't, because of the lack of snow. I ran into a log and broke my leg. I think I was about ten years old. Norquay was a great hill to grow up on. No matter where you went in the world everything after Norquay seemed flat.

"I remember trips to Jasper; we had to get a permit to drive the road. Doug Robinson was our coach, but John Hartefeld, who was our shop teacher in school, was very supportive in many ways. On one trip after leaving Lake Louise, John stopped the van, got a rope out and let us ski-jore down the road. What fun that was!

"I started coaching in 1969. I found both racing and coaching gratifying. The sport gave me an education. Working for Bob Lange led me to a business career in Colorado. My brother Wayne was offered a coaching position in Alaska, which also

Scotty Henderson National Team, 1966.

let him use the degree he had in civil engineering. He still loves to race. I saw him last week at Winter Park competing in a Master's Race. I don't really race, but I enjoy coming to this race and supporting Ken Read and his efforts to raise money for Cystic Fibrosis."

RALPH SCURFIELD (Ralph is the owner of Sunshine Village.)

"I remember skiing Norquay when I was a kid, possibly ten years old. At that time it was known as 'Tough or Tender.'

"My more recent recollection was about four years ago when I was asked by the Alberta Treasury Branch to submit a bid on the Norquay Ski Area as it had gone into receivership by the previous owners. It was a strange process. After submitting the first bid they came back to us and requested a second bid. I was away on business at the time and didn't really have time to plan the second bid. Before I knew it, it was over and the new owners were Kika Grandi and Peter White.

"I would like to say that Pat Coté, the Norquay manager, has done an excellent job in turning Norquay around."

DIANNE LEHODEY (Trained at Norquay while in her teens before making Canada's National Team. Now returns with her eight-year-old girl and six-year-old boy as they ski with the Quikies.)

"Norquay has grown, but I still enjoy the run off the Big Chair. I think it is unequaled anywhere, in Canada or Europe. And this year they opened those chutes they haven't opened for years, it was just awesome. As a memory I still reflect on the day our coach Ottmar Setzer let the girls go off the 'B' jump. I barely cleared the brow, even now when I go up the chair and look over there I have those memories of going off that jump. I skied with Wendy Robinson and stayed with their family when I was in town. I also skied with Loni Klettl and Chris McCready, with good memories. One more memory: I was 12 when I watched Gustavo Thoeni in the World Cup here in 1972. Down at the finish line where he had just completed a fantastic slalom run, he spotted me as a young fan and he gave me his toque. And that great Italian racer just swept me off my feet, I was hooked from then on."

NORM RAULT (An Edmonton skier who along with Bob Freeze of Calgary was instrumental in starting the Alberta International Intercollegiate Ski Meet in 1947, which ran for 26 years. In the 1940s Norm was one of Alberta's top slalom skiers.)

"I competed at Norquay in the Dominion Championships of 1940. That was before Norquay even had a rope tow, but it was a great meet. Art Coles of Vancouver won the slalom and Ted Paris of Banff won the downhill. I came ninth in the slalom. It was the first time I saw a lady skiing in a skirt; that lady was Peggie Johannsen, daughter of the famous Jackrabbit Johannsen.

"Talking about skiing in the 1930s, they were depression years and there wasn't much to do. I remember a ski program at that time in Edmonton that brought out about 2,000 skiers when Edmonton's population was around 50,000."

JIM READ (Calgary skier who skied on Canada's National Team from 1981 to 1989, then raced professionally in the United States until 1995.)

"Norquay was so challenging, it made you a good skier. There was a group of us who attacked the run off the Big Chair, down the Bowl and over the 'B' jump, maybe twenty times a day, and running gates off the Memorial, and doing run after run, after run. Competing on the National Team I was better in GS, but with equipment changes while pro-racing I became better in slalom."

Cameron Barnes and Jan Hudec at the 2000 Pontiac Cup.

JOHNNY PRISTOV (Was on the Norquay Ski Patrol when it was still operated by the Warden Service. He then became a ski instructor and operated his own school. Born in Slovenia, 1932.)

"One of my best skiing days at Norquay was the year we had the earliest opening ever. That was 1966 when skiing started with three feet of snow in mid October. Doug Robinson was managing the hill that year. Everything happened just right, Doug had groomed the slopes that fall hoping we would have an early dump. A storm from the north hit Norquay with more snow than the rest of the Rockies. It was a year that saw Norquay open before Sunshine and Lake Louise.

"When I was still on the ski patrol for the Warden Service (the government discontinued this service to the ski area in 1966) I was called to help a very heavy man than was having trouble on the upper slopes. After checking him I decided to call for a toboggan to take him down. Jim Davies came up with the toboggan. The man was so big we decided to use two men to take him down. Jim was on the front and myself with a rope, on the back. Normally the best procedure is to have just one person operating the toboggan from the front. Because of the snow conditions we decided to take a route on the ridge that divides the North American run from a major avalanche slope. Suddenly the whole avalanche area gave away. I managed to jump to the stable side holding on with the rope to the toboggan and Jim, who now was sitting on the other side, on nothing but grass, while the

Paul Stutz at the 2000 Pontiac Cup.

First ski train leaves Edmonton for Banff 1937.

s Who in Skiing Around Edmonton

NORMIE RAULT BILL HALIBURTON GEORGE HARRIS REG RAULT STAN WARD WALLY STAUFFER HOWARD HODGSON

MEET THESE RENOWNED SKIERS ON THE SKI TRAIN

The number of Edmonton skiers grew rapidly once they discovered Norquay.

avalanche roared down into the canyon below. Our lives were saved that day, but about two weeks later the skier we were taking down was killed in an auto accident near Lake Louise.

"We could always tell when the season was going to end at Norquay. In late March or early April a golden eagle would arrive above the upper slopes. When that happened we knew we had ten days to two weeks before the season ended."

ROB BOSINGER (The family arrived in Banff from Rossland in 1982. Rob and his brother Peter would make Canada's National Team. Rob was on the team from 1987 to 1993.)

"Doing big GS turns down the Bowl or Lone Pine in fresh snow is one of my favourite runs in the world. It was great to have Norquay in our backyard."

RACING SCENE 1973 (The Alberta Cup Finals were about to be held at Norquay in March of 1973. These are the standings going into that race.)
George Motter of Calgary and Joanne Becker of Banff take slim leads into the Men's and Women's section of the Alberta Cup Final. George Motter is six points ahead of early leader Mike Irwin, who is recovering from an injury. John Hilland is in third spot. Joanne Becker is only one point ahead of her teammate from the Banff Ski Runners, Joan Tittemore. In third place is Loni Klettl of Jasper. In fourth place is Pat Gordon of Banff and Dianne Lehodey, of Calgary, is in fifth position. In the Boy's, fourth and fifth places are held by Mark Bowman of Calgary and Banff's Phillip Monod.

The Sunday races will feature an innovation in competitive skiing, with the best slalom skiers in the province racing head to head in a dual slalom.
Dual slalom is the invention of Bob Beattie, former U.S. Alpine Director, who is using the format successfully on the U.S. professional tour.

RESULTS

When this weekend was over Loni Klettl and John Hilland had come out of their third positions to win the Alberta Cup Championship.

13-year-old Loni won both Slaloms. Hilland had returned from the U.S. Junior Nationals at Crystal Mountain, Washington, to win the Sunday slalom and the Alberta Cup. Banff's Joan Tittemore ended up in second position. In third place was 13-year-old Dianne Lehodey of Calgary. 16-year-old Phillip Monod of Banff finished in second place over-all. Third spot went to George Motter of Calgary, Mike Irwin, Calgary, 4th and Keith Humphrey, Calgary, was 5th.

Two Banff girls placed 4th and 5th; they were Joanne Becker and Pat Gordon. The Alberta Cup was conceived by Leo Berchtold and Brian Becker of Banff and Gerry Hood of Calgary. It was an all-Alberta competition. The organizers believed the Alberta Cup advanced the competitive atmosphere in Alberta. This proved to be true as several of these young skiers, and many that followed, went on to compete on Canada's National Team.

Ski Patrolman Bob Meggs easing the pain, 1967.

BOB MEGGS (Bob worked on the Norquay Patrol eight years and was an instructor with the Heinz Vifian school at Norquay.)

"My first thoughts are with the Ski Patrol and the years I worked with John Wackerle. He demanded such a high standard of operation from the patrol members that worked for him, and it showed in the respect we received in turn from the skiing public. People looked up to us, there were times when I felt like a hero. In the early years the patrol was responsible for the grooming of the slopes. This was accomplished by hours of tramping on our 220 cm skis. We were employed by the Parks Warden Service, but there were people in town at the Administration building who didn't look upon us as professional patrol people, they thought we were on the slopes just to run powder. To help deflate those thoughts we would start our tramping on the North American slope that was visible from town. Park Superintendent Harry Dempster left his skis at Norquay. He would from time to time inspect the slopes, which always coincided with fresh snow. One day after a good fall of snow when we were sure Harry would appear, we doped his skis with a base wax and then added a spray wax so he wouldn't notice it. We went with him up the chair and jumped into the beautiful powder, as did Harry, only after two turns he came to a grinding stop. We went on to do other work. It seemed like hours before Harry cursed his way into our Patrol Hut. Dempster was a good guy; he was one of the few government people you could kid with. We were always playing tricks on one another.

"I remember the day Bruno was going to take a picture of Johnny Pristov and me. I was to do a left turn around a tree and Johnny was going to do a right turn. (I know it sounds like a plot for disaster, and it was.) I ran over his skis, but Bruno got a great shot of Johnny 'crashing and burning,' as we used to say in the old days.

"I worked for George Encil, Walter Fisher and Bill Herron. They were all good to work for, but each one had a very different personality. George liked to be around talented people. He admired good skiers, artists, hunters, musicans, photographers and so on, but he didn't excel in any of these professions himself. He could talk with people in the arts, but when it came to talking with workers, he didn't communicate well at all. We thought perhaps he didn't understand the personalities of western Canadians, but it was probably his aristocratic upbringing in Europe that caused the gap.

"Walter Fisher, whose family had worked with George's family before the war in the textile business, his being knitted material and Encils (the Eisenschiml family) leather, had similar childhoods, in fact they had gone to school together. Walter had good ideas as did George, but his communication with workers was not always too good. Doug Robinson understood him and they accomplished much together, but with many employees he preferred to write them a note rather than enter into a verbal discussion.

"Bill Herron was eager to talk to his staff and know what was going on. He was always on the scene, whereas the two previous owners were often absent. If the three owners had anything in common it was probably their reaction and conflict with the policy of the government. Fisher and Encil had both threatened to close down Sunshine and Norquay at different times if the government didn't co-operate more. This generally involved plowing the roads. Bill Herron also had his conflict with the Parks people, but it was different in most cases. Bill had built a large work shed well ahead of Government approval. His order of a double chairlift was also a year or two premature, he couldn't understand how long it took them to approve the obvious. He had also questioned the government on their road clearing priorities.

"Not related to Norquay directly, but Andy Anderson who headed the Ski Patrol for a while had the smartest dog I have ever seen. When Andy left his dog, 'Bow' at home the dog would run out to the overpass on the highway and wait for a green government truck to come by at which time he would bark madly until the driver took him up to see Andy at Norquay. Andy thought he lost him at one time to a pack of coyotes, but Bow survived intact. There were several chocolate brown coyotes seen the following year, a similiar brown to Bow's colouring."

MIKE MISKOW (Born in Canmore in 1944 and lived in Banff most of his life. Excellent skier, powder and cross country. Won Canadian Men's Master Championship, with gold in 15 and 30 km, plus a silver in the 50 km. Was honored with an Alberta Achievement Award, given to athletes of outstanding ability.)

"Where do I start! I have skied Norquay so much. The early seventies come to mind, I was part of the 'Rusticana Club.' Six of us lived in the house called 'Rusticana.' (It was a non-winterized summer house where you could count on the pipes freezing on most days.) There was John Heinz, Steve Orchin, Ian Wilson, Bobby Crone, Noldie Keach, myself, plus any guests that might have stayed over, and for a while Jerry and Anne Goulet parked their camper outside when they first arrived into town. We started the day by going to 'Jeannies' on Banff Avenue for breakfast. Following that we would all climb into the old car we had, trying to get in too many bodies wearing ski boots, with the skis and poles generally hanging outside the windows, and up to Norquay we would go where most of us worked at that time. We never did have a ski rack.

"Norquay has always been fun for me. I admit I was always one of the 'first track people.' We would wait in minus 30°C, for the lift to start, just to get on that mountain to make those first marks, then rush back looking for new tracks on the second run and so on. What did I ski on? In the early 1970s the 'K shorts' were popular. Remember everyone said they made the moguls too small and pointed? Then I believe it was Heads, next came the Dynamic VR 17s; they were a good ski. If I had to ski on those old skis today, I couldn't do it. Today's parabolic and fat skis are so much easier on the knees.

"In the winter of 1971/72 there was so much snow you could ski anywhere, the snow just kept coming, every day we were out for first tracks. I still do that, I'll be there an hour before the lift opens, there is nothing like going for first tracks. It was in the winter of '72 when we had the World Cup following the Olympics. All these fabulous skiers were here going wild in the deep powder; you looked up the mountain and all you could see were heads weaving above a cloud of snow.

"I remember a costume race we had at Norquay during the winter carnival that was always fun. I guess one of the wildest races (which still runs) during the winter carnival was the 'Mountain Madness.' I, along with John Heintz, Steve Orchin and Jerry Tucker, initiated the race in 1977. It starts with a downhill racer from the top of the Big Chair. Near the Timberline Hotel the skier hands off to a runner. The runner takes it to Echo Creek by the railway tracks. From there a snowshoer shoots off to a waiting skater on the Bow River. Following the skater a cross country skier completes the final leg of the race to the finish line.

"The early 'Mountain Madness Relay' races started with a mass start. You would get forty or fifty downhill skiers pushing off as one from the top of the Big Chair, all trying to be the first to hand off to their team mate waiting about a mile away, and over 2000 vertical feet below at the Timberline Hotel. It was crazy. I recall Paul Stutz saying 'It was the scariest and the most thrilling thing I have ever competed in, I was that tight all the way down.' We won the second running of that race. Our team was made up of Jerry Goulet, downhill skiing, Ian Wilson, the runner, Mike Goulet, on snowshoes, Carl Chwachka did the skating and I finished with the cross country skiing. Our time for the five events from the top of Norquay was 27:40. We were about two minutes ahead of second place."

"There are some things not related to skiing. I was at the top of the mountain when a large ram charged his reflection in the Tea House window.

"From by-gone years I can still see Johnny Monod skiing the mountain with his boys, Phil, Peter and Nicky following close behind. I can see George Geber skiing with his boy Klaus. I can see the Ski Patrol out looking for false teeth, lost by an elderly lady. I can see Morgan Davies riding on the shoulders of ski instructors when his Mom Siri was an instructor at Norquay. I remember my burning legs after snowplowing the length of the mountain in a torchlight parade. Johnny Pristov always led the torchlight descent.

"There was a lady who arrived for a little sightseeing. Because it was a warm day she went up the lift in street clothes, a dress and high heel shoes. At the top she got too close to the edge and slid down the Bowl. She survived, but when the patrol finally got to her, she was minus most of her clothing. Her high heels were probably the first to go. Although unhurt she was in an extreme state of shock. She was a lucky lady to survive that run.

"Then there was a lady taking a group lesson over on the Wishbone Slope. She had a sudden call of nature. Because of the distance to the lodge she decided to go into the woods. Unfortunately while in a crouched position with her pants down she coasted out onto the open slope and full view of her waiting classmates."

DAVE SPENCE (Western President of the Canadian Amateur Skiing Association from 1946 to 1956. A fighter for western skiers at a time when the east dominated politically the selection of Canada's National Team.)

"I moved the family to Banff in the late 1940s, but I had assisted in competitions at Norquay in the 30s. Norquay was Canada's leading ski area in 1937, probably the best mountain for competition in North America. That was a couple of years before Sun Valley even opened for skiing. It was difficult to convince eastern Canada to hold a national title in the west. Sydney Dawes, the national president of the C.A.S.A. was a reasonable man and I did enjoy working with him. He realized the hills in the east were not much of a challenge for a national championship.

"I have good memories of Norquay. I remember they had the first lady on their ski patrol in the early 1950s. Her name was Mary June Miles and she married my old friend Cam Mitchell, who was the President of the Calgary Ski Club."

Fred Hudson and Dave Spence, jump officials at the 1948 Dominions.

NORQUAY NEWS FOR 1999/2000

The Cascade double chair is being replaced by a new fixed-grip Quad. The location of the new lift has been moved slightly to the north. This move will offer a gentle start for the skier and snowboarder at the top terminal, avoiding the steep slope encountered at the top of the old Cascade chair. The Snowboard Park has been moved to the south. The old location will now become open slope for skiing and riding, joining in with the old Terrain Park. The avalanche mounds previously known as the Valley of the Ten have been reclaimed. This area will become a more usable beginner slope that feeds back to the base of the new Cascade Quad. Also new for your up-hill riding pleasure will be a 64-meter Magic Carpet. This should eliminate the humorous shuffle and slide routines generally encountered by

Large crowds enjoying 1948 jumping.

beginners on skis and boards when getting on the old platter lift. (There goes another phase of humour on snow.) The location of the carpet will be near the start of the old Cascade Chair. Sundance is a good name for the carpet as you should be able to dance on it.

There are many major events scheduled for the winter of 1999/2000. Some being competitive for young skier and snowboarders, some being fund-raisers for charities. Special events for locals and visitors include a "locals free" night on January 19th and the ever-popular Torchlight Parade will wind its way into the year 2000. Clarke Lefaivre will once again head the Ski School along with his talented wife Maureen, who specializes in programs for the young and very young. For the young who want a competitive style of skiing, Norquay has given birth to the new 'Avalanche Racing Club.' The director and head coach is Marty Hansen. The very energetic Nikki Hansen looks after the entry level or Nancy Greene program.

The well known Banff Alpine Racers (BAR) will have Jim Davis as Program Director for 1999/00. John Evely will coach Kinder 2 (13 and 14 years), while Mike Necesanek will handle the Juniors (15 to 18 years).

BANFF BOYS MEMORIAL RACE 1980 (This was a Banff Ski Runners race keeping alive the memory of four Banff boys killed in an air crash in May 1975, Tom Kelly, Jim Peyto, Greg Henderson, and Dave Howell.)

Girls: 1st Lorraine Robinson, 2nd Louise Knight, 3rd Shelley McLennan.

Boys: 1st Kurt Ritcey, 2nd Kevin Hann, 3rd David Schellenberg.

CLIFF WHITE (Cliff's father was a pioneer skier and photographer who was instrumental in establishing the early ski scene at Mt. Norquay and Skoki. Cliff purchased Sunshine Village from George Encil in 1960 and was involved with that area until 1977. His sons have carried on the White tradition; Brad in skiing and photography and Cliff Jr. in skiing and environmental concerns.)

"I was carried to Norquay in a small basket before I had any idea where I was going. In the years that followed, my brothers Pete, Donald and myself would master the skills of skiing on those slopes. The excitement experienced by my Dad Cliff, and his brothers Jack and Peter in 1927/28 when they built the first cabin, has been shared by my family, Tara, Tristan, Brad and Cliff Jr, and now my grandchildren.

"There were times we would get out of school to help tramp new snow on the jumps at Norquay. I also remember offering to carry the jumping skis of Earl Pletch to the top of the inrun; he had lost an arm in a railway accident. He had been one of our best jumpers and still continued to compete after his accident.

"I remember the crowds that showed up to watch the North American Championship of 1950. I was driving a bus for Brewsters. We were still taking people up when the jumping was almost over. The people going up couldn't get out of the bus because of the people trying to push their way in to go down.

"Skiing has undergone many changes since my Dad, his brother and Cyril Paris started at Norquay. As an area owner at Sunshine I had to be aware of these changes as they applied to the public, the government and the conservationists.

"To make a ski area a viable business involves many factors, which include nature, your appeal to the public and keeping that appeal current. If the public enjoys your area they naturally come in growing numbers, so you add lifts and facilities to accommodate these people. How do you do that without spoiling the natural beauty that attracted them in the first place? This was brought home to me shortly after purchasing Sunshine Village. I attended a public hearing to let the government and the public know of my expansion plans. During a question period a Mountie asked me 'What are you going to do about the Trans Canada Highway?' I didn't know how to respond to the question as Sunshine was about fifteen miles from the highway. He repeated his question, 'What are you going to do about the accidents and fatalities I have to look after each year with cars trying to turn off the highway to get to Sunshine. Now you want to increase that traffic?' I began to realize my plans, as modest as they were to me, would reach out to other areas I never even thought of. In time that problem was solved as they twinned the highway, but at great expense in dollars and environmental impact. To ski resorts in most areas of the world this would appear completely normal, but we are looking at a ski area in a National Park. It's true the Government of Canada encouraged, even sponsored skiing in the parks in the early years. There were good reasons for development at that time, but now I believe we have reached a period of no further growth.

"In later years a government official told me, 'If we had been thinking back in 1960 when Sunshine was up for sale, we could have purchased it at a modest price and closed it down; it would have eliminated many problems we now have.' I dare say if that had been done it would have caused many problems with the public, but that was his comment.

"At one point in our operation, to comply with a 'no growth policy,' we proposed a plan that would limit the number of people coming to Sunshine. We would increase the cost of an annual pass to a limited number of people. The Superintendent of the Park at that time, Steve Coon, said, 'You can't do that, this is a National Park open to all people of Canada.'

Cliff White Sr. at the Norquay cabin he helped build in 1928.

Little Cliff about the same time trying to get ahead.

CLIFF WHITE Jr. (Cliff is a Consulting Biologist for Parks Canada.)

"I understand my grandfather's need to make dull inactive winters into something more enjoyable. Also wanting to bring people to Banff to enjoy the mountain experience, along with the Banff people. However with him being creative as he was, and with the ski area owners that followed, came problems. As the areas improve and grow, so does the number of people using them. The growing number of people demand more space and some of this space is at the expense of the wildlife and their natural living patterns: their lives are thrown off balance. Because of the presence of people, the open areas we create encourage some animals; the elk in Banff are an example of this. Now we have too many elk and not enough predators to control them. The large numbers of elk eat everything; this affects the growth of berries, flowers, grass and some timber.

Cliff (left) does get ahead in 1960 when he purchased Sunshine Village from George Encil.

"I understand the developers wanting to create growth, but now we have to define that growth and reach a balance suitable for humans and animals. You look at places like Denver, Colorado, and the mountain area that leads west from that city. You see eight-lane highways leading into their mountain valleys. Would you want to see something like that leading from Calgary, to possibly Golden, B. C.?"

NORQUAY POW WOW TENT, February 4, 1938

This was a tent borrowed from the Trail Riders of the Canadian Rockies to be used during carnival time. It was needed as the Norquay cabin had burnt down a month earlier.

RALPH HARVEY (February 10, 1938)

Mr. Harvey as treasurer of the Banff Ski Runners asked the government's permission to charge visitors to watch the Ladies' Dominion Ski Races. It wasn't approved.

CRAG & CANYON, January 1953.

Fly to Assiniboine with Al Gaetz, $10 per person.

AL GAETZ, killed in auto accident, March 16, 1953. Al had been taking pieces of his small plane to Calgary for repair following an emergency landing at Lake Louise. While driving his truck, 29 miles west of Banff, he skidded on a patch of ice. Al was thrown from his vehicle, which then rolled over him.

BERNIE SCHIESSER (Born in Golden, B. C. Lived in the Banff area almost forty years. Skier, Warden, man of the forest, teacher of mountaineering and respect for the mountains, to young people. Bernie has done it all, including a little inspiration to Sid Marty when they both worked Lake O'Hara as Wardens in the mid 1960s.)

"I remember an early October storm on Norquay. Friends gave me a call to say they were going to run the lift, a wonderful day of early powder.

"I did the clearing, me and a D7-Cat, on the new Mystic area of Norquay in 1989/90. We ended up with 90 logging trucks of timber (1400 Cords). There were some good logs suitable for building, but the Parks people said, 'Cut it up for firewood.'"

JOHN WATTS (Attended High School in Banff. Worked for Banff National Park until 1967, and Kootenay Park as General Works Director until 1972 when he was transferred to the West Coast.)

"I worked with the German jump designer, Heine Klopher, in 1955/56 when the government brought him over to plan the 70 and 90 meter jumps for Norquay. That was about the time Banff started making plans for the Winter Olympics. Klopher had been cited by Hitler as one of Germany's outstanding athletes in their Winter Olympics of 1936. I also worked with another German, Franz Bayer, who was employed by Parks to design the judges' towers, which still stand at Norquay.

"My Norquay memories include skiing with my Calgary friends whom I knew before moving to Banff; Peter Matthews, Dick Moore, Stu Miller, Bill Trigg and Dean Fry. They would arrive each weekend by train, before they became car owners. Then there was the best gal skier in the Calgary Ski Club who was to become my wife, Fran Harris.

"One great day on Norquay turned into my worst day on Norquay. I was skiing with Fran, Bill Trigg, Bill Heywood and Frank Gourlay. On this particular day the avalanche slope, just north of the lift, looked extra appealing. Unless you're a skier standing there, this is difficult to explain.

Anyway, we started on this forbidden slope. Frank and Bill had gone first. I had made a couple of turns and stopped just off the main slope when the whole area seemed to let out a big sigh and started sliding. I hardly moved, but was left standing on rocks. I looked up the slope but Fran and Bill Trigg were nowhere in sight. Frank Gourlay and Bill Heywood had finished their run safely. Fran was thrown out of the slide about two-thirds of the way down, unhurt. Bill Trigg was further down the slope, but had a broken leg. The next day, because Frank Gourlay and myself were employed by the government, we were called into 'Bim' Strong's office (the Park Superintendent), to explain our actions, which wasn't easy to do. I just agreed with him, it was a very stupid thing to do. Shortly after that the Wardens, who operated the Ski Patrol, started fining skiers who were caught skiing on avalanche slopes. This would have presented a problem as Frank Gourlay was on the patrol at the time."

DEAN FRY (A Calgary skier who terrorized the slopes and the town of Banff in the late 1940s and early 50s. Dean had a sense of humour dryer than any powder that ever fell on Norquay.)

"It was New Year's Day in the early 50s. It also happened to be the temperature that day, 50° below. Bob Freeze, Bill Trigg and myself went up Norquay. There was no one skiing, it was too damn cold, but we talked Red Crozier into cranking up the lift. He started us up the mountain, but half way up he turned it off and left us swinging until he figured we had succumbed to the elements. He had a weird sense of humour.

"Another time I saw John Southam of Southam newspapers, and President of the Calgary Ski Club at that time, rolling down the Bowl. I can still see him; he was wearing a big Hudson Bay coat. I was on the chair, but I could hear him talking to himself, 'John you're going to die this time, you're going to die this time.'"

NORQUAY CUTS LINE-UPS TO NIL (News item in a Calgary paper, November 18,1966.)

An all new, high speed, high capacity chairlift will grace the slopes of Mt. Norquay this winter. The new lift which has been in operation all summer as a cable-car gondola will, when converted to chairs for winter use, have a capacity of 600 skiers per hour. Assistant manager Doug Robinson said "Just let us say that there will be no lift lines. The ride to the top is expected to take less than five minutes."

BANFF WINTER CARNIVAL, February 1940 (newspaper report)
5000 Spectators at Norquay for the final ski competition.
A forerunner to the Dominion Championship which will take place next week. Earl Pletch, youthful Revelstoke flier combined leaps of 132 and 147 feet to win the jumping event. Second place went to Bill Copley, Banff boy who is one of western Canada's most promising young jumpers. Hans Gunnarsen of Revelstoke, who placed fourth behind Art Johnson of Revelstoke, actually had the longest jump, a leap of 179 feet. However, Pletch was the winner because of his superior style.

Peter Vadja, a former Swiss university star, now skiing for the Edmonton Ski Club

Rudi Gertsch makes the big curl from the Big Chair, 1967.

Not everyone made the same curl, 1967.

was first in the Slalom and third in the Downhill. Art Coles of Vancouver won the Downhill and was sixth in the Slalom. Rob Crosby of Banff, just out of the junior ranks, finished fourth in Slalom and Downhill. Twelve seconds in penalties cost Crosby second place in the Slalom. Junior Bud Gourlay won the Downhill and placed second in the Slalom.

BUCK DAY AT NORQUAY
To all Banff staff. Ski Norquay, lifts, rentals, lesson, plus a fun race all one buck each. On December 16th and 18th, 1975.

Adult prices

Ski Big 3	Lake Louise	Sunshine	Norquay
$525	$370	$390	$275 day&night
(Sr. $260)	(Sr. $185)	(Sr. $95)	(Sr.$105)
			$210 day only

KINSMEN SKI SCHOOL 1972
169 children enroll for classes $1 a week.

CHATEAU LAKE LOUISE NOW OPEN WINTER AND SUMMER, 1983.

GORDIE MORRISON (Banff's first male alpine skier to be chosen for Canada's Olympic Team, Oslo, 1952.)
Gordie had recived his PhD in civil engineering. He was doing consulting work and teaching in 1972. While on a consulting trip near Chetwynd B. C. his small plane crashed and Gordie was killed.

CARRIE HUBBARD (Carrie, from Ontario, was in charge of the Day Care Centre in 1999 at Norquay.)
"We take children from 19 months to 6 years of age. It is a provincially licensed Day Care Centre. These kids are getting so smart. The other day a little guy told me, 'You can't go for a lunch break, I'm going for my lunch break.' When I told him you don't get paid when you're on a lunch break he said, 'Okay you go.'"

GORD VINCENT (Writing in the Calgary Sun at the time the expansion for Norquay was approved in 1989/90.)
Norquay has served Banff like a corner pub. Every child in Banff has taken first falls off the gentle bunny slopes of Mt. Norquay. The towns hottest skiers have taken the big curl down from the top in relative obscurity, but what a ride; especially back in the mid-70s when the front moguls were 12 feet high and anything under a 205 cm ski virtually outlawed. Lift lines? Forget it."

PAUL LANG (Superintendent of Banff National Park in the late 1970s)
Mr. Lang was responding to a letter sent to him by Bill Herron, owner of Mt. Norquay. He had thanked Bill for the letter and proceeded to tell him the Park policy in regards to clearing snow: first the Trans Canada Highway, second would be the Fire Roads "…and the ski hills are third, but we make every effort to clear the ski hill roads especially on Sundays when heavier traffic is expected."
This was in response to Bill's letter, which was rather aggressive. It had stated, "With severe displeasure I would like to say I have spent the last four hours pulling cars out of parking lot No. 3, which wasn't cleared. In fact only lot No. 1 was cleared. People who pay Park fees should have the right to park their cars like anyone else."

Josee and Murray McCullough, the class of 1958.

SKI COUNT, THREE AREAS: (This is a skier count, January 24 to 30, 1966.
Lake Louise at that time was two areas, Temple and Whitehorn.)

Norquay	3,648
Temple	225
Whitehorn	1,482
Sunshine	2,476

ALVIN HAMILTON (Northern Affairs Minister, February 3, 1960)
Authorized the charging of admission for special ski events in the Park if the race was sanctioned by the Canadian Amateur Ski Association. Ralph Harvey of the Banff Ski Runners had asked for this in 1938 and it was not approved.

MURRAY McCULLOUGH (Murray grew up in Banff and lived in the area until the early 1960s. A successful artist now living in California and Vancouver Island.)

"I'm afraid I have an image of Norquay I would gladly erase if I could. It was the day Herman Fuhrer was tragically killed in an avalanche. I can still see his little boy waiting alone outside the Ski Patrol hut while they were trying to revive his Dad who had been buried for about an hour."

GLORIA BURDETT (Grew up in Banff, still resident.)

"Norquay! Well, I did a lot of skiing there with my friends and I actually represented Mt. Norquay as Princess Norquay during a Banff Winter Carnival in the early 1950s. My Dad Giovanni Riva, who spoke six languages, was an interpreter for Zeno Colo the Italian skiing ace during the North American races held at Norquay in 1950."

MOE VROOM (Moved to Banff as a young girl, still lives here.)

"I was working for Superintendent Harry Dempster in 1961 when the Austrian Olympic star Toni Sailer came to town. Harry was on his way to Norquay to greet him. I wanted to go along to see this attractive man who had won three gold medals in the 1958 Olympics. Mr. Dempster said, 'No,' but he brought me back an autographed picture.

"I also remember shortly after I arrived in Banff and my skiing was still improving, Ross Maxwell, who was probably the best skier in Banff at that time, stayed behind to help me with my run off the Big Chair when all my friends had left me.

"Years later, a group of us were soaking in a beautiful spring sun and a little wine, our thoughts reflecting on a great winter. But also on the action of the owners who had frosted the lodge windows to prevent people from sitting in the lodge with just a cup of coffee watching the action on the hill. This one girl in our group got so mad just thinking about it, in a moment of revenge she broke one of the windows. It was an action not reflecting her true personality. Although not seen by Mr. Fisher at that time, he must have phoned the police. They stopped us when we were driving to town, but of course we didn't know anything about it."

JIM BEATTIE (The Beatties: An early century family of Banff. Jim, his sister Ruth and brothers Rock and Don, were amongst the early skiers on Norquay.)

"I worked for a while at the top of the Big Chair. I was there the day the Waterworth girl fell off at the top. I have heard other stories of a Waterworth girl falling off of the chair who was knocked unconscious. This girl, 'Bunty,' just caught her pole in the net and it pulled her off, she was unhurt. I remember her saying, 'I think I've stretched a couple of inches.'

Were there two Waterworth girls that fell from the lift or is my memory, or someone else's, playing tricks after all these years?"

Ski Joring in style and Hudson Bay coats, 1925.

SKI JORING (A sport generally run on the river during the Banff Winter Carnivals of the 1930s.)

Jennie Edwards of Banff was defending champion and holder of the Brewster Cup. Other top competitors, Edith and Lorna Wellman, Ethel Knight, Elsie Brown, Pat Stirling, Ruth Lane and Mrs. Bessie Harvey. In the men's races the big threat came from Rupe Edwards, Cyril Paris, Jack Brown, Philip Ashton and 'Chuck' Learn.

These races were run in two ways; one where there was a rider on the horse leading the skier and in the other the skier had to control the horse.

SCOTTY HOLLAND (Golf Professional, skier and punster.)

"George Raham has been skiing so long he remembers it when it was black and white."

BILL TRIGG (Calgary skier and golfer. [Sometimes got the two sports mixed up.] Frequent visitor to Norquay along with other young men starting out in Calgary's oil business in the late 1940s.)

"I got caught in a small avalanche while skiing on the avalanche slope north of the Lone Pine. I broke my left leg and spent some time in the Banff Mineral Springs hospital. Also in there at that time was George Encil, 'Mr. Norquay.' He had broken a leg while skiing in the Bowl. When I was released I returned to Norquay for a visit. Red Crozier the lift operator made me sit at the bottom of the Big Chair with a sign around my neck saying, 'Don't let this happen to you.'"

ANDY ANDERSON (Park Warden who worked with the Ski Patrol at Norquay and Lake Louise in the 1950s and 60s. Now retired on Vancouver Island.)

"When I worked on the Ski Patrol, Parks were still doing the grooming for the ski areas. I recall one area owner asking me to cut the grass on the slope so he might open earlier after a fall of snow; it was four inches long. Howard Srigley would visit the three areas with a Tucker Sno-Cat and we did the rest on skis. In time we cut out the grooming, then members of the ski patrol and finally the avalanche control. I

Walter Perren, the man who established the high standards for mountain rescue in Banff National Park.

remember working with avalanche guns that resembled an automatic baseball-pitching machine. They were tricky when it came to judging the distance the charge was going to carry. I heard one had blown up in Utah killing two men."

WALTER PERREN (Swiss Montain Guide. Technical officer of Mountain Rescue for Banff National Park, one of the world's finest mountain rescue organizations.) Walter Perren, born in Zermatt, January 13, 1914; passed away in Banff, December 1967.

JOE HALSTENSON (Long time resident of Banff now living on the coast.)

"When I was about ten years old, it must have been the year the Big Chair opened up in late 1948, I tried to ski it on old wooden skis with no edges. It must have taken me a couple of hours, but eventually I got it down to about two minutes. I also remember skiing with George Capel and Jim Davies when I got my lift ticket taken away by the Wardens for skiing under the lift."

(Joe later became a Park Warden.)

SOME 1968 RACE RESULTS:

NANCY GREENE wins second World Cup Crown 1968 and Gold and Silver medals in Giant Slalom and Slalom at the 1968 Olympics.

SCOTTY HENDERSON wins U.S. Combined title, 1st in Downhill, 2nd in Giant Slalom, and 4th in Slalom.

WAYNE HENDERSON 4th in Downhill, 7th in Giant Slalom and 7th in Slalom.

STEPHANIE TOWNSEND 7th in slalom March 1968.

JENNY GOURLAY Midget Champ, 1st in Downhill, 2nd in Slalom.

NORQUAY 1950:

If you would like to volunteer for weekend Ski Patrol see Jim Masterson, Phone 211, ring 2 long, 1 short.

ROD ADAMS wins Morrison Trophy, 1950.

COAL SHORTAGE IN TOWN:

Banff temperature hit minus 51° Fahrenheit on January 2, 1950, 34 inches of snow to date. The January 25th temperature hit -60°F with 25 inches of new snow.

CRAG & CANYON SKI COLUMN 1950

"Skiers of Norquay, please fill in your bathtubs and refrain from

Catharine Whyte winning her race in Bruno Engler's 1970 veteran's competition.

schussing when the hill is crowded."

BRUNO'S VETERANS AND MASTERS RACE 1970

Winners: Catharine Whyte, Rob Crosby, Carmen Robinson, Carol Hann, Mel Ferrari, Leo Berchtold, Fred Wonnacott.

TOMMY KELLY wins Dual Slalom at Canada Winter Games, 1971.

BRENT MARSHALL

A Calgary member of the Alberta Ski Team who died in the summer of 1981 from lung cancer. The Brent Marshall Memorial slalom was held in April 1982 at Mt. Norquay.

On the podium at the Brent Marshall Memorial race (L to R) Camilla Burks, Polly Lumby, Vania Grandi, 1982.

JOHN MAUDSLEY (A Toronto resident still living with the images of his descent from the Big Chair 45 years ago.)

"In the winter of 1954 I was working with a survey crew in the Banff area. On our day off my friends showing western hospitality said they would take me to ski Norquay. My home slope would be about 10°. What is Norquay, 45° or vertical! Anyway it really got my blood flowing, which went right through my socks. It really did; my boots were too big and after sidestepping the length of the mountain my blisters were bleeding pretty good. My new bride Ruth, was the one who needed the Ski Patrol when she saw me, which was handy, as they had brought me home."

SALLY TRUSS (A child singing star on Calgary TV in the early 1960s. Had been touring North America singing and playing guitar, when burnout finally hit in 1971.)

"I came to Banff for a little 'R&R.' While trying to relax, a good friend, Pat Brewster, suggested I might feel better if I took a job. He suggested Mt. Norquay. It happened to be the World Cup year of 1972. It was great therapy, kidding and singing with the international crowd. I worked out of the kitchen for a while: the chef made some amazing apple strudl. The competing skiers really went for it. I told them not to take more than their share and tried to save some for the staff. Because of that the racers started to call me 'Dragon Lady.' I wrote a couple of songs during that time, 'Green Jade' and 'Snowbound.' Banff really was snowbound that winter. I stayed with a great friend that winter, Marilyn Kelly."

MURRAY PRIDHAM (A native of Vancouver Island. Murray heads the academic program at the Banff Mountain Academy. Information obtained March 1999.)

"The Academy has been going for nine years. We have had our classes at Norquay for the last three years and we are very happy to be here. We can be very flexible, have classes in the morning and ski in the afternoon, or ski in the morning and have afternoon classes. The students really enjoy being on the hill, from the classroom to the hill is about fifteen minutes. Students in our program skiing at the NorAm level

Murray Pridham from the Banff Mountain Academy gives a helping hand with the numbers game to Avalanche Club director Nikki Hansen, 1999.

might miss 20 days a year; in a regular classroom they would probably miss 60 days. We have also expanded into what we call 'Alpine Adventure.' We have some kids working with one of our alumni, Paul Norrie, who was here our very first year. He is now a guide in the Park and he is doing our 'Alpine Adventure' Program.

BYRON TARCHUK (Banffite from age six. Excellent skier, downhill and freestyle. Even with all his talent, Byron has managed to have two broken legs, a broken collarbone, dislocated shoulder, dislocated hip, etc.)

"I was probably about ten when I dislocated my hip. The patrol had picked me up on the Lone Pine. The person taking me down had his binding release. I might add he was a volunteer patrolman. While he was checking it out, the toboggan with me in it took off. It went straight for a while and then did a few lateral flips, followed by several spins and rolls. Leo Berchtold, who watched most of my freestyle toboggan run said I even flipped end-to-end, at which point he rushed to my rescue; so he tells me now. If nothing else the patrolman must have tied me in pretty good because I rode it to the bottom of the slope.

When I heard they were going to take me down to the Timberline on the toboggan, I staggered to a phone and called my parents to come and get me. My children handle Norquay much better. Josh, 18, is hopefully going to be called for the team going to World Junior Boardercross. Ashley, 16, is a member of the Banff Alpine Racers; nationally she is rated very high in her age group."

"Friends dont let friends ride junk?" Ratso Hallam, 2000.

RON 'Ratso' HALLAM (Co-owner of the "Ski Stop" sport shop with his school buddy from Ontario, Dick 'Dik' Walmsley. If these guys had to "stop skiing" they would never make it.)

"Powder! Why do the powder days stay in my mind? It was probably the winter of 1971/72, John Heinz, Jerry Goulet and myself were first in line; this happened quite often that winter. John and Jerry were on chair one, I was on chair two (they were bigger than me). When we reached the top they cut down the Bowl, that was fine, I didn't want to follow their dust. I headed for the Lone Pine in about three feet of powder, just me and several billion flakes of friendly powder. I still feel that ride.

"I recall another similiar day not too many years ago. The Park had received a big dump. Many of my friends thought it might be deeper at Lake Louise or Sunshine, so off they went. Eddie Coté, Bill Dennis, Rob Tooke and myself, having local knowlege, we headed for Norquay - wise choice. It was all ours and the snow kept falling.

Ski Stop gang arrive for demo challenge day 2000.

"Another great pleasure was the weekly 'Race For The Sun' at Norquay. A group of us would get together for an early breakfast, a different host each week, then compete with about sixty other gals and guys in that dual slalom. After the race, wondering why we weren't faster, we would join Ray Seguin's Rut Runners to learn a few tricks on improving our racing technique."

Irwin Tontch skiing for sheep and Bruno in the Norquay film *Ski Spree*, 1969.

SKI SPREE

Author's Note: Ski Spree *is a short promotional film I shot for Bill Herron in 1969. Edited by Bob Willis, a Calgary film maker, it won an award at the Seattle*

Film Festival.

Although the scenes in this film are over thirty years old it is a kick to look at old friends and the styles of that time. Stretch pants were tight and slim, ski suits for the gals had wild patterns. Boots were still leather; better skiers still used long-thong bindings and the safety binding of that time had limited safety features. In most cases the ski didn't leave the skier but would get involved in the fall and probably inflict a wound on other parts of the body while saving a twisted knee or ankle. Norquay had the Memorial rope tow at that time plus two Poma Lifts side by side. They were soon to be replaced by the Cascade Chair. The Big Chair was the challenge and supplied any skier with all they could handle. It was either creep or steep. Some of the skiers in powder: Heinz Vifian, Sepp Renner, Noldie Keach, John Pristov, George Geber, Roy Andersen, Siri Davies. Sitting watching the gals go by in stretch pants, wearing a pin that stated he was an 'Offical Stretch Pant Watcher' was Bob Meggs of the Ski Patrol. (Carol Herron had the tightest pair.) There were many young Banff skiers: naturally I put my daughters Mystee and Kendall in a few scenes. A very small Brad White was there competing in a race, his body almost covered by his racing bib. Nancy Greene was there training with the Henderson brothers, Scotty and Wayne, along with the National Team. Ken Waterhouse and his band, with long hair and matching sideburns, were playing for an Intercollegiate Ski Meet dance.

One scene I recall shooting had a special effect as though one were skiing in a "powder dream." The sequence wasn't planned. I was on the mountain looking for action as was Bruno Engler who was shooting "stills." The snow conditions were perfect. All of a sudden we stopped on the upper slopes of the North American when a beautiful ram confronted us. Not a common area for sheep at that time of year. Bruno was so excited at the prospects of the picture he was about to get he started telling us where the picture was going to be sold. "This is going to be the greatest shot! All ski magazines will want it, all wildlife and probably the National Geographic magazine will buy it, what a windfall." He proceeded to tell Erwin Tontch, who was going to be the key figure with the ram, to do a left turn above the animal to force him to an area where he could compose a good shot. The only one not listening to Bruno's directions was the ram. So the action begins; Erwin has good speed, Siri Davies with her long hair trailing looks gorgeous, while several members of the ski school chase in a cloud of powder. I am filming. Erwin goes into his big turn, the ram looks and decides to get out of the way, the opposite way to which Bruno wanted him to go. It ruined his planned still picture. Because I was shooting a movie it didn't matter to me which way the ram turned, I was okay, but the ensuing dialogue given by Bruno on that day shouldn't be repeated here.

STU AND GERRY MILLER (Young Calgary skiers of the late 1940s and still young skiers in the year 1999.)

GERRY: "I remember the early ski train to Banff, like at 6 a.m. Quite often it started in Edmonton and stopped to pick up Calgary skiers before going on to Banff. It was a party train, at least from Edmonton to Calgary. When the day at Norquay was over we skied down the Gulley to the railway station."

STU: "The first rope tow at Norquay was a real test. Once you got a grip on it that was only the beginning, it would start twisting. They came out with a clamp that started you okay, but then you couldn't get it off at the top; they finally banned it. When the weather was warm the rope on the tow gave off a juice that was more like a dye. It ruined your clothes."

DONNA MILLICAN (Skied Norquay in the years following the building of the lift in 1948.)
"Dave Freeze broke his leg on the upper part of the mountain. Rather than take him down on a toboggan they decided to load him on the chair. While the chair was stopped for this (a fairly long period), Ethan Compton who was going up on the lift, decided he didn't want to wait until they had Dave loaded. I was watching from the bottom when Ethan took one ski off and dropped it, then the other. He lowered himself to the footrest and hung there for a while and finally dropped to the slope. He would have been okay, but it was a heavy snow year and when he landed he completely disappeared.
"On another occasion Fran Harris and I had crashed on the mountain, pretty close together. The ski patrol decided to take me down first, but as it turned out I just had a sprain and Fran had the broken ankle."

GWEN HANTHO (One of the active young Calgary skiers that skied Norquay following the war.)
"The learning years were so much fun for a city gal. My first trip up the Big Chair was suggested by Norm Russell. We rode up together, he skied down and I rode the chair back down. I have fond memories of later mastering that steep slope."

AL BAHAN (Skied Norquay in the mid 1950s. Lived in Calgary.)
"Besides the 10 cent beers in the Cascade with skiing buddies, Bill Trigg, Dick Moore, Gordon Batie and Harvey Glover, I remember taking a ski lesson from Lois Woodworth. On my first run from the Big Chair I fell near the top and slid all the way to the Cliff. I was so shaken I said, 'That's it, I'm through!' Lois, having been a racer said, 'You have to go back up -- NOW!' It was the right thing to do: on my second run I didn't fall at all. I felt pretty good about that."

GRAHAM MacDONALD (A teacher and local business man who has lived in Banff for over 30 years. His wife Chris and three girls, Beth, Brodie and Toby do it all, downhill, snowboarding and cross country.)
"Pinch me. Am I awake or is this a dream! Standing in fresh powder at the top of the challenging North American run. Blue skies above and below the town of Banff protected by the surrounding Rockies.
"Skirting the western ridge of the North American, along with your pals, hugging the boundary line, you eye the tempting slopes of the avalanche shoot, but think better of it. After some thigh-burning turns, or back-smacking falls, you would be on top of the Rock Garden. Here you make a few relaxed turns (who am I kidding, there were no relaxed turns). From three- quarters up the Rock Garden you let them run, over the Hogs Back to the top of the End of the World. Taking a deep breath you plunge into the vertical Widow Maker. From here down the Gulley it's a breeze to the Timberline Hotel. What a run, two kilometers of sheer joy. You grab a bus back

Rudi off the roof. Rudi Gertsch, the only one to make this jump off the Tea House, 1967.

to the lodge and repeat the run. No line-ups. The day ends sitting with your pals and the last sun rays of the day. You grab a beer and toast the thousands of skiers who were at Sunshine and Lake Louise, leaving us with our secret - Norquay."

RUDI GERTSCH (Owner of Purcell Helicopter Skiing from Golden, B. C. Rudi is an outstanding skier. He coached and instructed skiing at Norquay following his arrival in Canada from Switzerland in 1966. Rudi was a top prospect for the Swiss National Team, which would have meant specializing in one discipline. His free spirit wasn't prepared to do that; he liked all areas of skiing equally.)

"It was the winter of 1967. In conversation with Bruno Engler who was looking to shoot some action ski shots I decided to jump off the Tea House at the top of the Big Chair. No one had done it before. The growth of trees above the Tea House made it difficult to get a direct run. I had to come in at an angle to get enough speed and then do a turn on the roof. Without the speed I wouldn't clear the cabin and the railing that ran from the top terminal of the lift. Speed was critical, I didn't want to go too far, or worse, be short. Anyway I hit it right and Bruno got his picture."

EDDIE COTÉ (A spirited member of the "Ski Stop Gang." He was smiling when he arrived in Banff from his home in Montreal. Today, 23 years later he is still smiling and skiing more.)

"Norquay! I simply…like it! I like being at the top looking down on that great view in the Bow Valley. I like meeting new and old friends there, you can always do that, and it has a nice blend of all ages. And it's a quiet area."

TRUDY WILSON (Trudy arrived in Banff in 1977 from her home east of Kingston, Ontario. Today she skis with her teenage daughter Laurel, and her two boys 7-year-old Malcolm and 5-year-old Reid. Trudy and her late husband, Ian Wilson, both very talented skiers, have tamed the worst Norquay can offer and enjoyed the best.)

"The best day that comes to mind for skiing was the opening of the 1995 season. The area had just received a couple of feet of new snow. The day before the opening on December 7th, the lodge burnt to the ground. There goes the opening and some great skiing, or so we thought. But a few of us had heard they were going to start the Big Chair anyway. There must have been only about twenty or so there for that start. But then they had a mechanical and the lift wouldn't start, so they said they would start the Mystic chair. Ian and I were off and got the first chair and the first tracks in those beautiful conditions. We skied there for about an hour when word came they got the Big Chair going. Once again Ian and myself raced for the first chair. (I must admit some of our friends were on snowboards. When you're travelling across the mountain with some climbing involved you're much faster on skis.) So we had the first tracks off the Lone Pine. The numbers hardly increased, I don't believe we ended up with more than thirty or forty people enjoying this wonderful day, while the lodge, completely flattened, still gave off little puffs of smoke. One hot night for the lodge turned into one hot day for a few skiers. I am glad Ian and I were two of them."

IAN WILSON (Ian and Trudy Wilson, along with children Laurel, Reid and Malcolm loved their active outdoor life in Banff. They were successful business partners together, their latest being the "Coyote Cafe." Ian's sudden illness took his life in the spring of 1999. The following is part of a newspaper article that appeared in 1987.)

Ian Wilson was a ski technician for Canada's National Ski Team. For four years he did an outstanding job. In 1987 the Canadian Amateur Ski Association honoured Ian for his contribution to the team.

This past week, Bruce Henry, coach of Canada's National Ski Team, presented on behalf of the Canadian Amateur Ski Association, a plaque to Ian Wilson for his outstanding contribution to Canadian downhill racing.

Ian was a ski technician on Canada's National Team for four years. It was a demanding job. It meant always being aware of snow and course conditions. What ski is going to be the best with which wax? Checking equipment for the best result in the past, will it work today? Then video the runs on the many European and North American courses. Plus the packing and unpacking of all the equipment for the next race.

Looking back on some of his highlights, Ian remembers the American Nationals at Copper Mountain, Colorado in 1985. It was near the end of the season and the team was looking for a lift. Ian gave it to them when he came up with the right skis and wax to place three Canadians in the first five and six in the top ten. It was definitely an equipment technician's victory and it really rocked the Americans to be scooped on their own mountain.

Ian said "It's difficult to get technical information from the European ski manufacturers and the Europeans still get the best skis."

Ian Wilson's hard work, extensive testing and observations certainly helped to even the score. Ian added "You have to love the job and you don't count the hours."

"We talked the university and the Alberta government into an annual ski meet just so we could get to Banff for some skiing." Clarence Haakenstad.

City skiers from Calgary and Edmonton join Banff skiers for competitions following the building of the chair lift in 1948.

2 Bill Armstrong, 3 'Hak' Haakenstad, 4 Jack Blackstaff, 5 Doug Lemmon, 6 Dave Freeze, 7 Norm Rault, 8 Bud Gourlay, 9 Bill Robinson, 10 Stu Rosmond, 11 Bob Freeze, 12 Gerald 'Cocky' Locke.

CLARENCE HAAKENSTAD (Edmonton born racer [1924]. Clarence was one of the members that made up the first University of Alberta Ski Team in 1945/46. He was instrumental in starting the International Intercollegiate Ski Meet that ran annually in Banff for 26 years.)

"When I was a student at the University of Alberta in Edmonton, we were always looking for ways to go skiing. Probably the best idea Norm Rault, Bob Freeze and I had was to talk the university and the government into a college ski meet. We figured that would get us to Norquay and they would pay for it. Some of the skiers that made up the U. of A. team in the late 1940s: there was Bill Robinson, Doug Lemmon, Bob Jackson, Bill Armstrong, Bob Freeze, Norm Rault, Bob Sutherland, Bill Mustard, Don Link, Bob Turner, Jack Blackstaff, Stu Rosamond, and myself. We didn't have a coach, but Don Smith was our adviser/manager/coach. There were only four schools attending the first meet in 1947: the University of British Columbia, Montana State, University of Manitoba and our team from U. of A. For the boys from Manitoba, Norquay was more than they had thought it might be, they never returned. But the meet grew each year with the top schools from all over Canada and the United States competing at some point during the next 26 years. The meet died following the 1972 competition when the Lougheed government decided to drop the funding. Bill Herron at Mt. Norquay was willing to continue as was Dave Leighton, Director of the Banff Centre, who had assisted with accommodation and meals, as had Senator Cameron before him from the meet's inception, but it wasn't enough to keep it going.

"Looking back it was gratifying to see how successful it had been. It was one of the major ski meets of North America. The quality of skiing, especially for a four-way competition, was very high. In most cases they were Olympic skiers or would become Olympic skiers. Not only Canadian and American, but also several competitors were from Scandinavian countries that were students in the United States. Personally I have great memories of the first meet in 1946, the sight of Jack Davis schussing the Bowl with his jacket wide open, but mostly of my ski buddies and the good times we had."

SEAN HABING (9-year-old Sean Habing is a student at the Mountain Gate School in Canmore. He received top marks for his "Legend of the Mt. Norquay Imps." This is part of his story about the little men who have lived there for centuries. To the untrained eye you might think you are looking at a fungus growing on a tree, but if you look closer you will see it's the beard of an 'Imp.')

"…Before skiers were on Mount Norquay the Imps were miners. They have hundreds of tunnels under the slopes of Mt. Norquay. Now, they use pickaxes to chop out the plastic from the bottom of skis from skiers passing overhead. While collecting the plastic, the Imps usually trip the skiers sending them crashing down the hill. The skiers call them Snow Snakes because they don't know anything about the Imps. They have a storage room where they keep the plastic bits from the skis.

"In the spring Santa comes and gets the plastic with his sleigh, so he can make Game Boys and other stuff…"

BETH WOOLLEY (This stylish lady switched from skis to a snowboard about five years ago. Married to Phil Monod, she adds a new dimension to legend of the Banff Monods.)

"On my way back from a California trip, I stopped in to have a coffee with a friend in Banff before returning to my home in Montreal. That was 23 years ago. I am still here. Yes, I snowboard, but it doesn't matter to me as long as I'm on the mountain sliding. Call it a millennium project, but I'm going to do a little skiing as well this coming winter. I speak both languages, skiing and riding. How about 'claw the dog' or is it 'pat the dog'?"

DON FINDLAY (In 1978 Don was graduating from the University of Manitoba with a masters degree in geology. A call from André Schwarz in Banff suddenly changed his direction in life. André wanted him to coordinate the newly formed Club Ski program at the Banff Springs Hotel. Don's ever-open mind thought it over for three seconds. He agreed, and told himself he could write his thesis just as easily in Banff. In the 1980s with thesis completed, Don commuted to Calgary and work in the oilpatch. In 1983 Betsy (Dr. Elizabeth Hall) and Don were married. In 1990, after extensive research, he created the Banff Mountain Ski Academy. Now ten years later Don is stepping down to enjoy more time with his family, Jamie 15, David 14 and 12-year-old Elise.)

"For myself the Academy has been a roller coaster ride, but it was always exciting. To create something from nothing was gratifying. While I was involved we supplied a majority of the skiers on the Provincial Team.

"We have had some excellent coaches. Marty Hansen, who has a passion for the sport, started with us. We lost him for a while when he chased Nikki, the love of his life, to Australia, but now they're both back with our racing program, which is called Avalanche and is operated by Mt. Norquay. Mark Sharp, along with his wife Sigrid, brought new ideas to our program. John Evely was an excellent coach, especially with the younger racers. Rob and Peter Bosinger have added to our success. We have survived because of so many people that have made it work. All levels of the staff have taken it on as their own personal goal. Rachel Fernandes, our business manager, has no boundaries when it comes to the jobs she will take on. Peter White and Kika Grandi added greatly to our success when we moved up here four years ago (1995). At that time our classrooms needed new lighting, plumbing and general updating, which cost $180 000. This was eased greatly when Peter White offered us a building for a $1 a year. Murray Pridham, the school Principal, has been a big part of our success. He not only discovered our classrooms, he also discovered the mountain had been hard-wired for timing. This was a great discovery after race people had carried equipment through trees and over slopes for six years, unaware of the wiring that had been completed during Norquay's expansion in 1990. My point is, the people working for the Academy are all for the Academy and its success.

"I had started the Academy when I realized many members of our National Team, at the age of 20 or 21 had only received, on average, a grade 10 education. I figured the Academy would supply the necessary schooling and training. In time I formed The Western Canada Ski Foundation, with the assistance of Marty Von Neudegg. This encouraged sponsors and allowed them to get a tax credit for their donation. Now almost ten years later I am ready to pass it on to Brian Rhodes who will be chairman, and Peter White will be co-chairman.

"This isn't related to the Academy, but my last year here was almost my last year anywhere, or so I thought. In late May of this year (1999) I had parked my car at the Timberline Hotel and walked up to my office at Norquay. On the return walk I was skirting the swampy section of the Gulley, trying to keep my feet dry. I heard this funny sound; it was a sound I didn't recognize, then I saw these two small grizzly cubs, very young, and very cute. Then I saw their mother. My immediate thought was I am much too close. When the cubs ran back to her she was now up on her hind legs. When she came down she charged me. She had hit top speed in a fraction of a second and crossed the width of the Gulley to where I was in another two seconds. I didn't know what to do. When she was about seven metres away, I did the only thing I could do; I yelled at the top of my voice 'NOOOO…' and to my surprise she stopped. She was now about three metres away. She turns around and goes back to the cubs. For whatever reason I kept talking to her in a low voice, then she turns and rushes me again. I thought this is it, I'll never bluff her again, but it's the only thing I could do, so once again I give a loud yell and she stops. Then she starts to return to the cubs. My thinking now is I have probably used up all my lives allowed for this situation, so I run into the woods and look for a tree I can climb quickly. I am half way up a tree when she comes screaming back. I am maybe fifteen feet up when she gets to the base of the tree. In my haste I realize I haven't chosen a very good tree, it was leaning and dead. If that grizzly wanted to, it would have been no problem for her to knock both of us to the ground. If that happened I knew it would be the end of me, or at least I would be so carved up life wouldn't be much fun. Fortunately the cubs had followed her back. She gave them a look, gave me another look and sauntered off into the woods. I am still trying to control my breathing, but I'm not moving for awhile. When I do decide to come down I realize how much I have scraped my stomach and legs going up that little tree, but I am still alive. I pick up the papers

I had been carrying, now lying over much of the Gulley. Then I cautiously make my way back to the Timberline and my car. I was so lucky, I believe the cubs being so small might have had something to do with her taking them away. It is a vivid memory and I haven't walked that trail since that day. So that's my story of 'Me and the Three Bears' - now I can kid about it."

ALEX EMOND: (A Banff artist, skier. Originally from Cornwall, Ontario. Had an outstanding show at the Whyte Museum of the Canadian Rockies in the summer of 1999, the title being "The Trail to Skoki." When this book was being researched, Alex kindly supplied ski material from the early days.)

"I'm not your average Norquay skier, but perhaps I ski more like the original skiers that skied Norquay in the 1920s. I like to telemark. What does that make me, a traditionalist? I love the mountains and all they give me. Cross country skiing gives me a little more time to enjoy their gift. There is probably more humour around the lift areas. I remember the days when Norquay had massive lift lines on the old chair, there was always a guy who would appear yelling 'single', fully expecting to be called to the head of the line."

RACHEL FERNANDES (Hard working Business Manager for the Banff Mountain Academy. Originally from Ontario.)

"What can I say! I love working with the kids. As we start the winter of 1999/2000 I have 33 students enrolled, their ages being from 12 to 18. Our classrooms are practically on the slopes, just minutes from science to skis. I am busy all year with a variety of projects including fund raising for the school. Ski, I get some time to ski, but I'm not a racer."

CARSTEN SORENSEN (Carsten is a Banff business man, active in sports as is his family: wife Karen and young boys, Eric and Conner. Carsten relates an experience which ended worse than Don Findlay's encounter with the grizzlies in the same Gulley. Carsten's pain lives on 26 years later. The accident cut short a very promising hockey career at that time.)

"The year was 1973, the 19th of January, but it was now the 20th, as it was after midnight when we started down the Gulley from Norquay on a large tire tube, under a full moon, Barry Stafford, Dave Sevick and myself. Three teenage boys out for a little fun. We had tied two tubes together, which meant the three of us could ride together with greater speed. The speed we got. I was riding in a position with a lot of snow flying in my face and that is the last thing I remember until I woke up a week later in the Mineral Springs Hospital. I didn't hear Barry yell 'jump.' After they bailed out I went off a cliff area and was thrown high into a tree, apparently just the drop from the tree to the ground was enough for severe damage. I was unconscious when either Barry or Dave ran down to the Timberline to get the car to drive to Norquay for a Ski-doo, and then come down the Gulley to pick me up. They said I was mumbling in Danish, but I don't remember anything. A couple of people saved my life that night. If I had been left on the slope much longer I would have died as I had extensive internal bleeding. Dr. Costigan saved my life by operating when I arrived at the hospital. When I woke up a week later I had lost thirty pounds. Four operations followed: one operation led to another when my body rejected a steel support that had been placed in my femur. I was confined to bed for about two months. Today, 26 years later, I still have problems. My next operation will be on my hip."

DON BRIDGES (Quebecker now living in Ontario, worked on the Ski Patrol in 1952/53. Still active skiing the major resorts of North America.)

"It was a good year for snow and Norquay did a lot of good for my skiing, or it might have been skiing with guys like Jack Pugh, Jimmy Innes and Peter Van Wagner that helped my skiing. Because the Patrol was operated by the Warden Service, Herb Ashley our boss had us working on the hill dismantling the old log jump. We were shown how to pry the logs apart and stack them. We were then left alone; Ashley would go back to town. The job was going to take several days. Ashley would come back from time to time to check our progress. Not long after we started we discovered the structure had been made in sections. All we had to do was remove a section in a fraction of the time it was taking to pry the logs loose individually. On a visit, Ashley said, 'You guys are really fast.' We didn't tell him how we were doing it. So each day we worked for awhile and then went skiing. The boss still thought we were doing it log by log in record time."

CHRISTL AND GEORGE GEBER (George arrived from Germany in 1956, Christl in 1959, the year they were married. Excellent skiers with their sons, Klaus and Chris, who are also into guiding.)

George: "Christl and I have both been part-time instructors on Norquay. Christl, mostly with the children's programs from Calgary, but I worked as a certified instructor with the Heinz Vifian Ski School on weekends. I started doing that back in the 1960s. As is the case with most Banff families, the boys skied the Big Chair when they were about four years old. Both boys broke their legs at about the same age."

BOB AND MAJA GEBER (Bob arrived from Germany in 1957, Maja arrived from Switzerland in 1970. Both are excellent skiers; Maja raced in Switzerland and Bob has been guiding with CMH as a heli-skiing guide since 1965. Their children, René 21 and Audrey 20, were both on the Alberta Ski Team: they now attend university in Calgary.)

BOB: "We were a Norquay skiing family. I did have a bad day back in the winter of 1961/62. I broke my leg while skiing the Bowl. Johnny Pristov and another guy were going to take me down on the toboggan. I had a feeling they might go over the Cliff area into the Memorial run: I honestly didn't trust them that much. In the past I had worked on mountain rescue and these two guys didn't impress me, so I made them take their skis off and walk the toboggan down the traverse under the jump. John Wackerle, their boss, had a big laugh over that when we got down to the patrol hut.

"I was at Norquay in February of 1965 when Herman Fuhrer was caught in the avalanche. In fact I was on the probe line. When we found him he had been covered for about an hour, it was too late to save him. Herman had come from near Adelboden, Switzerland, to Canada in 1953. Herman's brother, Hans Fuhrer and his wife Lilo, live over in Edgewater, B.C."

INTERSKI 1987 (On January 18, 1987, a demonstration which included several members of the local Alpine Racers and Quikies Ski Club performed during the opening ceremonies at Mt. Norquay. The fourteen member team included: Jamie Rosewosne, Gord Brown, Justin Brask, Chad Mullen, Nils Preshaw, Joanna Magee, Trevor Jensen, Grant Rutherglen, Dave Lech, Caslo Bastolacc, Jesse Seguin, René Geber, Jim Kirby and Ray Seguin.

The Quikies Ski Club in April 1987 had 97 racers between the ages of 4 and 18. Among coaches winning awards that year was Dave Bradley, most enthusiastic coach. Ken Vogel, Ski Club Director, won an award for his dedication.

CRAG & CANYON June 9, 1971. (On the front page of the 'Crag,' there stand three skiers who have been summer skiing at Norquay: Rick Ralf, Ken McRitchie and Pete MacLean. Howard Srigley, Area Manager said as season ticket holders, their pass was good up to October. There was also summer skiing in 1972. The winter of 1971/72 had a record snowfall of 437 cm.)

Caroline Wilson and Alan Deane win the Gordie Morrison Memorial 1978.

MORRISON MEMORIAL 1978 (This was a two-day slalom held at Norquay, a memorial race for Gordie Morrison who had lost his life in a plane crash.)

First race: Caroline Wilson, Banff, followed by Judy Fergstad, Calgary.

Second race: Polly Lumby, Calgary, second place Caroline Wilson.

Caroline Wilson won the Combined. Alan Deane won the Men's Combined.

CRAG & CANYON

Back in the 20s the weather must have been just as moody as it is in the 80s. In 1923 there wasn't enough snow to hold most of the events at the winter carnival. In 1924 the temperature dropped to minus 60°F and minus 67°F at Lake Minnewanka. There was eight feet of snow in front of the Cascade Hotel on Banff Avenue.

HANS GMOSER, December 1965.

Hans will be showing his latest ski film at the Banff High School on Thursday, December 30th. In the tradition of his earlier films (that have included the climbing of Mt. Logan in the Yukon and the leading of a party of eight on the first ascent of 20 300 ft. Mount McKinley's north face, the highest snow and ice wall in the world), this year he and five companions, Jim and Glen McConkey, Mike Wiegele, Scotty Henderson and Erwin Tontch, pioneer a new high level route from Lake Windermere to the Bugaboos.

GLEN TOOKE, January 1966

A photo in the *Crag & Canyon* shows Glen, Shirley and five-year-old Rob Tooke looking at a luge, the type used for Olympic competition. Excitement was running high at this time with the anticipation of Banff getting the games for 1972. (Later that year the games were given to Japan.)

LONNIE ANDERSON (Attended elementary school in Banff during the 1930s to mid 40s. Until retirement he was a television engineer in Calgary. Lonnie's dad had the first restaurant to sell hamburgers in Banff, the New Spot, probably 1931/32.)

"It didn't happen a lot, but if there was a good fall of snow just before a weekend they would get us out of school to go up and tramp the hill for the people coming in from Calgary on the ski train. They didn't give us anything; there was nothing to give. There were no lifts at that time, but they let us go in the cabin and eat our lunch. I believe they had thought of charging people to use the cabin at one time."

JIMMY DEEGAN (Jimmy became a Warden after years of packing into Skoki in the 1940s and 50s. He also published a book of poems. Possibly his first poem is remembered by a fellow grade five student, when he wrote:

"I'm going up to the Norquay camp,
    I'm going to tramp,
        tramp,
           tramp,
                Until I get a cramp, cramp, cramp."

HARRY GRIESSER (Harry came to Banff in 1990 from his home in Landeck, Austria. He is Manager of the Bistro Café in Banff.)

"I was skiing Norquay with a couple of my European buddies, Reno Sommerhalder and Gilbert Skrienig. Conditions were good and we were looking for a little variety, so we decided to jump off the bank that sits above the Cascade Chair. I didn't think we were going to bother anyone, but the Ski Patrol told us, 'You do that again I'm taking your lift ticket away.'"

DAVE FREEZE (Stylish Calgary skier, skied Norquay in the 1940s and was on the first University of Alberta Ski Team to compete in the Intercollegiate Ski Meet of 1947, along with his brother Bob Freeze.)

"I can still hear Victor Kutschera yelling 'Get those poles back.' He being Austrian naturally favoured the 'Arlberg' style of skiing which seemed to have the greatest influence on Canadian skiers in the 1930s and 40s.

"And the early Banff skiers, Gordie Hoggard, Don Lewthwaite, Gerry Locke and just before them Ted Paris and Norm Knight and Rupe Edwards: Banff had some wonderful skiers. Then there were the inter-city races we [Calgary] had with Edmonton; I think they might have even beaten us once."

Jim Brewster Memorial race held at the Columbia Icefields 1947. 1st. Bob Sutherland(centre), 2nd. Gordie Morrison (right), 3rd. Eddie Hunter (left).

BREWSTER MEMORIAL (This was a summer race held at the Columbia Icefields in June 1947. It was a Jim Brewster Memorial; his daughter Fern Brewster and his widow Del presented the awards. The Chief of Race was Bruno Engler. The course was set on Mt. Athabasca and ran only two years, 1947 and 1948.)

Bob Sutherland, Gordy Morrison and Eddie Hunter place one, two and three in the Jim Brewster Memorial Summer Race. The course which was set at about the 10 000 foot level with a vertical of over 2500 ft., was more than what you might expect from a summer race. The course started in winter temperatures and ended with small streams cutting through the gates of the modified Downhill/Giant Slalom. The race was Morrison's to win, but he lost several seconds on a near fall on the lower part of the course. Gordy in the next three years would be named to Canada's National Team.

Times for the race: Sutherland 1:36, Morrison 1:40, Hunter 1:42. Eleanor Boyle of Lake Louise was the only lady entrant, her time was 1:55.

In 1948 the race had several top skiers including Harvey Clifford of Canada's Olympic Team, along with Gene Gillis and Herbert Schneider of the American National Team. Also in the race was Toni Matt. The race was divided into two groups. Harvey Clifford won the pro race. In the amateur division the winner was Don Hayes.

RECORD SNOWFALL 1971/72

Town of Banff: Oct. 50.4 cm, Nov. 23.9 cm, Dec. 81.3 cm, Jan. 83.6 cm, Feb. 142.2 cm, March 37.9 cm, April 18.7 cm, for a total 438 cm.

Norquay: October, not recorded (estimated 70 cm), Nov. 22 cm, Dec. 95 cm, Jan. 121 cm, Feb. 182 cm, March 64 cm, April, 47 cm. Total 601 cm

In all recordings Norquay received about 20 to 30 percent more snow than the town of Banff. While in November Norquay shows less, this discrepancy was probably due to the fact they didn't take measurements until well into November, as in October when they didn't take any.

(From these figures Banff would have received almost 15 feet of snow and Norquay about 20 feet.) The previous year, 1970/71 had also been a good snow year with Norquay receiving about 400 cm; Sunshine Village that year received 791 cm. You talk to people in 1999, most will mention the good old days of heavy snowfall. It depends what you are calling the good old days. If you're looking at the figures above that is true. But records going back into the 1930s, 40s and 50s do not show heavy snowfalls. In many cases it was much colder than we have been experiencing from the 1970s to the end of the century, however official figures from 1941 to 1960 show an average snowfall of 160 cm. The highest during that period was in 1950/51 when there was 220 cm during the ski season. These recordings were taken at Anthracite that would have received less snow, but still there is nothing to show we had more snow "in the good old days." Some years there was less than 80 cm (approximately 33 inches).

It may have looked like more when you consider there would have been a fraction of today's skiing population messing it up. In downtown Banff the snow was generally left on the streets. Today they hustle it out of town as quickly as they can (if you get my drift).

To go back even further, I quote from the Government Meteorological Office for the winter of 1900:

"Many people while admitting the fact that we have an almost ideal summer climate are not aware that the winter climate is even superior. For further proof we called on N.B. Sanson, meteorological officer to make the following synopsis, a careful perusal of which will convince the most skeptical that the winter climate of the eastern Rockies is more salubrious than that of any western point.

"January 1900: This month was noted for its general mildness; for fourteen days the sky was clear or mostly clear all day. The most snow on the ground at any one time was seven inches on the 6th which gradually decreased till on the 31st, only one and three fourths inches remained. A chinook wind on the 17th carried off most of the snow, leaving only patches. Several northwest crows remained here throughout the winter, on the 29th finches were seen and a few American magpies wintered here."

The report goes on to call February as having about the same type of weather. Let's hope the 21st Century doesn't start as did the 20th.

HENRY NESS (Born in Bankhead, Alberta, 1908. Henry operated an electrical business in Banff for almost thirty years. Still lives in Banff, 1999.)

"Ralph Harvey who was the president of the Banff Ski Runners in 1936 asked me if I would run a telephone wire up the downhill course to be used in timing the race. I didn't figure it to be a problem, but as you know it is a steep hill and it was a good distance from the finish line near the old well to the little cabin they had at the top of the downhill. I had good friends, Herb Paris and 'Steam'Watt, help me string that line which must have been over 400 meters. For doing it the Ski Runners gave my wife Ann and myself a membership in the ski club."

LAKE LOUISE 1960

The 'Lake' had the new Eagle Poma Lift, plus an old Poma. The summer sedan was used to get skiers to the new lift. You could ski down to Temple, but not get back as there was no lift back to the Whitehorn area at that time. Buses were used to go into Temple from the Post Hotel. The ski school director was Franz Haas.

SUNSHINE 1960

Cliff White Jr. had just purchased Sunshine. At that time there was a platter-pull lift (four rides for $1.50) and snowmobiles that ran up Brewster (75 cents a ride or three for $1.25). Ski school director was Ted Clark.

NORQUAY 1960

Walter Fisher had purchased Norquay from George Encil. Norquay had the chair and rope tows; twin tows toward the Lone Pine area, and the Memorial tow. A day ticket for all lifts was $4, for rope tows only, $2. The ski school was run by Jerry Johnston.

BOBBY CRONE (Started his professional skiing at Gray Rocks, Quebec. Taught skiing at Norquay in 1972 with Heinz Vifian, John Heinz, Noldie Keach, Scotty Grub, and Sandy Howard.)

"At that time in 1972 it was still very quiet during the week, we had a lot of time for free-skiing. The ski packages out of eastern Canada were just starting. (Skifari started in 1972.) As instructors we were paid on a monthly basis. We made extra money on private lessons. The director took 60% and we received 40%.

"I found most people take lessons to improve, which enables them to enjoy their new skills on a greater variety of runs. This can backfire at times, especially at the Norquay of 1972 when intermediate slopes didn't really exist. I remember one gentleman I was giving a private lesson to, he wanted to ride the Big Chair. I didn't feel he was really ready. So I suggested we ski the lower slopes. Doing a few turns on the lower part of the Lone Pine I could see his confidence level could have been better, but on the lower slopes if you miss a turn you can recover on the easy outrun. This gentleman was a doctor and he was determined to have a run off the top. He said, 'I have paid for a private lesson to go to the top and that's what I want to do.' So what do you do? I agreed to take him up. I had it in my mind to make it as easy as possible with lengthy traverses. I explained to him, 'we will just do three or four turns and stop and make sure you complete your turns.' I did my turns and told him to come down. On his third turn he lost it and crashed and slid down the length of the Bowl. When I caught up to him he told me he thought he had dislocated a shoulder. Being a doctor he recognized that rather quickly. So there was an example of someone who wanted to tell his friends he had skied the Big Chair and it ended with a toboggan ride by the Ski Patrol and a visit to the hospital. It's good for a person to want to improve by pushing themself, but you still have to recognize your abilities.

"Even when you have the confidence you have to keep your eyes open. One morning Rick Powell and myself were cruising down the Lone Pine. We were the only two skiing it. We were more or less side-by-side but a good distance apart. Near the bottom we both spotted a little rise that would end the run with a jump. By the time we realized it we were both heading for the same spot and about to hit. It was too late and we ended that run with arms extended for a big hug. But that was fun and no harm done."

RACE RESULTS, NORQUAY 1939

John Bird wins Alberta Slalom title, 2nd 'Wildman' Lewis Davis, 3rd Chess Edwards, 4th Bob Freeze.

Junior race: 1st Don Lewthwaite, 2nd Rob Crosby, 3rd Gordie Hoggard.
Eleanor Boyle of Lake Louise won both Slalom and Downhill. Ila LaCasse, Lake Louise was second in both races.

The Men's Downhill was won by 'Wildman' Davis followed by John Bird and Stan Ward, of Banff. Ward and Freeze were members of the Varsity Ski Team. 'Wildman' was from Vancouver, B. C.

(John Bird joined the Air Force and was one of the first from Banff to be killed in the war. Chess Edwards, living in the B. C. interior, said in a 1999 interview, "I was third in the slalom, but I didn't get a medal because the guy from Calgary making the presentation dropped my medal and they never found it. They ended up by giving me a written note saying I had come in third.")

RACE MARCH 1947

Frank Gourlay wins Memorial Trophy with a victory in weekend Giant Slalom. This follows his previous victory in the Slalom.

In a Junior Downhill, the winner was Keith Schneider, followed by Roy McCowan and Bob Neish.

Lois Woodworth won the Junior Girls Downhill; Sally Becker, second; Yvonne Legace, third and Barb Whyte, fourth.

RACE FEBRUARY 1968

Banff's Danny Wilson captures the Southern Alberta Junior 'C' Slalom.

Jenny Gourlay wins Midget Girls' race. Gerald Costigan, second in Midget Boys.

Jackie Wilson, was second in Girls' Slalom, 3/100 of a second behind Barbara Cheher of Calgary. Pat Adams of Banff was second to Danny Wilson in the Junior 'C' Slalom.

LOIS WOODWORTH WINS U.S. COMBINED SKI CHAMPIONSHIP
(March 1950)

Lois Woodworth became the first of the post-war school of Banff skiers to capture a major North American ski title. Her combined points in Slalom (4th) and Downhill (3rd) nosed out the pre-race favorite and Olympic winner, Janette Burr of the U.S.

Also in March of 1950, Lois Woodworth returned to Banff to compete in the first North American races held in Canada, at Mt. Norquay. This time the competition was much tougher with the best from Europe competing. Only three Canadians competed in the Women's races. Sandra Tomlinson of Vancouver was third in the Downhill, a race won by the American Janette Burr; Lois was 9th. The other

Norquay Ski School 1959/60
(L to R) Malcolm Cullen, Jay Kellum, Doug Robinson, Fri Rodley, Peggy Telfer, Fritz Frey, Jerry Johnston, Heinz Vifian.

Canadian was a young Rosemary Schultz who would go on to make Canada's National Team in a couple of years. Dagmar Romm of Austria won the Ladies' Slalom, followed by teammate Erika Mahringer and Italy's Celina Seghi.

Lois Woodworth was probably the only woman to schuss the Bowl. On March 11, 1951, while free skiing with Bob Dawson and Gordie Morrison, the three of them schussed the length of the Bowl. They had to stay high on the right side as they neared the Cliff to make the traverse under the jumps. Woodworth said, "On one of my runs that day I hit one of the young Neish kids who was standing on the Cliff right on the traverse, he just seemed to freeze when he saw me coming, but the Bowl that day was perfectly smooth and ideal for schussing." That year they held the Olympic trials in Banff but due to a dental problem Lois didn't make it to all of the trial races and failed to make Canada's Olympic Team. Gordie Morrison made the team as did Bob Dawson, but he couldn't go for financial reasons as the National team at that time only paid a part of the competitor's expenses.

FRITZ FREY (Outstanding all around skier from Switzerland. Fritz was on the Ski Patrol in the early 1950s. He had the Ski School at Norquay from 1954 to 1959. He also competed in major ski meets during that period. Fritz now (1999) lives in Sun Valley, Idaho.

"I was on the Ski Patrol with Frank Gourlay and the first lady on the Norquay patrol, Mary June Miles. I did well in competitive skiing, but I believe what I really like is the simplicity of skiing. When you have good friends and good snow that is what I really enjoy. For an instructor, Norquay in the 50s was a challenge. It was really too steep off the chair to give a good lesson to most people, but personally for my own skiing I loved it."

CALGARY HERALD SKI RESULTS, by Jock Osler
Western Canadian Championship, Mt. Norquay, 1957.
Fritz Frey popular Banff Head Ski Instructor skied off with the Alpine Combined title Sunday after a win in the Senior Men's Downhill. Fritz also won the Brewster Memorial Giant Slalom. Runner up to Frey in the combined was Bill Stevens of Rossland, B. C., followed by Pete Miller of Vancouver.

John Platt of Vancouver won the Senior Slalom.

Alpine Combined Junior Women: Ginger Edwards of Rossland, Lorna Becker of Banff was second. Mickey Johnson of Rossland won the Junior Men's Downhill and Slalom.

The Junior Women's Downhill was won by Banff's Lorna Becker. Barbara Pugh of Banff was second in the Ladies' Senior Slalom, behind Carmen Johnson of Vancouver, B. C. Dennis Smith of Banff placed fourth in the Downhill. Mary Lee Mather of Banff placed third in the Junior Slalom.

The Banff Ski Runners were the host club.

Jean (Kelly) Shafto (second from the left) and the skiing nurses of 1946.

Club president Imo Von Neudegg and assistant Lada Vrany co-ordinated the events.

Author's note: Skiers from B.C. almost dominated these races, especially the skiers from Rossland, B.C. Most would go on to Canada's National Team: Ginger Edwards, Bill Stevens, Mickey Johnson, Vern Anderson, Pat Nora, Doug Bowtry and Gary Kemp, Marvin Kempston and Sandra Osborne.

JEAN (KELLY) SHAFTO AND KAY WATT (Jean and Kay came to Banff in 1946. They were nurses at the Banff Mineral Springs Hospital. Kay married Bob 'Steam' Watt, a well-known Banff skier. In November of 1999 they were having coffee together.)

KAY: "I remember the Sisters of the hospital were not too happy with the fact that so many of the nurses were skiers, but I don't recall any of us losing a shift because of any injury we had."

JEAN: "They were such good years. If you were on an evening shift we would ski Norquay in the morning and ski down the Gulley in plenty of time to go on shift at three o'clock. Lorna Pirie was an avid skier. She would come to work so pumped from her day on the hill, the Sisters realized skiing was a good thing for their nurses. In later years, do you remember the stores in town would close on Wednesday afternoons, and just about everyone would go up to Norquay? There were the Hendersons, Wonnacotts, Mary and Cyril Paris, the Hansens, Mary and Pat Costigan, the Charltons; it was just the thing to do."

KAY: "I can remember the first lesson I had from Bill Wellman at Norquay. There was only one rope tow at that time in 1947. I would still be skiing if it weren't for my darn shoulder. Jean you're still skiing, that would be over 50 years on skis for you!"

JEAN: "A couple of years ago I skied a lot, in fact I think I was skiing the best I have ever skied."

JOHNNY MONOD (Born in Geneva, Switzerland, 1912. Arrived in Banff December 1947. The Monod family are one of Banff's top racing families. In 1999 the family business is still headed by Johnny Monod. They have five winter outlets, in Banff, Norquay and Lake Louise.)

"I arrived in Banff in December 1947. My first trip to Norquay was shortly after when Bruno Engler took me to the mountain. I still remember how beautiful the Rockies were. The only lift at that time was one rope tow. Skiing in Europe had started earlier as a serious sport. For several years the lifts that had been used to carry summer tourists were used for winter skiing in some areas, but they were not always covering slopes good or safe for skiing. It was in Megève, France in 1934 when they decided to make their lifts suitable for skiers. Following that my good friend Fred Islen and myself helped the Chamonix area plan for the winter trade, where we also had a ski shop. From this you see, the difference would have given Europe a fifteen to twenty year advantage over Banff that didn't have a lift until the winter of 1948/49.

"I actually started my first sport shop in Canada at Sunshine when I realized many people were ill equipped. That was the year the owner Jim Brewster died, but his daughter Fern Brewster was very helpful. The year was 1948.

"Banff was very quiet in those days. I remember Mr. Frank Hayes, the Brewster agent who sat in the Mount Royal Hotel all winter with nothing to do but smoke his pipe. If the hotel bus came back with more than one or two people from the railway station it was almost headline news in the *Crag & Canyon*. There wasn't much unity in the town at that time as far as trying to create more winter business. I tried and I am glad I stayed with it. We just celebrated fifty years of ski shop business in Banff.

"What ski comes to mind? I think the 'Strato' by Rossingol was one of the finest skis ever made. It came out in 1968. It had a wood core with fiberglass covering. The first step-in binding I remember was made by Cubco in 1951. Today, you would have to ask my boys, Phillip, Peter and Nicky what skis and snowboards are the best, they run the business now, at Norquay and also in Banff and Lake Louise."

LEAGH KENDAL (Born in Banff 1928. Leagh has been successful in several real estate holdings through the years including the present Sundance Mall on Banff Avenue. His entrepreneurial skills started at a very young age.)

"In 1942 when I was fourteen years old we were right in the middle of World War II. There were service men coming to Banff on leave, many of them Air Force personnel from Australia and New Zealand. My Dad, Pete Neish, gave me the idea to

Boardercross Champion, Candice Drouin of Banff had an outstanding 1999/2000 season. Candice won gold at the Goodwill Games in Lake Placid, New York. She won the Rocky Mountain series with a convincing win at Sunshine Village, followed by another gold performance at the North American Championship at Whistler in late April, 2000.

rent skis and boots to them. He gave me a loan to buy a half a dozen pairs of skis and boots and I rented them out of our home on Beaver Street. The number quickly grew and I remember staying up all night putting edges and bindings on skis at a time when I was still going to school. Then I realized it would be better to rent them from Banff Avenue, so I took space in the Rocky Mountain transport garage. (The present 'Grizzly House' restaurant.) I stayed there until 1956 before going on to other things. In the beginning I rented skis, boots and poles for $1.50 a day."

CANDICE DROUIN (Candice is a 23-year-old Banff snowboarder on Canada's National Boardercross team. Toronto born, Candice has lived all but a few early years in Banff.)

"When I was ten years old and still a skier with the Quikies, I remember the dual slaloms we had at Norquay on Wednesday nights. The Banff Alpine Racers would be there as well and we could challenge anyone we wanted to ski against. It was great fun.

"It's difficult to compare skiing and snowboarding. I enjoyed the downhill speed of skiing and holding an edge on an icy slope, just as I enjoy the speed on my board in powder, which gives a great surfing feeling."

JACK GORMAN (A newspaperman, Jack challenged the *Crag & Canyon* in the late1960s with a Banff newspaper called *The Summit News*. It was a good paper, however local advertisers stayed with the *Crag & Canyon*. His star reporter, Carrie Hunter covered the winter opening of the Banff Springs Hotel in December of 1969. It was a great boost to Banff's winter season. The front-page photo shows Marion Leigh, the Festival Queen, jumping out of a giant snowball to officially open the hotel. Jack currently lives in Calgary and Arizona.)

Blessing the teams as they prepare to ski the Mt. Everest Challenge, a fund raiser for the Red Cross and the Banff Centre, 1999.

"Man, do I remember Norquay! And I'm sure Norquay remembers me. I was never what you might call Olympic material, but I recall the weekly challenge I had with Wayne King and Jimmy Tighe. They were both bartenders (I have no idea how I would have met them), but anyway each Sunday, their day off (as bars didn't stay open on Sundays at that time), we would drop from the Big Chair and race for the lodge. The loser would buy the pie and coffee. It's not the winning or the losing that counts, but how quickly you pay the bill."

TIM AUGER (A Banff National Park Warden. Tim was a member of the Canadian Everest 1982 Expedition that put the first Canadian on the summit. He presently manages the visitor safety program for the Warden Service in the Banff area. This service issues a daily report on backcountry avalanche conditions, written and audio on phone number 762-1460.)

"Norquay has always been a major concern when we are talking avalanches and skier safety. Much of what produces the danger is not skied upon at Norquay. The danger comes from the cornices, plus the snow that blows over the summit of Norquay and lands in great depth just below the cornices, but above the ski slopes. This buildup can release into the open chutes and skiing area.

"When snow comes off that face it is really moving. One year I took our video operator, Jim Martin, up to tape an avalanche we released from the top. To stand there and experience a wall of suffocating snow coming at you is, to say the least, a very compressing experience. The audio comments picked up as that wall came rushing toward us were priceless. They can be humourous, but only at times like that when it is a controlled situation. The reality is that they can easily kill you.

"When Art Haenni was at Norquay he brought Willi Garanti over from Europe to discuss a method of stabilizing an avalanche slope. It was a method called a 'Bomb Tram' (something like a chair lift). Basically it was a bomb carried on a stationary line over an avalanche area, which then would be detonated in the desired area. It is used in Europe, but it was an expensive method, too expensive for here.

"I have worked with some wonderful people while learning about avalanche safety. Keith Everts was one of those men. His knowledge, leadership and intelligence were always inspiring to me.

"My Norquay memories don't go back too far: I came to Banff in the mid 1970s, but my parents told me about their great trips on the special ski trains from Calgary to Banff, for skiing at Norquay. That would have been over fifty years ago."

MARY JUNE MILES (Mary June was the first lady member of the ski patrol at Norquay in the winter of 1950/51.)

"The people I remember? There was Father McGuiness who really didn't like skiers coming in for morning mass at six o'clock with their noisy ski boots. At Norquay, Red Crozier was a big rough guy but always friendly with a ready joke. Franz Gabl always helped me with my skiing, who could be better. There was Fritz Frey and Frank Gourlay who headed the patrol. I seem to recall we skied no matter what the weather was like, it was never too cold to go for a run. The lodge would be full of people and you knew them all. A little later I met my husband, Cam Mitchell. As President of the Calgary Ski Club he had been working with Dave Spence, Director of the Canadian Amateur Ski Association on racing programs. Cam celebrated 50 years of skiing in the spring of 1999. About 30 skiing friends turned out to mark the occasion. I couldn't ski at the time because I was about to receive a new artifical ankle, the first in Alberta."

KEVIN HANN (Number three son of Bob and Carol Hann in between Andy, Greg and the youngest, Brian. Born in Banff 1960. Alberta Team member for four years. When a downhill accident cut his chances of making the National Team, Kevin turned to the professional circuit and raced North America and Japan for seven years. Won the Pacific Pro Tour one year and was runner-up the following year. As a junior he had won the Canadian Geländesprung Championship.)

"The day before an Alberta Cup slalom I was free skiing off the Big Chair. It was an unusual day in that there was a heavy fog. Coming off the Lone Pine I started to cut under the Cascade Chair. I thought I was on a lower slope where it is gentle, but I was actually much higher up and I suddenly dropped off a 15-foot cliff and went straight into the slope. I'm not sure if my head shot down to my ski tip or if it was the broken tip flying up to my face. I was waiting for the pain to hit me, I thought something had to break. There was a great break, but fortunately it was mostly my boot. The sole of the boot was still in the binding, my foot had come out with the liner but the two top buckles were still holding on to my foot, if you can picture that.

When the Ski Patrol arrived I was still moaning, but being 14 years old I wasn't ready to be taken down on a toboggan. They took my broken equipment and I started down the hill on one ski; that's all I remember, the next thing I knew they were wiping my face in the Ski Patrol Hut. They say I made it down there by myself, but I don't remember doing it. I raced the next day and just missed the podium by one placing.

"I remember Larry Bakstad and his dog 'Rocky.' Larry was a good freestyle and downhill skier. He went off the Big Chair as fast as anyone and his dog was just as fast. I don't know how he did it, but that dog, I think he was a black Lab., would keep up with him no matter how many runs Larry made. He did it for a few years before the management decided it wasn't a good idea. I also remember one of my first coaches, Marilyn Kelly, she made skiing fun."

Eight year old Kevin Hann wins Gelundy competition, 1968.

MADELINE CRILLEY (A gal that came to the Rockies from Glasgow, Scotland in 1965. Married notorious Park Warden Keith Everts in 1967. In Sid Marty's publication *Switchbacks*, 1999, he dedicated the book to his wife Myrna and to the memory of his fellow warden, Keith Everts, who suffered a fatal heart attack in March 1999. Keith was 54.)

"I remember, not with pleasure, the old Poma lifts they had at Norquay in the late 60s. I remember, with pleasure, taking lessons on the special 'ladies' day', I believe it was the Heinz Vifian ski school. Keith enjoyed skiing powder. He had spent so much time in the Rogers Pass area where the snow is so deep. He always came home with funny stories after skiing a day with Bruno Engler at Norquay."

PETER FUHRMANN (Parks Alpine Specialist, Western Region since 1968, retired 1991.)

"Myself and pilot Eddie Aman were the first to stabilize an avalanche slope by bombing from a helicopter in the winter of 1969/70. We did it by throwing a CIL Nitron charge. It is against regulations to carry a high explosive in the air, but a Nitron charge was considered a blasting agent, which technically was approved. Ed, who had worked mountain rescue in Europe, had an idea to make a hole in the bottom of the helicopter to drop the charge, but we decided against it as it was more accurate and safer to throw it onto the slope. We could bomb the Wishbone and then stabilize it further by skiing the area. You can't do that with most of the avalanche slopes on Norquay.

"On another flight, I believe Jim Davies was now the pilot, we had a bit of a surprise. Normally the western wind coming down over Norquay causes a down-draft on the upper slopes above the ski area which forces the helicopter to be sucked down. On this occasion we were almost at the top of the lift ready to bomb the open slope that lies just to the north of the Tea House. We had already made certain all skiers were off the slope or in the Tea House. Just as we released the bomb the helicopter hit an unusual up-draft. It looked like the bomb would land right on the roof of the Tea House. Perhaps there was another current of air, or an angel of mercy that just carried it to the slope at which we were aiming, but it was awfully close."

CAMILLA BURKS (Outstanding Banff skier. Six years on the Alberta Team and four years with the National Development Team. Raced all major North American competitions.)

"I have good memories of skiing with my friends, but the first one that comes to mind was a little touchy. I was training with my friend Vania Grandi. It was the first time we had used break-away gates. Ray Seguin, our coach, showed us how to hit them, but at the time we didn't have the proper padded equipment. Hitting those gates can really hurt, so Ray had us improvise with cottage cheese and yogurt containers cut to the shape of our arms. We combined them with a little foam rubber. It seems funny now, but it helped. It makes me feel like a ski pioneer."

GEORGE RAHAM (A Toronto skier who first viewed Mt. Norquay from a passing train in 1953. He couldn't believe there was a lift up that mountain. After moving to Calgary in 1960, he proceeded to conquer those slopes on his skis and every slope that got in his way. Forty winters later, George is still doing it. If he fails to win Bruno's Veterans and Masters Race in his class this year it will be because he didn't show up.)

"Where do I start? I have so many Norquay memories that are all advancing in my mind, and not only my memories. Like the day my son Dave, who along with his friends Morgan Grant and Roland Fuhrmann, made 45 runs off the top in one day that still stands as a record. That would be something like 58 000 vertical feet, twice the height of Mt. Everest.

"In Doug Godfrey's 'Mountain Smoker,' my wife Marian and I went up to watch our son compete. If you remember, it was the wildest race. You skied non-stop for three hours. When they came into the lift area they banked off a sheet of plywood put there by the management, and then just threw themselves at the lift. It was our plan to hand Dave nourishment as he completed each run. We ended up feeding everyone until Klara Huser, the area manager, came out to the rescue and took over that service.

"I skied Bruno's 25th Veterans and Masters Race. I think that would have been about 1991, in my equipment from the 1950s: wooden skis, leather boots and 35 year-old pants and jacket. Yes, they still fit.

"Another thought from the 70s. Bill Herron put up an equipment building in one day. It was called a 'fold-away.' It was surprising to see such a large building go up so quickly, but the most surprised people were the Park officials, as Bill didn't have authorization to build."

LADD SNOWSELL (Kelowna, B. C. native came to Banff in 1979. Ladd is presently the General Manager of Ski Banff/Lake Louise. He has an active skiing family with his wife Sheila and children, Ian 13, and 11 year-old Lauren.)

"My thoughts go back to the winters of 1979 to 1981. As a member of 'Club Ski,' the three area ski school, we would have a wind-up dinner at the old Norquay lodge for our ski week clients every Friday night. During the evening the instructors would ride the Big Chair and perform a Torchlight Parade down to the Lone Pine, which was right in front of the lodge. Our classes would gather in front of the lodge to cheer us on. In the still of the night they could hear all the chatter and laughter we made as we snaked our way back to the base where we had dinner with our classes and presented them with their diplomas. It always ended up being a great evening for everyone involved. Who do I remember? There was Geoff Booth, Neil Tanner and Don Findlay to name a few who are still in the area. They were great evenings until the numbers got too big for the old Norquay Lodge of that time."

Friends who don't ride junk. (L to R) Dana DeGeer, Nicky de Champlain, Ladd Snowsell, Viki Walmsley, Wilson Walmsley, 2000.

MARILYN HORN (Historical art consultant for Chateau Lake Louise. She skied Norquay in the early days.)

"Someone told me the fastest way to the pub was to ski the Gulley. In my haste I crashed but I was still able to lift a beer. And by the way, I am still looking for the mitts that were twisted from my hands by that old rope tow. Who did I ski with? Well I remember the English gal by the name of Derith Mottershaw and also Gerry Cole."

DON WATERS (Park Warden. Don supplied some early photos of the Norquay parking area in the late 1930s.)

"I remember runs down the North American to the Timberline Hotel and returning by bus for repeated runs. The best ones were made with my friend Norm Murray, he was an enthusiastic skier. That would have been in the early 1980s."

Don also said the Park Wardens stopped their avalanche control within the ski boundary in the winter of 1992/93. He added that Tim Auger is now the avalanche safety manager. He puts out a daily bulletin that covers avalanche danger in the back country.

RACE FOR THE SUN 1980
Mark Bennett edges Larry Bakstad.

RACE FOR THE SUN 1987
Dave Spence wins 'A' class and a trip to Hawaii. Curtis Vigh wins 'B' group and a trip to Mexico. Spence was followed by Dean Moffit, Ken Ross, Jim Uffelmann, Ron Hallam and Scott Holland.

CANADA GAMES 1987
Three Banff skiers go to the Canada Games in Cape Breton, Jason Santa Lucia, Michelle Wiegele and Cary Mullen.

GERALD COSTIGAN (Banff born and grew up on the slopes of Norquay skiing with his sister Peggy and brother Norman.)

"I remember the well scene when Marty Von Neudegg and I couldn't get out for an hour or two. But that wasn't as bad as the time my brother Norman disappeared one afternoon, only to be found about two hours later unconsious in the housing that contained the bullwheel of the old Memorial rope tow. His jacket was in shreds. Walter Fisher bought him a new jacket."

CHARLIE LOCKE (I caught up with Charlie on his cell phone in the spring of 1999 as he was driving past Banff on his way to Kimberley, B. C. to part of his skiing and golfing empire. He owns six ski areas in the west, the largest being Lake Louise, and two in eastern Canada.)

I told Charlie that I was doing research on the Mount Norquay ski area. I thought he might say "Oh! That's the one I don't own, but almost did." Rather than saying that, he told me how he skied Norquay as a ten-year-old with his brothers and sisters. In later years he came to the area from Calgary and would stay at Ma Ruby's for $3 a night. He also remembers the line-ups on the single Norqauy chair, never dreaming that one day he would be developing ski areas to eliminate similar line-ups. It was also a surprise to him when in 1995 he was asked to bid on the Norquay area. The winning bid went to Peter White and Kika Grandi as they offered $50 000 more than the highest bid. Mr. Locke wasn't critical of the process as conducted by the Alberta Treasury Branch, but he didn't think it was very ethical either.

BRUCE MCGAVIN (A skier who led Edmontonians to Norquay in pre chair lift days. Bruce was an outstanding skier in cross country, jumping and downhill. He was a member of the Ryerson ski team that defeated McGill in 1957.)

"My first ski train ride from Edmonton was in 1946. We left Saturday night at 11:55 p.m. and arrived in Calgary at 6:30 a.m. There we waited for a troup train that was travelling from Toronto to Vancouver. They tacked us on to the back and dropped our cars off in Banff. We were bussed to Norquay where we skied our brains out on the rope tow that went up a section of the Lone Pine. This mountain skiing was much different than our 200-foot vertical slope in Edmonton. And all for the inclusive price of $10.50.

"I, along with Banff characters Stan Peyto and Fred Wonnacott, was a jumping judge during the intercollegiate meets of the 1960s and 70s. Each team had to have a minimum of three jumpers. One or two might be Norwegian exchange students that would end up on Olympic teams, but to meet the three-jumper requirement, they would add a downhill skier who had very little, if any, experience. How do you judge a jumper who leaves the take-off area only to land on the brow of the landing area where he is reborn into the air again? Which jump do you judge? The one from the jump, or the second take-off from the brow. The solution came easily in the form of Fred's rum-bearing thermos. Thanks to his generosity and the warmth of the liquid, by the time the last jumper came down we judges were in perfect accord with our judging decisions. Aided of course by Stan's expertise in judging."

HEINZ VIFIAN (An innovative ski instructor who had the Norquay Ski School from 1961 to 1974. His ski school set a Norquay record when they gave 750 lessons in one day. This included the thirteen bus loads of people from Calgary.)

"In 1958 I took my Ski Alliance exam at Jasper, Bob Dawson was the examiner. After taking over the ski school at Norquay I joined Norm Russell and also managed the ski shop. I did several things to encourage business. I believe it was the year 1963 that I started a kid's program which became the Kinsmen Ski School. I had the very best instructors and it cost the parents about $1 a week. Jerry Johnston and Mike Wiegele and I started a three-area ski school which was a forerunner to Club Ski. I also started a Saturday night fashion show in the Voyager Inn. Three weeks after it started you couldn't get in. Of course it helped the hotel, Russell's Ski Shop and Mt. Norquay.

"I remember Klara Huser starting at Norquay. She worked so hard looking after kids on a small-handled rope tow, and later worked her way up to a managerial job.
"It was a very quiet day (we had many quiet days) and I was in the ski shop when a nurse came in with a bent ski. She said she had had a bad fall on the Lone Pine and had also lost her false teeth at the same time. I told her I could probably straighten the ski out while she went for coffee. A few minutes later a snowy Bob Meggs came in to the shop. 'You won't believe this,' he said, 'but I took a real duster on the Lone Pine and when I opened my eyes this set of teeth was grinning back at me.' Bob returned them to a happy nurse who was in the lodge trying to drink a cup of coffee with some difficulty.

"Yes, I had a good working relationship with Walter Fisher: he did many good things for the area. One more thing I remember. There was so much snow in 1972, that instead of reaching up for the ski school bell, we had to reach down."

EDDIE HUNTER (Born in Edmonton, 1926. The family moved to Banff in 1934, where I discovered skiing is actually done on a slope. I have lived in Banff 65 years minus about 10 while working in Calgary TV, and a few more at Squaw Valley, California.)

"Perhaps I should have given my 'need to write' (not to be confused with the Banff National Park regulation, 'need to reside') in this book earlier, but then I thought what a wonderful opportunity to have the last word. That also means everyone has gone and no one is listening or reading, but that's okay, I just hope someday my grandchildren, or their children will read it and say, 'Gee our family has skied here a long time.'

"They might have trouble imagining my pine skis, back in the 1930s, with nothing but a toe strap and a heavy rubber band cut from an old tire tube holding the ski to a snowboot. I hope they understand it was as much fun as any hi-tech ski or board they may be riding, perhaps more. My mother and father skied Norquay in the 30s, but I believe I skied there before they did.

"I'm crossing my fingers as I say this, but, 'I have never really hurt myself skiing, well, hurt yes, but never broken anything.' In a race down the old North American I went off the 'end of the world' and landed upside down in a tree. I hung there like a Christmas decoration until help came. I probably should have died that day. It was pre-helmet days, plus long-thong bindings that refused to part with the boot unless you snapped your leg off at the ankle.

"Just for my grandchildren I would like to say, 'Gramps won a few races in Canada and California. I was doing well in Europe when I heard someone yell 'track.' In Canada that meant get out of the way, but over there it meant cablecar track, which I managed to hit with very noisy results.

"As I mentioned earlier, Norquay was really our backyard playground. Then it became a playground for my children, Mystee and Kendall. Both girls became excellent skiers. In the early years I had signed Mystee up for the Nancy Greene league. She asked, 'Dad, is that where you go through gates and someone times you'? I said, 'yes' and she said, 'I don't want to do that.' When she was thirteen she skied the Norquay Challenge, which was 27 runs off the Big Chair in one day. Kendall was a strong skier and she liked competitive skiing, however a case of 'mono' at a critical time when she was training with the Alberta Team in France real-

ly hurt her chances of staying with the team. Mystee did compete eventually and won a few races, and that is what she wanted to do. Kendall had also won races, and that is what she wanted to do. She would have won more if she hadn't wanted to win so badly. Sometimes competitive skiing can make you better, but not when the pressure tightens your mind and body. As a family, Carrie, myself and the girls made it a small tradition to leave the gifts of Christmas and overeating, to make our way to Norquayj0

for a few runs and a sharing Christmas Day. Now, years later, I join my daughter Mystee, and her husband Rick Maisonet and their two boys, Jake and Noah, to build new memories and relive earlier years, wishing at the same time Kendall, now living in Switzerland, and her daughter Sadie, and husband Alex Maycock were with us.

The sweater promised. Eddie Hunter and Ted Paris in 1938.

... daughters. One year old Kendall ... four year old Mystee, 1966 and ... years later.

"In researching this book I have realized what Norquay has meant to other families and individuals: the sharing and community feeling of Norquay. I also found individuals who may have arrived twenty or thirty years ago still share with skiing buddies memories of special days. Memories that grow as the years pass. I was told most of those days were spent in the powder off the Big Chair. I had grown up on that mountain, taking each slope as my ability increased. I never looked at the big turns off the top as a special world, as did the skiers who were adults when they moved to Banff and mastered the same runs. Their appreciation was much more intense than mine was. I realized that when I spoke with Jerry Goulet, Steve Orchin, Ratso, Mike Miskow, Trudy Wilson, and a few others. To be the first in line on a freshly powdered mountain was to win the lottery. In recent years snowboarders have been sharing their new approach to a winter on Norquay, promoting friendship and a whole new set of memories.

"I have been fortunate to experience practically the whole life that has been Norquay, which includes the people who built the first cabin and all the wonderful people that I have worked and skied with through the years. Thirty years ago I made a promotional film for Bill Herron and now I have the privilege to work on this book for Kika Grandi and Peter White. I am pleased with the people I have revisited in doing this book, and sorry when I think of so many more that should have more of a voice here. I would have liked to have more on Dave Spence Sr. who worked so hard for Western Canadian skiers in the 1940s and 50s, Don Becker who was always a top supporter of skiing events, along with his talented skiing family and Stan ...to, a man who conveyed the strength and will of a mountain along with our heritage, plus ... gifted boys who excelled in four-way skiing. I would have liked to have more on Walter ...ren and John Wackerle. Also the countless number of parents who couldn't always afford ...put their children on the hill, but managed somehow, and then stood out there shivering ...gatekeepers to support their kids.

'I thank the people at the Whyte Museum and Archives, Don Bourdon, Lena Goon and ...ry Andrews for their support and photographs. I want to thank Jon Whelan, historical ...earcher, for his help and encouragement also Charlie Zinkan, Superintendent of the Banff ...tional Park and the office of Dave Millard for their co-operation. I am indebted to Anne ...ely for reading, editing, indexing and proof-reading the manuscript. And I thank so many ...er people who donated photos, with their Norquay memories. I skied with too many ...nds to thank them all for for my memories, but in the early years there was Lois ...odworth, Donnie Hayes, Whitey Andersen, Zeke Robley, Gordie Morrison, 'Socs'

"Lets go Gramp!" Noah Maisonet. 1996

"Get your board Gramp!" Jake Maisonet. 2000

Andrews, Ross Maxwell, Peter Van Wagner, John Holland, Peter Matthews, Dean Fry, Bob Dawson, Barb Whyte and Bruno Engler. My year skiing with Emile Allais (the French Olympic skier who introduced the French method of skiing) at Squaw Valley, California is a great memory, and of course the thousands of people I have skied with and filmed through the years. Watching people like Hans Gmoser and Mike Wiegele make it big in the heli-world of skiing, and the passion shown by Jerry and Anne Johnston in their many years with disabled skiers. I could go on for pages naming people who have been a credit to this wonderful sport in the past, and of course in the present. Today's coaches who are dedicated to teaching in the local clubs of the Banff Alpine Racers, Quikies, and the Norquay Avalanche Club, Coaches: Duane Baird, Jordy Burks, Jim Davis, John Evely, Marty Hansen, Mike Necesanek, Wade Rettie, Richard Semenchuck and Ryan Whetung. And the young skiers of the Bow Valley:

Jeffrey Crompton, Colin DeGeer, Katie Fukushima, Jan Hudec, Dustin McLeary, Ania Morton, Pierre Héry, Kathleen Shaw, Andrew Sheppard, Brad Spence, Paul Stutz, Ashley Tarchuk, Kristen Tarchuk, just to name a few. Not forgetting the older crowd with Ray Seguin's and Bruce Henry's Rut Runners, and their star performer, Bonnie Wiegele. Plus Bruno's even older crowd of skiers like Frank Gourlay and Rob Crosby. Their combined time on skis would be at least 140 years, just for Frank and Rob. Adding new spirit to the mountain are the snowboarders in the Halfpipe and Boardercross events: Candice Drouin, Andrew Hardingham, Sara Jordan, and Jim Theys. All had an excellent year. I don't mean to honour only skiers who compete. The Norquay Ski School headed by Clarke Lefaivre will instruct hundreds of skiers and snowboarders daily who will never have their names mentioned on a sporting page. One event which more or less combines skating and skiing skills with a social tone is the annual 'Mountain Madness.' In 1999, the 23rd 'Mountain Madness' was won by a team called 'Owe My Mom Big' with members Jake Howe, Marilee Howe, Davin MacIntosh and Paul Watson. (Thoughts of this race go back several years to when Rod Adlington competed as a one-man team in the five required disciplines.)

"You might think I am just another senior roaming through the lodge area running into other seniors that have also forgotten where they left their skis….(or did I bring my snowboard today?). Anyway, it's a pleasant way to meet people.

"I do have one wish. As we enter a new Century, it is my wish that there will be greater understanding between the area owners/skiing public, and the extreme groups that would have ski areas removed from the Park. A compromise which will allow our children to continue to ski in this valley and share it with the wildlife.

"My memories as a kid, skiing the trail to town with friends; trying to ski like Ted Paris and chasing the sweater he promised I could have when he was done with it. Skiing with my aggressive little daughters, Mystee and Kendall; they both started when they were a year and a couple of months, frozen diapers helping to keep them in an upright position. And now runs with grandsons Jake and Noah, through the trees on our way to a hot chocolate, and chatter you wouldn't believe. It doesn't get any better.

> I love the world when I stand on skis,
> surrounded by sunny peaks or snow giving clouds.
> The gift of motion from mountain slopes that
> look up to greet my turns.
> The flight of snow particles back-lighting my descent,
> the joy in my body riding skis and snow
> to anywhere I want to go-
> a celebration of freedom!
> The Rockies fulfill people in many ways,
> I am glad this is mine.

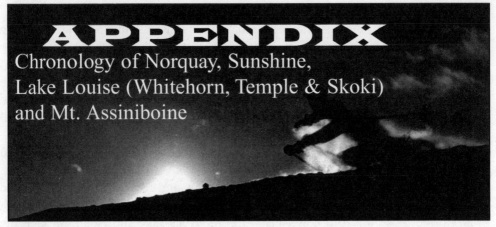

APPENDIX
Chronology of Norquay, Sunshine,
Lake Louise (Whitehorn, Temple & Skoki)
and Mt. Assiniboine

NORQUAY
1920s	Skied by Gus Johnson and young Banff skiers.
1928	Cabin built, a town effort led by the White brothers and Cyril Paris.
1938	Cabin destroyed by fire.
1940	New lodge funded by shares sold to Banff and Calgary skiers.
1946	George Encil takes over Norquay. First chair built in 1948.
1960	Encil sells to Walter Fisher.
1968	Fisher sells to Bill Herron.
1978	Herron sells to Art Haenni (Sulphur Mountain Gondola).
1989	Dave Morrison (Brewster Transport) joins Norquay for major 1990 development.
1995	Peter White and Kika Grandi outbid Charlie Locke and Ralph Scurfield for Mt. Norquay. Lodge destroyed by fire in December 1995.
1996	New lodge opens.
2000	New Cascade chair and Magic Carpet for beginners.

SUNSHINE
1934	Brewsters lease trail riders cabin. In 1936, Brewsters purchase and develop area for skiing. First vehicle driven to the area in 1941 by Lloyd Hunter.
1952	George Encil buys Sunshine and renames it Sunshine Village.
1960	Cliff and Bev White purchase and develop the area further.
1965	Power Corporation acquire Sunshine.
1972	Sunshine sold to Warnock Hersey. Gondola replaces buses in 1980.
1981	Ralph Scurfield buys Sunshine after being outbid by Charlie Locke in an effort to buy Lake Louise.

LAKE LOUISE (WHITEHORN, TEMPLE &SKOKI)

1930   Cliff White, Cyril Paris, Fulton Dunsmore and Tex Woods explore the Little Pipestone area, 12 miles from the present village of Lake Louise.

1931   Log cabin built at Skoki.

1931   First guests arrive. Two more cabins were built (his and hers) at Skoki, plus the Halfway Cabin in the Ptarmigan. Most of the expense was covered by Catharine and Peter Whyte who also managed the lodge in 1932 and 1933. Jim Boyce was the next manager. The next addition to the lodge in 1938 was paid for by an English visitor, Sir Norman Watson.

1938   Lodge built at Temple.

1940   Lake Louise ski lodge was built; later renamed the Post Hotel.

1942   Lizzie Rummel managed Skoki until 1949.

1951   Jack McDowell arrived from England to manage Sir Norman Watson's interests. He managed the ski hill until 1968, and the Post Hotel until 1972.

1959   Gondola opened in late August. The Eagle poma lift in 1960.

1981   By this time Sir Norman Watson had sold all his shares and the Post Hotel. A testy bidding battle between Ralph T. Scurfield and Charlie Locke for control of the 1.3 million shares finally ended with Locke the winner. Rodney Touche, a shareholder, played a major role at this time and stayed on to work with Charlie Locke until 1984. In 1990 he wrote a book on the fifty years of Lake Louise (*Brown Cows, Sacred Cows*).

MT. ASSINIBOINE

1928   Erling Strom and Marquis degli Albizzi arrive with the first organized ski group from the eastern United States. Strom leased the cabin for a couple of years and then purchased and operated it for 50 years along with a variety of people including Larry Boyd, Veijo Tiesmaki and Benny Judah.

1950   Lizzie Rummel operated her Sunburst lodge at Assiniboine until 1970.

1970   The government of British Columbia purchased Assiniboine. Since 1983 Sepp and Barbara Renner, along with their children, have leased and operated Assiniboine Lodge

INDEX

Hunter, Eddie, 10, 74, 114, 116, 117, 178, 192-195
Hunter, 'Jungle' Jim, 52, 103, 109, 132, 137
Hunter, Kendall, 58, 59, 60, 109, 132, 136, 138, 192-195
Hunter, Lloyd, 196
Hunter, Mystee, 58, 60, 134, 136, 192-195
Hunter, Ted, 28
Huser, Klara, 39, 45, 68, 145, 188, 191
Hutchins, 'Hutch', 88
Hutchison, J. A., 29
Iles, David, 74
Iles, Jack, 74
Innes, Jimmy, 34, 90, 175
Interbourse , 53, 76, 133
International Intercollegiate Ski Meet, 27, 71, 101, 103, 147
Interski 1987, 87, 102, 176
Ironleg Triathlon, 89
Irwin, Bill, 107
Irwin, Bill (Calgary), 109, 133
Irwin, Dave, 108, 109, 122, 146
Irwin, Dean, 107
Irwin, Joe, 73, 97, 133
Irwin, Mike, 76, 133, 149
Islen, Fred, 183
Iverson, Dolly, 84
J2 racer (unknown), 83
Jackson, Bob, 171
Jacobitz, Al, 124
Jacobs, Brothers, 80
Jacobs, Dave, 98
Jacobs, Pete, 26, 73
Jeannie's, 151
Jeffrey, Doug, 62
Jeffrey, Vern, 62
Jennings, K., 10
Jennings, P. J., 14, 59
Joffe, Jay 33
Johannsen, Jackrabbit, 148
Johannsen, Peggy, 148
Johnson, Art, 158
Johnson, Bill, 73
Johnson, Carmen, 182
Johnson, Charlie, 121

Johnson, F., 130
Johnson, Gus, 5, 6, 25, 53, 61, 62, 84, 196
Johnson, Gussie, 61
Johnson, Hux, 110
Johnson, Mickey, 182, 183
Johnson, Peter, 88, 116
Johnson, Ron, 73
Johnston, Anne, 88, 95, 194
Johnston, Jerry, 32, 34, 88, 95, 101, 130, 179, 181, 191, 194
Jordan, Sara, 194
Jost, Karl, 52, 72, 121
Judah, Benny, 88, 197
Kain, Conrad, 4
Kappler, Heinz, 108
Kaserer, Monika, 70
Kayhko, Tauno, 40
Keach, Noldie, 128, 151, 167, 179
Keely, Bill, 6
Keith, Ted, vii
Kellam, Jay, 88, 93
Kellam, Terry, 88, 93
Kellum, Jay, 181
Kelly Family, 29, 135
Kelly, Fran, 69
Kelly, Hilda, 93
Kelly, Jean (Shafto), 93, 182, 183
Kelly, Marilyn, 94, 99, 135, 164, 187
Kelly, Tom, 135, 154, 164
Kemp, Gary, 183
Kempston, Marvin, 183
Kendal, Leagh, 184
Kennedy, 'Doc', 6
Kennedy, Bud, 10
Kennedy, Percy, 81
Kent, Betty (Leper), 95, 103, 139
Kent, Chris, 122, 133, 146
Kent, George, 96, 103, 139
Keys, Bill, 110
Keys, Toby, 110
King, Wayne, 185
'King Eddie', 88
Kinsmen Ski School, 94, 103, 130, 132, 160, 191
Kirby, 176
Kirby, Mike, 137

Matthews, Peter, 88, 157, 194
Maudsley, John, 164
Maxwell, Elaine, 94
Maxwell, Ross, 88, 94, 99, 127, 161, 194
Maycock Family, 193
McCall, Captain P., 7, 69
McCartney, Ian, 88
McCaw, Jodi, 133
McConkey, Glen, 176
McConkey, Jim, 26, 118, 130, 176, 199
McCowan, Connie, 130
McCowan, Roy, 130, 181
McCrea, Bill, 18, 63
McCrea, Don, 18, 63
McCready, Chris, 108, 109, 147
McCullough, Murray, 161
McDonald, Bill, 63
McDonald, J., 130
McDonald, Jim, 18, 63
McDowell, Jack, 197
McGavin, Bruce, 116, 190
McGuiness, Father, 186
McKeen, Shirley, 116
McKenzie, Mike, 110
McKenzie, Ralph, 129
McKinnon, J. A., 26
McLeary, Dustin, 194
McLennan, Shelley, 154
McLeod, Pat, 145
McManus, Derek, 110
McManus, Doug, 110
McMurdo, Chris, 69
McMurdo, Martina, 69
McRitchie, Ken, 176
Medic, Mel, 64
Meggs, Bob, 34, 73, 150, 167, 191
Memorial Bowl, 105, 116
Memorial Tow, 67
Merriam, Rick, 103
Michaels, Dorothy, 17
Miles, Mary June, 34, 153, 182, 186
Millard, Dave, 193
Miller, Gerry, 88, 167
Miller, Pete, 182
Miller, Stu, 88, 157, 167
Millican, Donna, 168

Mills, Ike, vii, 6, 114
Mills, Mark, 128
Miskow, Mike, 111, 125, 127, 151, 193
Mitchell, Cam, 153, 186
Mobraaten, Tom, 11
Moffit, Dean, 190
Monod, Jerry, 27, 71
Monod, Johnny, 89, 101-103, 142, 152, 183
Monod, Kay, 115, 141
Monod, Matthew, 136
Monod, Nicky, 109, 136, 142, 184
Monod, Peter, 75, 99, 109, 117, 140, 141, 184
Monod, Phillip, 75, 99, 109, 117, 128, 141, 149, 150, 172, 184
Monod Family, 29, 152, 183
Mont Tremblant, 89
Montalbetti, Jim, 40, 45, 135
Moodie, Gordon B., 9
Moore, Dick, 64, 87, 157, 168
Moore, Pearl, 4
Moore, Ross, 119
Morin, J., 136
Morrison, Dave, 25, 42, 45-49, 54, 144, 196
Morrison, Gordie, 28, 72, 116, 120, 145, 160, 177, 178, 182, 193, 196
Morrison Family, 29
Morrison, Jim, 17, 82, 144
Morrison, Lee Lee, 109
Morrison, Margaret, 17, 145
Morrison Memorial (1978), 176
Morrison, Tom, 93, 116
Morter, Howard, 74
Morton, Ania, 194
Motter, George, 141, 1149, 150
Mottershaw, Derith, 189
Mount Assiniboine, 73, 115, 142, 157, , 196, 197
Mount Bulyea, 26
Mount Everest Ski Challenge, 53
Mount Norquay Racing Club, 48
Mount Royal Hotel, 88, 98, 112
Mountain Madness, 110, 122, 134, 136, 152, 194
Mountain Smoker, 128, 139, 188

THE SPIRIT OF NORQUAY

Copies of this book can be ordered from:

EDDIE HUNTER
403.762.0770
Box 1256
Banff, AB
T0L 0C0

BANFF MOUNT
NORQUAY
403.762.4421
Suite 7000
Box 219
Banff, AB
T0L 0C0
www.banffnorquay.com